PEACEABLE KINGDOMS

PEACEABLE KINGDOMS

AN ANTHOLOGY OF UTOPIAN WRITINGS

EDITED BY *Robert L. Chianese*

SAN FERNANDO VALLEY STATE COLLEGE

HARCOURT BRACE JOVANOVICH, INC.

NEW YORK   CHICAGO   SAN FRANCISCO   ATLANTA

ISBN: 0–15–569053–1

Library of Congress Catalog Card Number: 74-153749

Printed in the United States of America

COPYRIGHTS AND ACKNOWLEDGMENTS

For permission to use the selections reprinted in this book, the editor is grateful to the following publishers and copyright holders:

AMS PRESS, INC. For "Life Without Principle" from *The Writings of Henry David Thoreau*. Reprinted by permission of AMS Press, Inc.

BLACK PANTHER PARTY. For "Black Panther 1966 Party Platform." Reprinted from *The Black Panther* by permission of the Black Panther party.

RALPH H. BOWEN. For *A Supplement to Bougainville's "Voyage"* from *Rameau's Nephew and Other Works of Diderot*. Reprinted by permission of the translator.

HENDRICKS HOUSE, INC. For *The City of the Sun* from *Famous Utopias of the Renaissance*. Reprinted by permission of Hendricks House, Inc.

HOUGHTON MIFFLIN COMPANY. For "War" from *Emerson's Complete Works*, Volume XI. Reprinted by permission of Houghton Mifflin Company.

OXFORD UNIVERSITY PRESS. For "The Shepherd," "Night," "The Divine Image," "A Divine Image," "The Clod & The Pebble," "The Garden of Love," "London," "To Tirzah," *The Book of Thel* from *The Complete Poems of William Blake*. Reprinted by permission of Oxford University Press, London.

RUSSELL & RUSSELL. For *News from Nowhere* abridged from Volume XVI of *The Collected Works of William Morris* (1910–1915). Copyright © 1966 by Russell & Russell, New York.

THE BOBBS-MERRILL COMPANY, INC. For "Idea of a Universal History from a Cosmopolitan Point of View" from *Immanuel Kant: On History*, translated by Lewis White Beck, copyright © 1963 by the Liberal Arts Press, Inc. Reprinted by permission of the Liberal Arts Press Division of The Bobbs-Merrill Company, Inc.

THE NEW YORK REVIEW OF BOOKS. For "Ecological Armegeddon" by Robert L. Heilbroner from *The New York Review of Books* (April 23, 1970). Reprinted with permission from *The New York Review of Books*. Copyright © The New York Review.

THE VIKING PRESS, INC. For an excerpt from *Ovid: The Metamorphoses* translated by Horace Gregory. Copyright © 1958 by The Viking Press, Inc. Reprinted by permission of The Viking Press, Inc.

PREFACE

Man has always wanted to create a utopia. He has sought the Promised Land and yearned for Christ's earthly kingdom; he has tried to construct organized city-states and has dreamed of free societies based on love and friendship. These plans for the future have been designed by men who are not only visionary idealists but perceptive social critics as well.

The aim of this anthology is to encourage both the analytical and creative aspects of utopian thought. The utopian works reprinted here represent a major cross section of the tradition of utopian ideas. The headnotes and study questions focus attention on the definition of human nature that forms the basis of each writer's particular vision of utopia. By exploring these imaginary societies and by noting the different view of man at the core of each of them, we should learn to examine our own definition of man and to question our assumptions about the organization of society. The emphasis, then, is on aiding one to reach personal conclusions about the question of utopia, rather than on initiating academic research.

The works have also been selected because of their rhetorical and literary interest, and both the Introduction and study questions direct attention to elements of expression and form. With essentially complete texts of three utopian works in Part A, it is possible to examine the conventions of the utopia as a literary genre.

Finally, the anthology is designed to illustrate the direct points of comparison and contrast between individual selections, and each of the utopias presented can enrich and be enriched by other utopian views. For example, it is interesting to know that Denis Diderot's *Supplement to Bougainville's "Voyage"* closely resembles the early travel books that were obvious targets of Swift's satire in *Gulliver's Travels*. The Academy of Lagado in Book III of *Gulliver's Travels* might be viewed as an ironic reflection of Tommaso Campanella's *The City of the Sun*. In Part D of the anthology, suggestions for complementary readings are given. Designed in this manner, the anthology may profitably be used as the basis for courses in the broadened humanities curriculum.

I would like to thank Donald Livingston and Gerald Reeves for helping me with the choice of particular selections in the anthology and to acknowledge my indebtedness to Richard Stang for widening my view of the whole utopian tradition.

ROBERT L. CHIANESE

San Fernando Valley State College
Northridge, California

CONTENTS

INTRODUCTION

The times are comet-crossed. The list of crises grows, and human perfection edges forward only in political rhetoric. It is no surprise that utopia now seems more unobtainable than ever. The ecologists, now in their ascendancy, foretell of grim alternatives: we must either radically change the way we live or suffer the effects of planetwide environmental catastrophe. A dark irony, then, confronts us: science and its new prophets entreat us to do the impossible, to embrace the "unreal." The realities of a rapidly expanding population, industrial abuses, and a dying earth must give way to the fictions of the utopian life. If man is to ensure his future, we need a primer of instructive utopias.

No brief anthology could claim to be so comprehensive, since the necessary changes are too numerous and complex. There are a few aspects of this gigantic topic, however, that this short book can present. By bringing together selected utopias, utopian essays, and miscellaneous statements that form the background of utopian ideas, this anthology allows us to see that designing the ideal world for man requires a special kind of attention. In exploring these created worlds, we are forced to come to terms with our most basic assumptions about the nature of man and how he ought to live with other men. This requires an investigation of the fundamental aspects of human life, which in turn will lead us to reexamine ourselves and our society.

Suppose we contend that men are basically good and just and should therefore be able to rule themselves without external laws. This utopia of benevolent anarchists would certainly be freer than any society that ever existed. But would daily life be stimulating and interesting? If there were no marks of distinction between the goodness of one man and another, what would happen to individuality? Would each man reach his fullest, unique potential when free of the restraints of society, or would the urge for personal achievement die of disuse? When everyone follows his own inclination, and this inclination is good and just, we might perhaps find ourselves bored with voluntary goodness. Like some versions of heaven, our utopia could be a dull and stagnant place. We must be ready, then, to trace our beliefs to their logical outcome if we are to engage in utopian thinking. This is a highly philosophical approach to deciding how we should live, and it is not surprising that many utopian writers are philosophers: the list includes Plato, St. Augustine, More, Bacon, Campanella, Diderot, Rousseau, and Saint-Simon.

The purpose of this anthology, then, is to stimulate inquiry into some of the basic questions of human life that must be solved before we decide how man should live. To realize this goal, we should understand the primary philosophical conceptions that have informed ideal societies in the past. We should know the myth of the Golden Age, the Hebrew prophesies of the Promised Land, the radical altruism of Christ's earthly kingdom, as well as the attitudes toward love and freedom upon which idyllic visions of perfected relationships are based. All these ideas are major themes in utopian literature. Thus, Part C of this anthology includes extracts from writers who present these ideas, whether it be in the form of a sonnet, a sermon, or a political pamphlet. Each of these extracts has a number of connections with the three envisioned utopian communities presented in the anthology—Tommaso Campanella's *The City of the Sun*, Denis Diderot's *Supplement to Bougainville's "Voyage"*, and William Morris' *News from Nowhere*.

In selecting these particular utopias, a number of criteria have been used. First, these three works represent some of the major trends in utopian thought. Campanella's *The City of the Sun* demonstrates the planning mentality of utopian thinkers: every feature of life is commented upon, even the selection of genetically compatible mates. The *City* reflects the idea of society as a well-organized machine and has much in common with Plato's *Republic*, Bacon's *New Atlantis*, and More's *Utopia*. Also, the extensiveness of the controls in this society may impart to it an antiutopian cast. Much like Salomon's House in *New Atlantis*, the *City* divides life into corresponding mental and physical faculties, but Campanella's work is more elaborate, more complex, and more easily accessible than Bacon's. Further, it has a Baconian faith in progress, consistent with seventeenth-century optimism in the advancement of learning, but Campanella never forgets real human relations, and he deals at length with the problems of love and daily living.

Supplement to Bougainville's "Voyage" represents the other side of the tradition. Diderot's Tahiti is an open society, viewed as a huge family, impelled and guided by the power of love. All values lie in human beings themselves, who actually constitute the wealth of the society. These people are Rousseauian noble savages, whose wise innocence is informed by the experience of human life. They see progress and civilization as evils, and the French voyagers who invade the island represent the disease of culture. The view of utopia as a South

Sea island retreat is based not upon escape, but upon a confident rejection of civilization.

Morris' *News from Nowhere* offers a compromise, since his communal society is at once primitive and cultivated. In Campanella's world, work is an endurable requirement for everyone. In Tahiti, no one works in the normal sense but simply indulges in the pleasures of love and friendship. Morris, who resolves the contradictions between work and pleasure described later by Freud in *Civilization and Its Discontents*, makes work a pleasure by transforming most of it into art or craft. Thus, an aesthetic ideal converts society into a community of altruistic laborers.

Diderot's *Supplement* is brief enough to be reprinted here in its entirety. *The City of the Sun* and *News from Nowhere* lose little of their impact in their slightly abridged form. By presenting several complete or almost complete utopias rather than numerous short extracts, it is possible to study them as literary works and to examine the features that define the utopia as a literary genre: the dream of or voyage to the new world, the naive protagonist, the first greeting, the use of dialogue, and the dislocation that results from comparing the utopian world with the protagonist's own. This technique of comparison creates tensions that invite satire, an important feature of utopian writing.

With essentially complete texts, it is also possible to examine the language and structure of these works. While *The City of the Sun* lacks the structural complexity of More's *Utopia,* it is organized to reflect the hierarchy of importance in the society, everything taken up in its due time and place. The extensive range of topics is in itself a persuasive technique. Essentially, Campanella's work attempts to sway us to accept order, reason, and variety as ways of life by engaging us with its own order, good sense, clarity, and comprehensiveness.

Diderot's utopia is perhaps the most subtle rhetorically. The Tahitian episodes are framed by a discussion between two civilized Frenchmen, who often chat about topics that seem unrelated to the story. We must examine the connection between the "frame" and the story it surrounds, for Diderot is a master of irony that cuts in a number of directions. The work is composed of a series of dialogues or debates that invite rhetorical analysis.

Morris' work most closely resembles the novel in form. The question as to why utopian thinkers often prefer fiction as the framework for their social scheme, rather than the essay or formal treatise, becomes clear in *News from Nowhere*. The feasibility of a utopia is always in question without a sample of its daily life. The imagination rather than the logic of the utopian writer is therefore the key to our acceptance of his social plan, since so much of our interest is in the flavor or "feel" of the world we are asked to evaluate.

The essays chosen for Part B offer arguments supporting and denying the possibility of creating a utopia and may be used to comment upon the full-scale works in Part A. Kant's essay "Idea for a Universal History" suggests that utopia is inevitable, since the workings of certain cosmic laws ensure it. His essay is written in a systematic form of statement and proof, which serves as a model of argumentative clarity. Emerson's essay "War" examines two kinds of heroism: one martial, one pacific. He tries to persuade us to accept a different definition of masculinity as a first step to world harmony. The essay has an obvious relevance to the contemporary issues of war and passive resistance. Thoreau's essay "Life Without Principle" is a companion to *Walden,* but unfortunately less well-known. Thoreau's concept of self-reliance almost defies classification as a social theory, but his position is simultaneously utopian and antiutopian. Finally, Robert Heilbroner's review of a recent book by Paul and Anne Erlich, *Population, Resources, Environment,* offers a frantic hope for a utopian future: the crises in our environment will eventually burden world society with an unavoidable choice—massive changes in our attitudes toward profit and progress or destruction of the earth as an inhabitable planet. This contemporary hell vision of ecological disaster portends the most ironic end to the tradition of faith in science as a means of world salvation.

From the study and discussion of these works, which comprise only a portion of the history of utopian thought, each student should be closer to solving, at least for himself, the problem of how man should conduct his life.

PART *A*

THREE

UTOPIAS

TOMMASO CAMPANELLA (1568–1639) was born in the town of Stilo, in Calabria, Italy. At the age of fourteen he entered the Dominican order. His intellect soon landed him in prison, as his studies of natural science, astrology, and the occult, coupled with his inquiring mind, made him liable to the charge of collaboration with the Devil. But the major source of the almost relentless official harassment of Campanella was his sustained and scholarly disputes with established authority, both religious and civil. His beliefs led him to support the overthrow of Spanish rule in Italy, and he later worked to reform Catholicism so that it could incorporate all religions in a universal faith. He was often charged with heresy and conspiracy. His inquisitors tortured him to make him confess his loss of faith, but they were unsuccessful. Though Campanella was a defender and disciple of Bernardino Telesio's school of experimental philosophy, which sought truth and knowledge through sense experience rather than through following established principles, he never attacked the primacy of God, even in his bouts with authority.

The City of the Sun (1623), first published in Latin in Frankfort, is Campanella's only well-known work, though it is only one of a hundred works he wrote. The city, a model of social planning on a massive scale, suggests the work of a scientific mind dedicated to structure and utility. On the surface we see a hierarchical city-state, fashioned according to numbers, quantities, and symmetrical significances. The city itself is a well-designed, living machine that serves as school, fortress, activity organizer, and religious altar. Like Plato's philosopher-king, Campanella's learned metaphysician reigns by wisdom and not by political force. He shares his responsibility with three lieutenants: Pon (Power), who is defense chief; Sin (Sapience), who leads the practice of the arts and sciences; and Mor (Love), who conducts what we would now call an office of husbandry, genetics, and home economics. Through progressive screening of talents, the magistrates assign each citizen a task suited to his ability; he is then free to seek his own level on a hierarchy of merit. Though class-free and communal, the city recognizes and rewards differences in human worth.

The city is filled with imaginative practical features, such as educational murals, but Campanella suggests that a society geared primarily for efficiency may be detrimental to the happiness of the

7

individual. The Grandmaster rightfully balks at the matching of couples for selective breeding. It is not clear whether this idea is the serious notion of a celibate and inexperienced friar or the invention of a skillful satirist who exposes the dangers of an idea by pushing it to logical extremes. Our personal estimate of the city, however, should be influenced less by the value of its individual features than by the view of human nature at its heart. Campanella sees human life as competing, producing, and progressing toward perfection in obedience to laws ordained by what he believes to be the natural order of the universe. From this point of view, the city is a microcosm of the earth in its ideal form. Its name suggests this as well. Our own definitions of human nature will determine whether we judge the city as utopian or antiutopian.

Reprinted here is the slightly abridged translation by T. W. Halliday.

THE CITY OF THE SUN

A POETICAL DIALOGUE BETWEEN A GRANDMASTER OF THE KNIGHTS HOSPITALLERS AND A GENOESE SEA-CAPTAIN, HIS GUEST.

GRANDMASTER: Prithee, now, tell me what happened to you during that voyage?

CAPTAIN: I have already told you how I wandered over the whole earth. In the course of my journeying I came to Taprobane, and was compelled to go ashore at a place, where through fear of the inhabitants I remained in a wood. When I stepped out of this I found myself on a large plain immediately under the equator.

GRANDMASTER: And what befell you here?

CAPTAIN: I came upon a large crowd of men and armed women, many of whom did not understand our language, and they conducted me forthwith to the City of the Sun.

GRANDMASTER: Tell me after what plan this city is built and how it is governed?

CAPTAIN: The greater part of the city is built upon a high hill, which rises from an extensive plain, but several of its circles extend for some distance beyond the base of the hill, which is of such size that the diameter of the city is upwards of two miles, so that its circumference becomes about seven. On account of the humped shape of the mountain, however, the diameter of the city is really more than if it were built on a plain.

It is divided into seven rings or huge circles named from the seven planets, and the way from one to the other of these is by four streets and through four gates, that look towards the four points of the compass. Furthermore, it is so built that if the first circle were stormed, it would of necessity entail a double amount of energy to storm the second; still more to storm the third; and in each succeeding case the strength and energy would have to be doubled; so that he who wishes to capture that city must, as it were, storm it seven times. For my own part, however, I think that not even the first wall could be occupied, so thick are the earthworks and so well fortified is it with breastworks, towers, guns and ditches.

When I had been taken through the northern gate (which is shut with an iron door so wrought that it can be raised and let down, and locked in easily and strongly, its projections running into the grooves of the thick posts by a marvellous device), I saw a level space seventy paces wide between the first and second walls. From hence can be seen large palaces all joined to the wall of the second circuit, in such a manner as to appear all one palace. Arches run on a level with the middle height of the palaces, and are continued around the whole ring. There are galleries for promenading upon these arches, which are supported from beneath by thick and well-shaped columns, enclosing arcades like peristyles, or cloisters of an abbey.

But the palaces have no entrances from below, except on the inner or concave partition, from which one enters directly to the lower parts of the building. The higher parts, however, are reached by flights of marble steps, which lead to galleries for promenading on the inside similar to those on the outside. From these one enters the higher rooms, which are very beautiful, and have windows on the concave and convex partitions. These rooms are divided from one another by richly decorated walls. The convex or outer wall of the ring is about eight spans thick; the concave, three; the intermediate walls are one, or perhaps one and a half. Leaving this circle one gets to the second plain, which is nearly three paces narrower than the first. Then the first wall of the second ring is seen adorned above and below with similar galleries for walking, and there is on the inside of it another interior wall enclosing palaces. It has also similar peristyles supported by columns in the lower part, but above are excellent pictures, round the ways into the upper houses. And so on afterwards through similar spaces and double walls, enclosing palaces, and adorned with galleries for walking, extending along their outer side, and supported by columns, till the last circuit is reached, the way being still over a level plain.

But when the two gates, that is to say, those of the outmost and the inmost walls, have been passed, one mounts by means of steps so formed that an ascent is scarcely discernible, since it proceeds in a slanting direction, and the steps succeed one another at almost imperceptible heights. On the top of the hill is a rather spacious plain, and in the midst of this there rises a temple built with wondrous art.

GRANDMASTER: Tell on, I pray you! Tell on! I am dying to hear more.

CAPTAIN: The temple is built in the form of a circle; it is not girt with walls, but stands upon thick columns, beautifully grouped. A very large dome, built with great care in the centre or pole, contains another small vault as it were rising out of it, and in this is a spiracle, which is right over the altar. There is but one altar in the middle of the temple, and this is hedged round by columns. The temple itself is on a space of more than three hundred and fifty paces. Without it, arches measuring about eight paces extend from the heads of these columns outwards, whence other columns rise about three paces from the thick, strong and erect wall. Between these and the former columns there are galleries for walking, with beautiful pavements, and in the recess of the wall, which is adorned with numerous large doors, there are immovable seats, placed as it were between the inside columns, supporting the temple. Portable chairs are not wanting, many and well adorned. Nothing is seen over the altar but a large globe, upon which the heavenly bodies are painted, and another globe upon which there is a representation of the earth. Furthermore, in the vault of the dome there can be discerned representations of all the stars of heaven from the first to the sixth magnitude, with their proper names and power to influence terrestrial things marked in three little verses for each. There are the poles and greater and lesser circles according to the right latitude of the place, but these are not perfect because there is no wall below. They seem, too, to be made in their relation to the globes on the altar. The pavement of the temple is bright with precious stones. Its seven golden lamps hang always burning, and these bear the names of the seven planets.

At the top of the building several small and beautiful cells surround the small dome, and behind the level space above the bands or arches of the exterior and interior columns there are many cells, both small and large, where the priests and religious officers dwell to the number of forty-nine.

A revolving flag projects from the smaller dome, and this shows in what quarter the wind is. The flag is marked with figures up to thirty-six, and the priests know what sort of year the different kinds of winds bring and what will be the changes of weather on land and sea. Furthermore, under the flag a book is always kept written with letters of gold.

GRANDMASTER: I pray you, worthy hero, explain to me their whole system of government; for I am anxious to hear it.

CAPTAIN: The great rule among them is a priest whom they call by the name HOH, though we should call him Metaphysic. He is head over all, in temporal and spiritual matters, and all business and lawsuits are settled by him, as the supreme authority. Three princes of equal power—viz., Pon, Sin and Mor—assist him, and these in our tongue we should call POWER, WISDOM and LOVE. To POWER belongs the care of all matters relating to war and peace. He attends to the military arts, and, next to HOH, he is ruler in every affair of a warlike nature. He governs the military magistrates and the soldiers, and has the management of the munitions, the fortifications, the storming of places, the implements of war, the armories, the smiths and workmen connected with matters of this sort.

But WISDOM is the ruler of the liberal arts, of mechanics, of all sciences with their magistrates and doctors, and of the discipline of the schools. As many doctors as there are, are under his control. There is one doctor who is called Astrologus; a second, Cosmographus; a third, Arithmeticus; a fourth, Geometra; a fifth, Historiographus; a sixth, Poeta; a seventh, Logicus; an eighth, Rhetor; a ninth, Grammaticus; a tenth, Medicus; an eleventh, Physiologus; a twelfth, Politicus; a thirteenth, Moralis. They have but one book, which they call Wisdom, and in it all the sciences are written with conciseness and marvellous fluency of expression. This they read to the people after the custom of the Pythagoreans. It is Wisdom who causes the exterior and interior, the higher and lower walls of the city to be adorned with the finest pictures, and to have all the sciences painted upon them in an admirable manner. On the walls of the temple and on the dome, which is let down when the priest gives an address, lest the sounds of his voice, being scattered, should fly away from his audience, there are pictures of stars in their different magnitudes, with the powers and motions of each, expressed separately in three little verses.

On the interior wall of the first circuit all the mathematical figures are conspicuously painted—figures more in number than Archimedes or Euclid discovered, marked symmetrically, and with the explanation of them neatly written and contained each in a little verse. There are definitions and propositions, etc. On the exterior convex wall is first an immense drawing of the whole earth, given at one view. Following upon this, there are tablets setting forth for every separate country the customs both public and private, the laws, the origins and the power of the inhabitants; and the alphabets the different people use can be seen above that of the City of the Sun.

On the inside of the second circuit, that is to say of the second ring of buildings, paintings of all kinds of precious and common stones, of minerals and metals, are seen; and a little piece of the metal itself is also there with an apposite explanation in two small verses for each metal or stone. On the outside are marked all the seas, rivers, lakes and streams which are on the face of the earth; as are also the wines and the oils and the different liquids, with the sources from which the last are extracted, their qualities and strength. There are also vessels built into the wall above the arches, and these are full of liquids from one to three hundred years old, which cure all diseases. Hail and snow, storms and thunder, and whatever else takes place in the air, are represented with suitable figures and little verses. The inhabitants even have the art of representing in stone all the phenomena of the air, such as the wind, rain, thunder, the rainbow, etc.

On the interior of the third circuit all the different families of trees and herbs are depicted, and there is a live specimen of each plant in earthenware vessels placed under the outer partition of the arches. With the specimens there are explanations as to where they were first found, what are their powers and natures, and resemblances to celestial things and to metals: to parts of the human body and to things in the sea, and also as to their uses in medicine, etc. On the exterior wall are all the races of fish, found in rivers, lakes and seas, and their habits and values, and ways of breeding, training and living, the purposes for which they exist in the world, and their uses to man. Further, their resemblances to celestial and terrestrial things, produced both by nature and art, are so given that I was astonished when I saw a fish which was like a bishop, one like a chain, another like a garment, a fourth like a nail, a fifth like a star, and others like images of those things existing among us, the relation in each case being completely manifest. There are sea-urchins to be seen, and the purple shell-fish and mussels; and whatever the watery world possesses worthy of being known is there fully shown in marvellous characters of painting and drawing.

On the fourth interior wall all the different kinds of birds are painted, with their natures, sizes, customs, colors, manner of living, etc.; and the only real phoenix is possessed by the inhabitants of this city. On the exterior are shown all the races of creeping animals, serpents, dragons and worms; the insects, the flies, gnats, beetles, etc., in their different states, strength, venoms and uses and a great deal more than you or I can think of.

On the fifth interior they have all the larger animals of the earth, as many in number as would astonish you. We indeed know not the thousandth part of them, for on the exterior wall also a great many of immense size are also portrayed. To be sure, of horses alone, how great a number of breeds there is and how beautiful are the forms there cleverly displayed!

On the sixth interior are painted all the mechanical arts, with the several instruments for each and their manner of use among different nations. Alongside the dignity of such is placed, and their several inventors are named. But on the exterior all the inventors in science, in warfare, and in law are represented. There I saw Moses, Osiris, Jupiter, Mercury, Lycurgus, Pompilius, Pythagoras, Zamolxis, Solon, Charondas, Phoroneus, with very many others. They even have Mahomet whom nevertheless they hate as a false and sordid legislator. In the most dignified position I saw a representation of Jesus Christ and of the twelve apostles, whom they consider very worthy and hold to be great. Of the representations of men, I perceived Caesar, Alexander, Pyrrhus and Hannibal in the highest place; and other very renowned heroes in peace and war, especially Roman heroes, were painted in lower positions, under the galleries. And when I asked with astonishment whence they had obtained our history, they told me that among them there was a knowledge of all languages, and that by perseverance they continually send explorers and ambassadors over the whole earth, who learn thoroughly the customs, forces, rule and histories of the nations, bad and good alike. These they apply all to their own republic, and with this they are well pleased. I learnt that canon and typography were invented by the Chinese before we knew of them. There are magistrates, who announce the meaning of the pictures, and boys are accustomed to learn all the sciences, without toil and as if for pleasure; but in the way of history only until they are ten years old.

LOVE is foremost in attending to the charge of the race. He sees that men and women are so joined together, that they bring forth the best offspring. Indeed, they laugh at us who exhibit a studious care for our breed of horses and dogs, but neglect the breeding of human beings. Thus the education of the children is under his rule. So also is the medicine that is sold, the sowing and collecting of fruits of the earth and of trees, agriculture, pasturage, the preparations for the months, the cooking arrangements, and whatever has any reference to food, clothing, and the intercourse of the sexes.

Love himself is ruler, but there are many male and female magistrates dedicated to these arts.

Metaphysic then with these three rulers manage all the above-named matters, and even by himself alone nothing is done; all business is discharged by the four together, but in whatever Metaphysic inclines to the rest are sure to agree.

GRANDMASTER: Tell me, please, of the magistrates, their services and duties, of the education and mode of living, whether the government is a monarchy, a republic, or an aristocracy.

CAPTAIN: This race of men came there from India, flying from the sword of the Magi, a race of plunderers and tyrants who laid waste their country, and they determined to lead a philosophic life in fellowship with one another. Although the community of wives is not instituted among the other inhabitants of their province, among them it is in use after this manner. All things are common with them, and their dispensation is by the authority of the magistrates. Arts and honors and pleasures are common, and are held in such a manner that no one can appropriate anything to himself.

They say that all private property is acquired and improved for the reason that each one of us by himself has his own home and wife and children. From this self-love springs. For when we raise a son to riches and dignities, and leave an heir to much wealth, we become either ready to grasp at the property of the state, if in any case fear should be removed for the power which belongs to riches and rank; or avaricious, crafty, and hypocritical, if any one is of slender purse, little strength, and mean ancestry. But when we have taken away self-love, there remains only love for the state.

GRANDMASTER: Under such circumstances no one will be willing to labor, while he expects others to work, on the fruit of whose labors he can live, as Aristotle argues against Plato.

CAPTAIN: I do not know how to deal with that argument, but I declare to you that they burn with so great a love for their fatherland, as I could scarcely have believed possible; and indeed with much more than the histories tell us belonged to the Romans, who fell willingly for their country, inasmuch as they have to a greater extent surrendered their private property. I think truly that the friars and monks and clergy of our country, if they were not weakened by love for their kindred and friends, or by the ambition to rise to higher dignities, would be less fond of property, and more imbued with a spirit of charity towards all, as it was in the time of the Apostles, and is now in a great many cases.

GRANDMASTER: St. Augustine may say that, but I say that among this race of men, friendship is worth nothing; since they have not the chance of conferring mutual benefits on one another.

CAPTAIN: Nay, indeed. For it is worth the trouble to see that no one can receive gifts from another. Whatever is necessary they have, they receive it from the community, and the magistrate takes care that no one receives more than he deserves. Yet nothing necessary is denied to any one. Friendship is recognized among them in war, in infirmity, in the art contests, by which means they aid one another mutually by teaching. Sometimes they improve themselves mutually with praises, with conversation, with actions and out of the things they need. All those of the same age call one another brothers. They call over twenty-two years of age, fathers; those who are less than twenty-two are named sons. Moreover, the magistrates govern well, so that no one in the fraternity can do injury to another.

GRANDMASTER: And how?

CAPTAIN: As many names of virtues as there are amongst us, so many magistrates there are among them. There is a magistrate who is named Magnanimity, another Fortitude, a third Chastity, a fourth Liberality, a fifth Criminal and Civil Justice, a sixth Comfort, a seventh Truth, an eighth Kindness, a tenth Gratitude, an eleventh Cheerfulness, a twelfth Exercise, a thirteenth Sobriety, etc. They are elected to duties of that kind, each one to that duty for excellence in which he is known from boyhood to be most suitable. Wherefore among them neither robbery nor clever murders, nor lewdness, incest, adultery, or other crimes of which we accuse one another, can be found. They accuse themselves of ingratitude and malignity when any one denies a lawful satisfaction to another, of indolence, of sadness, of anger, of scurrility, of slander, and of lying, which curseful thing they thoroughly hate. Accused persons undergoing punishment are deprived of the common table, and other honors, until the judge thinks they agree with their correction.

GRANDMASTER: Tell me the manner in which the magistrates are chosen.

CAPTAIN: You would not rightly understand this, unless you first learnt their manner of living. That you may know then, men and women wear the same kind of garment, suited for war. The women wear the toga below the knee, but the men above. And both sexes are instructed in all the arts together. When this has been done as a start, and before their third year, the boys learn the language and the alphabet on the walls by walking round them. They have four leaders, and four elders, the first to direct them, the second to teach them, and these are men approved beyond all others. After some time they exercise themselves with gymnastics, running, quoits, and other games, by means of which all their muscles are strengthened alike. Their feet are always bare, and so are their heads as far

NO PRIVATE PROPERTY

as the seventh ring. Afterwards they lead them to the offices of the trades, such as shoemaking, cooking, metalworking, carpentry, painting, etc. In order to find out the bent of the genius of each one, after their seventh year, when they have already gone through the mathematics on the walls, they take them to the readings of all the sciences; there are four lectures at each reading, and in the course of four hours the four in their order explain everything.

For some take physical exercise or busy themselves with public services or functions, others apply themselves to reading. Leaving these studies all are devoted to the more abstruse subjects, to mathematics, to medicine, and to other sciences. There is continual debate and studied argument amongst them, and after a time they become magistrates of those sciences or mechanical arts in which they are the most proficient; for every one follows the opinion of his leader and judge, and goes out to the plains to the works of the field, and for the purpose of becoming acquainted with the pasturage of dumb animals. And they consider him the more noble and renowned who has dedicated himself to the study of the most arts and knows how to practise them wisely. Wherefore they laugh at us in that we consider our workmen ignoble, and hold those to be noble who have mastered no pursuit; but live in ease, and are so many slaves given over to their own pleasure and lasciviousness; and thus as it were from a school of vices so many idle and wicked fellows go forth for the ruin of the state.

The rest of the officials, however, are chosen by the four chiefs, Hoh, Pon, Sin and Mor, and by the teachers of that art over which they are fit to preside. And these teachers know well who is most suited for rule. Certain men are proposed by the magistrates in council, they themselves not seeking to become candidates, and he opposes who knows anything against those brought forward for election, or if not, speaks in favor of them. But no one attains to the dignity of Hoh except him who knows the histories of the nations, and their customs and sacrifices and laws, and their form of government, whether a republic or a monarchy. He must also know the names of the lawgivers and the inventors in science, and the laws and the history of the earth and the heavenly bodies. They think it also necessary that he should understand all the mechanical arts, the physical sciences, astrology and mathematics. (Nearly every two days they teach our mechanical art. They are not allowed to overwork themselves, but frequent practice and the paintings render learning easy to them. Not too much care is given to the cultivation of languages, as they have a goodly number of interpreters who are grammarians in the state.) But beyond everything else it is necessary that Hoh should understand metaphysics and theology; that he should know thoroughly the derivations, foundations and demonstrations of all the arts and sciences; the likeness and difference of things; necessity, fate, and the harmonies of the universe; power, wisdom, and the love of things and of God; the stages of life and its symbols; everything relating to the heavens, the earth and the sea; and the ideas of God, as much as mortal man can know of Him. He must also be well read in the Prophets and in astrology. And thus they know long beforehand who will be Hoh. He is not chosen to so great a dignity unless he has attained his thirty-fifth year. And this office is perpetual, because it is not known who may be too wise for it or who too skilled in ruling.

GRANDMASTER: Who indeed can be so wise? If even any one has a knowledge of the sciences it seems that he must be unskilled in ruling.

CAPTAIN: This very question I asked them and they replied thus: "We, indeed, are more certain that such a very learned man has the knowledge of governing, than you who place ignorant persons in authority, and consider them suitable merely because they have sprung from rulers or have been chosen by a powerful faction. But our Hoh, a man really the most capable to rule, is for all that never cruel nor wicked, nor a tyrant, inasmuch as he possesses so much wisdom. This, moreover, is not unknown to you, that the same argument cannot apply among you, when you consider that man the most learned who knows most of grammar, or logic, or of Aristotle or any other author. For such knowledge as this of yours much servile labor and memory work is required, so that a man is rendered unskilful; since he has contemplated nothing but the words of books and has given his mind with useless result to the consideration of the dead signs of things. Hence he knows not in what way God rules the universe, nor the ways and customs of Nature and the nations. Wherefore he is not equal to our HOH. For that one cannot know so many arts and sciences thoroughly, who is not esteemed for skilled ingenuity, very apt at all things, and therefore at ruling especially. This also is plain to us that he who knows only science, does not really know either that or the others, and he who is suited for only one science and has gathered his knowledge from books, is unlearned and unskilled. But this is not the case with intellects prompt and expert in every branch of knowledge and suitable for the consideration of natural objects, as it is necessary that our HOH should be. Besides in our state the sciences are taught with a facility (as you have seen) by which more scholars are turned out by us in one year than by you in ten, or even fifteen. Make trial, I pray you of these boys." In this manner I was struck with astonishment at their truth-ful discourse and at the trial of their boys, who did not understand my language well. Indeed it is necessary that three of them should be skilled in our tongue, three in Arabic, three in Polish, and three in each of the other languages, and no recreation is allowed them unless they become more learned. For that they go out to the plain for the sake of running about and hurling arrows and lances, and of firing harquebuses, and for the sake of hunting the wild animals and getting a knowledge of plants and stones, and agriculture and pasturage; sometimes the band of boys does one thing, sometimes another.

They do not consider it necessary that the three rulers assisting HOH should know other than the arts having reference to their rule, and so they have only a historical knowledge of the arts which are common to all. But their own they know well, to which certainly one is dedicated more than another. Thus POWER is the most learned in the equestrian art, in marshalling the army, in marking out of camps, in the manufacture of every kind of weapon and of warlike machines, in planning stratagems, and in every affair of a military nature. And for these reasons, they consider it necessary that these chiefs should have been philosophers, historians, politi-cians, and physicists. Concerning the other two triumvirs, under-stand remarks similar to those I have made about POWER.

GRANDMASTER: I really wish that you would recount all their public duties, and would distinguish between them, and also that you would tell clearly how they are all taught in common.

CAPTAIN: They have dwellings in common and dormitories, and couches and other necessaries. But at the end of every six months they are separated by the masters. Some shall sleep in this ring, some in another; some in the first apartment, and some in the second; and these apartments are marked by means of the alphabet on the lintel. There are occupations, mechanical and theoretical, common to both men and women, with this difference, that the occupations which require more hard work, and walking a long distance, are practised by men, such as plowing, sowing, gathering the fruits, working at the threshing-floor, and perchance at the vintage. But it is customery to choose women for milking the cows, and for making cheese. In like manner, they go to the gardens near to the outskirts of the city both for collecting the plants and for cultivating them. In fact, all sedentary and stationary pursuits are practised by the women, such as weaving, spinning, sewing, cutting the hair, shaving, dispensing medicines, and making all kinds of garments. They are, however, excluded from working in wood and the manufacture of arms. If a woman is fit to paint, she is not prevented from doing so; nevertheless, music is given over to the women alone, because they please the more, and of a truth to boys also. But the women have not the practice of the drum and the horn.

And they prepare their feasts and arrange the tables in the following manner. It is the peculiar work of the boys and girls under twenty to wait at the tables. In every ring there are the suitable kitchens, barns, and stores of utensils for eating and drinking, and over every department an old man and an old woman preside. These two have at once the command of those who serve, and the power of chastising, or causing to be chastised, those who are negligent or disobedient; and they also examine and mark each one, both male and female, who excels in his or her duties.

All the young people wait upon the older ones who have passed the age of forty, and in the evening when they go to sleep the master and mistress command that those should be sent to work in the morning, upon whom in succession the duty falls, one or two to separate apartments. The young people, however, wait upon one another, and that alas! with some unwillingness. They have first and second tables, and on both sides there are seats. On one side sit the women, on the other the men; and as in the refectories of the monks, there is no noise. While they are eating, a young man reads a book from a platform, intoning distinctly and sonorously, and often the magistrates question them upon the more important parts of the reading. And truly it is pleasant to observe in what manner these young people, so beautiful and clothed in garments so suitable, attend to them, and to see at the same time so many friends, brothers, sons, fathers and mothers in all their turn living together with so much honesty, propriety and love. So each one is given a napkin, a plate, fish, and a dish of food. It is the duty of the medical officers to tell the cooks what repasts shall be prepared on each day, and what food for the old, what for the young, and what for the sick. The magistrates receive the full-grown and fatter portion, and they from their share always distribute something to the boys at the table who have shown themselves more studious in the morning at the lectures and debates concerning wisdom and arms. And this is held to be one of the most distinguished honors. For six days they ordain to sing with music at table. Only a few, however, sing; or there is one voice accompanying the lute and one for each other instrument. And when all alike in service join their hands, nothing is found to be wanting. The old men placed at the head of the cooking business and of the refectories of the servants praise the cleanliness of the streets, the houses, the vessels, the garments, the workshops and the warehouses.

They wear white undergarments to which adheres a covering, which is at once coat and legging, without wrinkles. The borders of the fastenings are furnished with globular buttons, extended round and caught up here and there by chains. The coverings of the legs descend to the shoes and are continued even to the heels. Then they cover their feet with large socks, or as it were half-buskins fastened by buckles, over which they wear a half-boot, and besides, as I have already said, they are clothed with a toga. And so aptly fitting are the garments, that when the toga is destroyed, the different parts of the whole body are straightway discerned, no part being concealed. They change their clothes for different ones four times in the year, that is when the sun enters respectively the constellations Aries, Cancer, Libra and Capricorn, and according to the circumstances and necessity as decided by the officer of health. The keepers of clothes for the different rings are wont to distribute them, and it is marvellous that they have at the same time as many garments as there is need for, some heavy and some slight, according to the weather. They all use white clothing, and this is washed in each month with lye or soap, as are also the workshops of the lower trades, the kitchens, the pantries, the barns, the store-houses, the armories, the refectories and the baths. Moreover, the clothes are washed at the pillars of the peristyles, and the water is brought down by means of canals which are continued as sewers. In every street of the different rings there are suitable fountains, which send forth their water by means of canals, the water being drawn up from nearly the bottom of the mountain by the sole movement of a cleverly contrived handle. There is water in fountains and in cisterns, whither the rain-water collected from the roofs of the houses is brought through pipes full of sand. They wash their bodies often, according as the doctor and master command. All the mechanical arts are practised under the peristyles, but the speculative are carried on above in the walking galleries and ramparts where are the more splendid paintings, but the more sacred ones are taught in the temple. In the halls and wings of the rings there are solar timepieces and bells, and hands by which the hours and seasons are marked off.

GRANDMASTER: Tell me about their children.

CAPTAIN: When their women have brought forth children, they suckle them and rear them in temples set apart for all. They give milk for two years or more as the physician orders. After that time the weaned child is given into the charge of the mistresses, if it is a female, and to the masters, if it is a male. And then with other young children they are pleasantly instructed in the alphabet, and in the knowledge of the pictures, and in running, walking and wrestling; also in the historical drawings, and in languages; and they are adorned with a suitable garment of different colors. After their sixth year they are taught natural science, and then the mechanical sciences. The men who are weak in intellect are sent to farms, and when they have become more proficient some of them are received into the state. And those of the same age and born under the same constellation are especially like one another in strength and in appearance, and hence arises much lasting concord in the state, these men honoring one another with mutual love and help. Names are given to them by Metaphysicus, and that not by chance but designedly, and according to each one's peculiarity, as was the custom among the ancient Romans. Wherefore one is called Beautiful (Pulcher), another the Big-nosed (Naso), another Crooked (Torvus), another Lean (Macer), and so on. But when they have become very skilled in their professions and done any great deed in war or in time of peace, a cognomen from art is given to them, such as Beautiful, the great painter (Pulcher, Pictor Magnus), the golden one (Aureus), the excellent one (Excellens), or the strong (Strenuus); or from their deeds, such as Naso the Brave (Nason Fortis), or the cunning, or the great, or very great conqueror; or from the enemy any one has overcome, Africanus, Asiaticus, Etruscus; or if any one has overcome Manfred or Tortelius, he is called Macer Manfred or Tortelius, and so on. All these cognomens are added by the higher magistrates, and very often with a crown suitable to the deed or art, and with the flourish of music. For gold and silver is reckoned of little value among them except as material for their vessels and ornaments, which are common to all.

GRANDMASTER: Tell me, I pray you, is there no jealousy among them or disappointment to that one who has not been elected to a magistracy, or to any other dignity to which he aspires?

CAPTAIN: Certainly not. For no one wants either necessaries or luxuries. Moreover, the race is managed for the good of the commonwealth and not of private individuals, and the magistrates must be obeyed. They deny what we hold—viz., that it is natural to man to recognize his offspring and to educate them, and to use his wife and house and children as his own. For they say that children are bred for the preservation of the species and not for individual pleasure, as St. Thomas also asserts. Therefore the breeding of children has reference to the commonwealth and not to individuals, except in so far as they are constituents of the commonwealth. And since individuals for the most part bring forth children wrongly and educate them wrongly, they consider that they remove destruction from the state, and therefore, for this reason, with most sacred fear, they commit the education of the children, who as it were are the element of the republic, to the care of the magistrates; for the safety of the community is not that of a few. And thus they distribute male and female breeders of the best natures according to philosophical rules. Plato thinks that this distribution ought to be made by lot, lest some men seeing that they are kept away from the beautiful women, should rise up with anger and hatred against the magistrates; and he thinks further that those who do not deserve cohabitation with the more beautiful women, should be deceived whilst the lots are being led out of the city by the magistrates, so that at all times the women who are suitable should fall to their lot, not those whom they desire. This shrewdness, however, is not necessary among the inhabitants of the City of the Sun. For with them deformity is unknown. When the women are exercised they get a clear complexion, and become strong of limb, tall and agile, and with them beauty consists of tallness and strength. Therefore, if any woman dyes her face, so that it may become beautiful, or uses high-heeled boots so that she may appear tall, or garments with trains to cover her wooden shoes, she is condemned to capital punishment. But if the women should even desire them, they have no facility for doing these things. For who indeed would give them this facility? Further, they assert that among us abuses of this kind arise from the leisure and sloth of women. By these means they lose their color and have pale complexions, and become feeble and small. For this reason they are without proper complexions, use high sandals, and become beautiful not from strength, but from slothful tenderness. And thus they ruin their own tempers and natures, and consequently those of their offspring. Furthermore, if at any time a man is taken captive with ardent love for a certain woman, the two are allowed to converse and joke together, and to give one another garlands of flowers or leaves, and to make verses. But if the race is endangered, by no means is further union between them permitted. Moreover, the love born of eager desire is not known among them; only that born of friendship.

Domestic affairs and partnerships are of little account, because, excepting the sign of honor, each one receives what he is in need of. To the heroes and heroines of the republic, it is customary to give the pleasing gifts of honor, beautiful wreaths, sweet food or splendid clothes, while they are feasting. In the daytime all use white garments within the city, but at night or outside the city they use red garments either of wool or silk. They hate black as they do dung, and therefore they dislike the Japanese, who are fond of black. Pride they consider the most execrable vice, and one who acts proudly is chastised with the most ruthless correction. Wherefore no one thinks it lowering to wait at table or to work in the kitchen or fields. All work they call discipline, and thus they say that it is honorable to go on foot, to do any act of nature, to see with the eye, and to speak with the tongue; and when there is need, they distinguish philosophically between tears and spittle.

Every man who, when he is told off to work, does his duty, is considered very honorable. It is not the custom to keep slaves. For they are enough, and more than enough, for themselves. But with us, alas! it is not so. In Naples there exists seventy thousand souls, and out of these scarcely ten or fifteen thousand do any work, and they are always lean from overwork and are getting weaker every day. The rest become a prey to idleness, avarice, ill-health, lasciviousness, usury and other vices, and contaminate and corrupt very many families by holding them in servitude for their own use, by keeping them in poverty and slavishness, and by imparting to them their own vices. Therefore public slavery ruins them; useful works, in the field, in military service and in arts, except those which are debasing, are not cultivated, the few who do practise them doing so with much aversion. But in the City of the Sun, while duty and work is distributed among all, it only falls to each one to work for about four hours every day. The remaining hours are spent in learning joyously, in debating, in reading, in reciting, in writing, in walking, in exercising the mind and body, and with play. They allow no game which is played while sitting, neither the single die nor dice, nor chess, nor others like these. But they play with the ball, with the sack, with the hoop, with wrestling, and hurling at the stake. They say, moreover, that grinding poverty renders men worthless, cunning, sulky, thievish, insidious, vagabonds, liars, false witnesses, etc.; and that wealth makes them insolent, proud, ignorant, traitors, assumers of what they know not, deceivers, boasters, wanting in affection, slanderers, etc. But with them all the rich and poor together make up the community. They are rich because they want nothing, poor because they possess nothing; and consequently they are not slaves to circumstances, but circumstances serve them. And on this point they strongly recommend the religion of the Christians, and especially the life of the Apostles.

GRANDMASTER: This seems excellent and sacred, but the community of women is a thing too difficult to attain. The holy Roman Clement says that wives ought to be common in accordance with the apostolic institution, and praises Plato and Socrates, who thus teach, but the Glossary interprets this community with regard to obedience. And Tertullian agrees with the Glossary, that the first Christians had everything in common except wives.

CAPTAIN: These things I know little of. But this I saw among the inhabitants of the City of the Sun that they did not make this exception. And they defend themselves by the opinion of Socrates, of Cato, of Plato, and of St. Clement but, as you say, they misunderstand the opinions of these thinkers. And the inhabitants of the solar city ascribe this to their want of education, since they are by no means learned in philosophy. Nevertheless, they send abroad to discover the customs of nations, and the best of these they always adopt. Practice makes the women suitable for war and other duties. Thus they agree with Plato, in whom I have read these same things. The reasoning of our Cajetan does not convince me, and least of all that of Aristotle. This thing, however, existing among them is excellent and worthy of imitation—viz., that no physical defect renders a man incapable of being serviceable except the decrepitude of old age, since even the deformed are useful for consultation. The lame serve as guards, watching with the eyes which they possess. The blind card wool with their hands, separating the down from the hairs, with which latter they stuff the couches and sofas; those who are without the use of eyes and hands give the use of their ears or their voice for the convenience of the state, and if one has only one sense, he uses it in the farms. And these cripples are well treated, and some become spies, telling the officers of the state what they have heard.

GRANDMASTER: Tell me now, I pray you, of their military affairs. Then you may explain their arts, ways of life and sciences, and lastly their religion.

CAPTAIN: The triumvir, Power, has under him all the magistrates of arms, of artillery, of cavalry, of foot-soldiers, of architects, and of strategists, and the masters and many of the most excellent workmen obey the magistrates, the men of each are paying allegiance to their respective chiefs. Moreover, Power is at the head of all the professors of gymnastics, who teach military exercise, and who are prudent generals, advanced in age. By these the boys are trained after their twelfth year. Before this age, however, they have been accustomed to wrestling, running, throwing the weight and other minor exercises, under inferior masters. But at twelve they are taught how to strike at the enemy, at horses and elephants, to handle the spear, the sword, the arrow and the sling; to manage the horse; to advance and retreat; to remain in order of battle; to help a comrade in arms; to anticipate the enemy by cunning; and to conquer.

The women also are taught these arts under their own magistrates and mistresses, so that they may be able if need be to render assistance to the males in battles near the city. They are taught to watch the fortifications lest at some time a hasty attack should suddenly be made. In this respect they praise the Spartans and Amazons. The women know well also how to let fly fiery balls, and how to make them from lead; how to throw stones from pinnacles and to go in the way of an attack. They are accustomed also to give up wine unmixed altogether, and that one is punished most severely who shows any fear.

The inhabitants of the City of the Sun do not fear death, because they all believe that the soul is immortal, and that when it has left the body it is associated with other spirits, wicked or good, according to the merits of this present life. Although they are partly followers of Bramah and Pythagoras, they do not believe in the transmigration of souls, except in some cases, by a distinct decree of God. They do abstain from injuring an enemy of the republic and of religion, who is unworthy of pity. During the second month the army is reviewed, and every day there is practice of arms, either in the cavalry plain or within the walls. Nor are they ever without lectures of Moses, of Joshua, of David, of Judas Maccabeus, of Caesar, of Alexander, of Scipio, of Hannibal, and other great soldiers should be read. And then each one gives his own opinion as to whether these generals acted well or ill, usefully or honorably, and then the teacher answers and says who are right.

GRANDMASTER: With whom do they wage war, and for what reasons, since they are so prosperous?

CAPTAIN: Wars might never occur, nevertheless they are exercised in military tactics and in hunting, lest perchance they should become effeminate and unprepared for any emergency. Besides there are four kingdoms in the island, which are very envious of their prosperity, for this reason that the people desire to live after the manner of the inhabitants of the City of the Sun, and to be under their rule rather than that of their own kings. Wherefore the state often makes war upon these because, being neighbors, they are usurpers and live impiously, since they have not an object of worship and do not observe the religion of other nations or of the Brahmins. And other nations of India, to which formerly they were subject, rise up as it were in rebellion, as also do the Taprobanese, whom they wanted to join them at first. The warriors of the City of the Sun, however, are always the victors. As soon as they suffered from insult or disgrace or plunder, or when their allies have been harassed, or a people have been oppressed by a tyrant of the state (for they are always the advocates of liberty), they go immediately to the council for deliberation. After they have knelt in the presence of God that He might inspire their consultation, they do proceed to examine the merits of the business, and thus war is decided on. Immediately after a priest, whom they call Forensic, is sent away. He demands from the enemy the restitution of the plunder, asks that the allies should be freed from oppression, or that the tyrant should be deposed. If they deny these things war is declared by invoking the vengeance of God—the God of Sabaoth—for destruction of those who maintain an unjust cause. But if the enemy refuse to reply, the priest gives him the space of one hour for his answer, if he is a king, but three if it is a republic, so that they cannot escape giving a response. And in this manner war is undertaken against the insolent enemies of natural rights and of religion. When war has been declared, the deputy of Power performs everything, but Power, like the Roman dictator, plans and wills everything, so that hurtful tardiness may be avoided. And when anything of great moment arises he consults Hoh and Wisdom and Love.

Before this, however, the occasion of war and the justice of making an expedition is declared by a herald in the great council. All from twenty years and upwards are admitted to this council, and thus the necessaries are agreed upon. All kinds of weapons stand in the armories, and these they use often in sham fights. The exterior walls of each ring are full of guns prepared by their labors, and they have other engines for hurling which are called cannons, and which they take into battle upon mules and asses and carriages. When they have arrived in an open plain they enclose in the middle the provisions, engines of war, chariots, ladders and machines and all fight courageously. Then each one returns to the standards, and the enemy thinking that they are giving and preparing to flee, are deceived and relax their order: then the warriors of the City of the Sun, wheeling into wings and columns on each side, regain their breath and strength, and ordering the artillery to discharge their bullets they resume the fight against a disorganized host. And they observe many ruses of this kind. They overcome all mortals with their stratagems and engines. Their camp is fortified after the manner of the Romans. They pitch their tents and fortify the wall and ditch with wonderful quickness. The masters of works, of engines and hurling machines, stand ready, and the soldiers understand the use of the spade and the axe.

Five, eight, or ten leaders learned in the order of battle and in strategy consult together concerning the business of war, and command their bands after consultation. It is their wont to take out with them a body of boys, armed and on horses, so that they may learn to fight, just as the whelps of lions and wolves are accustomed to blood. And these in time of danger betake themselves to a place of safety, along with many armed women. After the battle the women and boys soothe and relieve the pain of the warriors, and wait upon them and encourage them with embraces and pleasant words. How wonderful a help is this! For the soldiers, in order that they may acquit themselves as sturdy men in the eyes of their wives and offspring, endure hardships, and so love makes them conquerors. He who in the fight first scales the enemy's walls receives after the battle a crown of grass, a token of honor, and at the presentation the women and boys applaud loudly; that one who affords aid to an ally gets a civic crown of oak-leaves; he who kills a tyrant dedicates his arms in the temple and receives from Hoh the cognomen of his deed, and other warriors obtain other kinds of crowns. Every horse-soldier carries a spear and two strongly tempered pistols, narrow at the mouth, hanging from his saddle. And to get the barrels of their pistols narrow they pierce the metal which they intend to convert into arms. Further, every cavalry soldier has a sword and a dagger. But the rest, who form the light-armed troops, carry a metal cudgel. For if the foe cannot pierce their metal for pistols and cannot make swords, they attack him with clubs, shatter and overthrow him. Two chains of six spans length hang from the club, and at the end of these are iron balls, and when these aimed at the enemy they surround his neck and drag him to the ground; and in order that they may be able to use the club more easily, they do not hold the reins with their hands, but use them by means of the feet. If perchance the reins are interchanged above the trappings of the saddle, the ends are fastened to the stirrups with buckles and not to the feet. And the stirrups have an arrangement for swift movement of the bridle, so that they draw in or let out the rein with marvellous celerity. With the right foot they turn the horse to the left and with the left to the right. This secret, moreover, is not known to the Tartars. For, although they govern the reins with their feet, they are ignorant nevertheless of turning them and drawing them in and letting them out by means of the block of the stirrups. The light-armed cavalry with them are the first to engage in battle, then the men forming the phalanx with their spears, then the archers for whose services a great price is paid, and who are accustomed to fight in lines crossing one another as the threads of cloth, some rushing forward in their turn and others receding. They have a band of lancers strengthening the line of battle, but they make trial of the swords only at the end.

After the battle they celebrate the military triumphs after the manner of the Romans, and even in a more magnificent way. Prayers by the way of thank-offerings are made to God, and then the general presents himself in the temple, and the deeds, good and bad, are related by the poet or historian, who according to custom was with the expedition. And the greatest chief, Hoh, crowns the general with laurel and distributes little gifts and honors to all the valorous soldiers, who are for some days free from public duties. But this exemption from work is by no means pleasing to them, since they know not what it is to be at leisure, and so they help their companions. On the other hand, they who have been conquered through their own fault, or have lost the victory, are blamed; and they who were the first to take flight are in no way worthy to escape death, unless when the whole army asks their lives, and each one takes upon himself a part of their punishment. But this indulgence is rarely granted, except when there are good reasons favoring it. But he who did not bear help to an ally or friend is beaten with rods. That one who did not obey orders is given to the beasts, in an enclosure, to be devoured, and a staff is put in his hand, and if he should conquer the lions and the bears that are there, which is almost impossible, he is received into favor again. The conquered states or those willingly delivered up to them, forthwith have all things in common, and receive a garrison and magistrates from the City of the Sun, and by degrees they are accustomed to the ways of the city, the mistress of all, to which they even send their sons to be taught without contributing anything for expense.

It would be too great trouble to tell you about the spies and their master, and about the guards and laws and ceremonies, both within and without the state, which you can of yourself imagine. Since from childhood they are chosen according to their inclination and the star under which they were born, therefore each one working according to his natural propensity does his duty well and pleasantly, because naturally. The same things I may say concerning strategy and the other functions.

There are guards in the city by day and by night, and they are placed at the four gates, and outside the walls of the seventh ring, above the breastworks and towers and inside mounds. These places are guarded in the day by women, in the night by men. And lest the guard should become weary of watching, and in case of a surprise, they change them every three hours, as is the custom with our soldiers. At sunset, when the drum and symphonia sound, the armed guards are distributed. Cavalry and infantry make use of hunting as the symbol of war, and practise games and hold festivities in the plains. Then the music strikes up, and freely they pardon the offences and faults of the enemy, and after the victories they are kind to them, if it has been decreed that they should destroy the walls of the enemy's city and take their lives. All these things are done on the same day as the victory, and afterwards they never cease to load the conquered with favors, for they say that there ought to be no fighting, except when the conquerors give up the conquered, not when they kill them. If there is a dispute among them concerning injury or any other matter (for they themselves scarcely ever contend except in matters of honor), the chief and his magistrates chastise the accused one secretly, if he has done harm in deeds after he has been first angry. If they wait until the time of battle for the verbal decision, they must give vent to their anger against the enemy, and he who in battle shows the most daring deeds is considered to have defended the better and truer cause in the struggle, and the other yields, and they are punished justly. Nevertheless, they are not allowed to come to single combat, since right is maintained by the tribunal, and because the unjust cause is often apparent when the more just succumbs, and he who professes to be the better man shows this in public fight.

GRANDMASTER: This is worth while, so that factions should not be cherished for the harm of the fatherland, and so that civil wars might not occur, for by means of these a tyrant often arises, as the examples of Rome and Athens show. Now, I pray you, tell me of their works and matter connected therewith.

CAPTAIN: I believe that you have already heard about their military affairs and about their agricultural and pastoral life, and in what way these are common to them, and how they honor with the first grade of nobility whoever is considered to have a knowledge of these. They who are skilful in more arts than these they consider still nobler, and they set that one apart for teaching the art in which he is most skilful. The occupations which require the most labor, such as working in metals and building, are the most praiseworthy among them. No one declines to go to these occupations, for the reason that from the beginning their propensities are well-known, and among them, on account of the distribution of labor, no one does work harmful to him, but only that which is necessary for him. The occupations entailing less labor belong to the women. All of them are expected to know how to swim, and for this reason ponds are dug outside the walls of the city and within them near to the fountains.

Commerce is of little use to them, but they know the value of money, and they count for the use of their ambassadors and explorers, so that with it they may have the means of living. They receive merchants into their states from the different countries of the world, and these buy the superfluous goods of the city. The people of the City of the Sun refuse to take money, but in importing they accept in exchange those things of which they are in need, and sometimes they buy with money; and the young people in the City of the Sun are much amused when they see that for a small price they receive so many things in exchange. The old men, however, do not laugh. They are unwilling that the state should be corrupted by the vicious customs of slaves and foreigners. Therefore they do business at the gates, and sell those whom they have taken in war or keep them for digging ditches and other hard work without the city, and for this reason they always send four bands of soldiers to take care of the fields, and with them there are the laborers. They go out of the four gates from which roads with walls on both sides of them lead to the sea, so that goods might easily be carried over them and foreigners might not meet with difficulty on their way.

To strangers they are kind and polite; they keep them for three days at the public expense; after they have first washed their feet, they show them their city and its customs, and they honor them with a seat at the council and public table, and there are men whose duty it is to take care of and guard the guests. But if strangers should wish to become citizens of their state, they try them first for a month on a farm, and for another month in the city, then they decide concerning them, and admit them with certain ceremonies and oaths.

Agriculture is much followed among them; there is not a span of earth without cultivation, and they observe the winds and propitious stars. With the exception of a few left in the city all go out armed, and with flags and drums and trumpets sounding, to the fields, for the purposes of plowing, sowing, digging, hoeing, reaping, gathering fruit and grapes; and they set in order everything, and do their work in a very few hours and with much care. They use wagons fitted with sails which are borne along by the wind even when it is contrary, by the marvellous contrivance of wheels within wheels.

And when there is no wind a beast draws along a huge cart, which is a grand sight.

The guardians of the land move about in the meantime, armed and always in their proper turn. They do not use dung and filth for manuring the fields, thinking that the fruit contracts something of their rottenness, and when eaten gives a short and poor subsistence, as women who are beautiful with rouge and from want of exercise bring forth feeble offspring. Wherefore they do not as it were paint the earth, but dig it up well and use secret remedies, so that fruit is borne quickly and multiplies, and is not destroyed. They have a book for this work, which they call the Georgics. As much of the land as is necessary is cultivated, and the rest is used for the pasturage of cattle.

The excellent occupation of breeding and rearing horses, oxen, sheep, dogs and all kinds of domestic and tame animals, is in the highest esteem among them as it was in the time of Abraham. And the animals are led so to pair that they may be able to breed well.

Fine pictures of oxen, horses, sheep, and other animals are placed before them. They do not turn out horses with mares to feed, but at the proper time they bring them together in an enclosure of the stables in their fields. And this is done when they observe that the constellation Archer is in favorable conjunction with Mars and Jupiter. For the oxen they observe the Bull, for the sheep the Ram, and so on in accordance with art. Under the Pleiades they keep a drove of hens and ducks and geese, which are driven out by the women to feed near the city. The women only do this when it is a pleasure to them. There are also places enclosed, where they make cheese, butter, and milk-food. They also keep capons, fruit and other things, and for all these matters there is a book which they call the Bucolics. They have an abundance of all things, since every one likes to be industrious, their labors being slight and profitable. They are docile, and that one among them who is head of the rest in duties of this kind they call king. For they say that this is the proper name of the leaders, and it does not belong to ignorant persons. It is wonderful to see how men and women march together collectively, and always in obedience to the voice of the king. Nor do they regard him with loathing as we do, for they know that although he is greater than themselves, he is for all that their father and brother. They keep groves and woods for wild animals, and they often hunt.

The science of navigation is considered very dignified by them, and they possess rafts and triremes, which go over the waters without rowers or the force of the wind, but by a marvellous contrivance. And other vessels they have which are moved by the winds. They have a correct knowledge of the stars, and of the ebb and flow of the tide. They navigate for the sake of becoming acquainted with nations and different countries and things. They injure nobody, and they do not put up with injury, and they never go to battle unless when provoked. They assert that the whole earth will in time come to live in accordance with their customs, and consequently they always find out whether there be a nation whose manner of living is better and more approved than the rest. They admire the Christian institutions and look for a realization of the apostolic life in vogue among themselves and in us. There are treaties between them and the Chinese, and many other nations, both insular and continental, such as Siam and Calicut, which they are only just able to explore. Furthermore, they have artificial fires, battles on sea and land, and many strategic secrets. Therefore they are nearly always victorious.

GRANDMASTER: Now it would be very pleasant to learn with what foods and drinks they are nourished, and in what way and for how long they live.

CAPTAIN: Their food consists of flesh, butter, honey, cheese, garden herbs, and vegetables of various kinds. They were unwilling at first to slay animals, because it seemed cruel; but thinking afterwards that it was also cruel to destroy herbs which have a share of sensitive feeling, they saw that they would perish from hunger unless they did an unjustifiable action for the sake of justifiable ones, and so now they all eat meat. Nevertheless, they do not kill willingly useful animals such as oxen and horses. They observe the difference between useful and harmful foods, and for this they employ the science of medicine. They always change their food. First they eat flesh, then fish, then afterwards they go back to flesh, and nature is never incommoded or weakened. The old people use the more digestible kind of food, and take three meals a day, eating only a little. But the general community eat twice, and the boys four times, that they might satisfy nature. The length of their lives is generally one hundred years, but often they reach two hundred.

As regards drinking, they are extremely moderate. Wine is never given to young people until they are ten years old, unless the state of their health demands it. After their tenth year they take it diluted with water, and so do the women, but the old men of fifty and upwards use little or no water. They eat the most healthy things, according to the time of the year.

They think nothing harmful which is brought forth by God, except when there has been abuse by taking too much. And therefore in the summer they feed on fruits, because they are moist and juicy and cool, and counteract the heat and dryness. In the winter they feed on dry articles, and in the autumn they eat grapes, since they are given by God to remove melancholy and sadness; and they also make use of scents to a great degree. In the morning, when they have all risen they comb their hair and wash their faces and hands with cold water. Then they chew thyme or rock parsley or fennel, or rub their hands with these plants. The old men make incense, and with their faces to the east repeat the short prayer which Jesus Christ taught us. After this they go to wait upon the old men, some go to the dance, and others to the duties of the state. Later on they meet at the early lectures, then in the temple, then for bodily exercise.

Then for a little while they sit down to rest, and at length they go to dinner.

Among them there is never gout in the hands or feet, no catarrh, nor sciatica, nor grievous colics, nor flatulency, nor hard breathing. For these diseases are caused by indigestion and flatulency, and by frugality and exercise they remove every humor and spasm. Wherefore it is unseemly in the extreme to be seen vomiting or spitting, since they say that this is a sign either of little exercise or of ignoble sloth, or of drunkenness or gluttony. They suffer rather from swellings or from the dry spasm, which they relieve with plenty of good and juicy food. They heal fevers with pleasant baths and with milkfood, and with a pleasant habitation in the country and by gradual exercise. Unclean diseases cannot be prevalent with them because they often clean their bodies by bathing in wine, and soothe them with aromatic oil, and by the sweat of exercise they diffuse the poisonous vapor which corrupts the blood and the marrow. They do suffer a little from consumption, because they cannot perspire at the breast, but they never have asthma, for the humid nature of which a heavy man is required. They cure hot fevers with cold potations of water, but slight ones with sweet smells, with cheese-bread or sleep, with music or dancing. Tertiary fevers are cured by bleeding, by rhubarb or by a similar drawing remedy, or by water soaked in the roots of plants, with purgative and sharp-tasting qualities. But it is rarely that they take purgative medicines. Fevers occuring every fourth day are cured easily by suddenly startling the unprepared patients, and by means of herbs producing effects opposite to the humors of this fever. All these secrets they told me in opposition to their own wishes. They take more diligent pains to cure the lasting fevers, which they fear more, and they strive to counteract these by the observation of stars and of planets, and by prayers to God. Fevers recurring every fifth, sixth, eighth or more days, you never find whenever heavy humors are wanting.

They use baths, and moreover they have warm ones according to the Roman custom, and they make use also of olive oil. They have found out, too, a great many secret cures for the preservation of cleanliness and health. And in other ways they labor to cure the epilepsy, with which they are often troubled.

GRANDMASTER: A sign this disease is of wonderful cleverness, for from it Hercules, Scotus, Socrates, Callimachus, and Mahomet have suffered.

CAPTAIN: They cure by means of prayers to heaven, by strengthening the head, by acids, by planned gymnastics, and with fat cheesebread sprinkled with the flour of wheaten corn. They are very skilled in making dishes, and in them they put spice, honey, butter and many highly strengthening spices, and they temper their richness with acids, so that they never vomit. They do not drink ice-cold drinks nor artificial hot drinks, as the Chinese do; for they are not without aid against the humors of the body, on account of the help they get from the natural heat of the water; but they strengthen it with crushed garlic, with vinegar, with wild thyme, with mint, and with basil, in the summer or in time of special heaviness. They also know a secret for renovating life after about the seventieth year, and for ridding it of affliction, and this they do by a pleasing and indeed wonderful art.

GRANDMASTER: Thus far you have said nothing concerning their sciences and magistrates.

CAPTAIN: Undoubtedly I have. But since you are so curious I will add more. Both when it is new moon and full moon they call a council after a sacrifice. To this all from twenty years upwards are admitted, and each one is asked separately to say what is wanting in the state, and which of the magistrates have discharged their duties rightly and which wrongly. Then after eight days all the magistrates assemble, to wit, Hoh first, and with him Power, Wisdom and Love. Each one of the three last has three magistrates under him, making in all thirteen, and they consider the affairs of the arts pertaining to each one of them; Power, of war; Wisdom, of the sciences; Love, of food, clothing, education and breeding. The masters of all the bands, who are captains of tens, of fifties, of hundreds, also assemble, the women first and then the men. They argue about those things which are of the welfare of the state, and they choose the magistrates from among those who have already been named in the great council. In this manner they assemble daily, Hoh and his three princes, and they correct, confirm and execute the matters passing to them, as decisions in the elections; other necessary questions they provide of themselves. They do not use lots unless when they are altogether doubtful how to decide. The nine magistrates under Hoh, Power, Wisdom and Love are changed according to the wish of the people, but the first four are never changed, unless they, taking counsel with themselves, give up the dignity of one to another, whom among them they know to be wiser, more renowned, and more nearly perfect. And then they are obedient and honorable, since they yield willingly to the wiser man and are taught by him. This, however, rarely happens. The principals of the sciences, except Metaphysics, who is Hoh himself, and is as it were, the architect of all science, having rule over all, are attached to Wisdom. Hoh is ashamed to be ignorant of any possible thing. Under Wisdom therefore is Grammar, Logic, Physics,

Medicine, Astrology, Astronomy, Geometry, Cosmography, Music, Perspective, Arithmetic, Poetry, Rhetoric, Painting, Sculpture. Under the triumvir Love are Breeding, Agriculture, Education, Medicine, Clothing, Pasturage, Coining.

GRANDMASTER: What about their judges?

CAPTAIN: This is the point I was just thinking of explaining. Every one is judged by the first master of his trade, and thus all the head artificers are judges. They punish with exile, with flogging, with blame, with deprivation of the common table, with exclusion from the church and from the company of women. When there is a case in which great injury has been done, it is punished with death, and they repay an eye with an eye, a nose for a nose, a tooth for a tooth, and so on, according to the law of retaliation. If the offence is wilful the council decides. When there is strife and it takes place undesignedly, the sentence is mitigated; nevertheless, not by the judge but by the triumvirate, from whom even it may be referred to Hoh, not on account of justice but of mercy, for Hoh is able to pardon. They have no prisons, except one tower for shutting up rebellious enemies, and there is no written statement of a case, which we commonly call a lawsuit. But the accusation and witnesses are produced in the presence of the judge and Power; the accused person makes his defence, and he is immediately acquitted or condemned by the judge; and if he appeals to the triumvirate, on the following day he is acquitted or condemned. On the third day he is dismissed through the mercy and clemency of Hoh, or receives the inviolable rigor of his sentence. An accused person is reconciled to his accuser and to his witnesses, as it were, with the medicine of his complaint, that is, with embracing and kissing. No one is killed or stoned unless by the hands of the people, the accuser and the witnesses beginning first. For they have no executioners and lictors, lest the state should sink into ruin. The choice of death is given to the rest of the people, who enclose the lifeless remains in little bags and burn them by the application of fire, while exhorters are present for the purpose of advising concerning a good death. Nevertheless, the whole nation laments and beseeches God that His anger may be appeased, being in grief that it should as it were have to cut off a rotten member of the state. Certain officers talk to and convince the accused man by means of arguments until he himself acquiesces in the sentence of death passed upon him, or else he does not die. But if a crime has been committed against the liberty of the republic, or against God, or against the supreme magistrates, there is immediate censure without pity. These only are punished with death. He who is about to die is compelled to state in the presence of the people and with religious scrupulousness the reasons for which he does not deserve death, and also the sins of the others who ought to die instead of him, and further the mistakes of the magistrates. If, moreover, it should seem right to the person thus asserting, he must say why the accused ones are deserving of less punishment than he. And if by his arguments he gains the victory he is sent into exile, and appeases the state by means of prayers and sacrifices and good life ensuing. They do not torture those named by the accused person, but they warn them. Sins of frailty and ignorance are punished only with blaming, and with compulsory continuation as learners under the law and discipline of those sciences or arts against which they have sinned. And all these things they have mutually among themselves, since they seem to be in very truth members of the same body, and one of another.

This further I would have you know, that if a transgressor, without waiting to be accused, goes of his own accord before a magistrate, accusing himself and seeking to make amends, that one is liberated from the punishment of a secret crime, and since he has not been accused of such a crime, his punishment is changed into another. They take special care that no one should invent slander, and if this should happen they meet the offence with the punishment of retaliation. Since they always walk about and work in crowds, five witnesses are required for the conviction of a transgressor. If the case is otherwise, after having threatened him, he is released after he has sworn an oath as the warrant of good conduct. Or if he is accused a second or third time, his increased punishment rests on the testimony of three or two witnesses. They have but few laws, and these short and plain, and written upon a flat table, and hanging to the doors of the temple, that is between the columns. And on single columns can be seen the essences of things described in the very terse style of Metaphysics—viz., the essences of God, of the angles, of the world, of the stars, of man, of fate, of virtue, all done with great wisdom. The definitions of all the virtues are also delineated here, and here is the tribunal, where the judges of all the virtues have their seat. The definition of a certain virtue is written under that column where the judges for the aforesaid virtue sit, and when a judge gives judgment he sits and speaks thus: O son, thou hast sinned against this sacred definition of beneficence, or of magnanimity, or of another virtue, as the case may be. And after discussion the judge legally condemns him to the punishment for the crime of which he is accused—viz., for injury, for despondency, for pride, for ingratitude, for sloth, &c. But the sentences are certain and true correctives, savoring more of clemency than of actual punishment.

GRANDMASTER: Now you ought to tell me about their priests, their sacrifices, their religion, and their belief.

CAPTAIN: The chief priest is Hoh, and it is the duty of all the superior magistrates to pardon sins. Therefore the whole state by secret confession, which we also use, tell their sins to the magistrates, who at once purge their souls and teach those that are inimical to the people. Then the sacred magistrates themselves confess their own sinfulness to the three supreme chiefs, and together they confess the faults of one another, though no special one is named, and they confess especially the heavier faults and those harmful to the state. At length the triumvirs confess their sinfulness to Hoh himself, who forthwith recognizes the kinds of sins that are harmful to the state, and succors with timely remedies. Then he offers sacrifices and prayers to God. And before this he confesses the sins of the whole people, in the presence of God, and publicly in the temple, above the altar, as often as it had been necessary that the fault should be corrected. Nevertheless, no transgressor is spoken of by his name. In this manner he absolves the people by advising them that they should beware of sins of the aforesaid kind. Afterwards he offers sacrifice to God, that He should pardon the state and absolve it of its sins, and to teach and defend it. Once in every year the chief priests of each separate subordinate state confess their sins in the presence of Hoh. Thus he is not ignorant of the wrongdoings of the provinces, and forthwith he removes them with all human and heavenly remedies.

Sacrifice is conducted after the following manner: Hoh asks the people which one among them wishes to give himself as a sacrifice to God for the sake of his fellows. He is then placed upon the fourth table, with ceremonies and the offering up of prayers: the table is hung up in a wonderful manner by means of four ropes passing through four cords attached to firm pulley-blocks in the small dome of the temple. This done they cry to the God of mercy, that He may accept the offering, not of a beast as among the heathen, but of a human being. Then Hoh orders the ropes to be drawn and the sacrifice is pulled up above to the centre of the small dome, and there it dedicates itself with the most fervent supplications. Food is given to it through a window by the priests, who live around the dome, but it is allowed a very little to eat, until it has atoned for the sins of the state. There with prayer and fasting he cries to the God of heaven that He might accept its willing offering. And after twenty or thirty days, the anger of God being appeased, the sacrifice becomes a priest, or sometimes, though rarely, returns below by means of the outer way for the priests. Ever after this man is treated with great benevolence and much honor, for the reason that he offered himself unto death for the sake of his country. But God does not require death. The priests above twenty-four years of age offer praises from their places in the top of the temple. This they do in the middle of the night, at noon, in the morning and in the evening, to wit, four times a day they sing their chants in the presence of God. It is also their work to observe the stars and to note with the astrolabe their motions and influences upon human things, and to find out their powers. Thus they know in what part of the earth any change has been or will be, and at what time it has taken place, and they send to find whether the matter be as they have it. They make a note of predictions, true and false, so that they may be able from experience to predict more correctly. The priests, moreover, determine the hours for breeding and the days for sowing, reaping, and gathering the vintage, and are as it were the ambassadors and intercessors and connection between God and man. And it is from among them mostly that Hoh is elected. They write very learned treatises and search into the sciences. Below they never descend, unless for their dinner and supper, so that the essence of their heads do not descend to the stomachs and liver. Only very seldom, and that as a cure for the ills of solitude, do they have converse with women. On certain days Hoh goes up to them and deliberates with them concerning the matters which he has lately investigated for the benefit of the state and all the nations of the world.

In the temple beneath one priest always stands near the altar praying for the people, and at the end of every hour another succeeds him, just as we are accustomed in solemn prayer to change every fourth hour. And this method of supplication they call perpetual prayer. After a meal they return thanks to God. Then they sing the deeds of the Christian, Jewish, and Gentile heroes, and of those of all other nations, and this is very delightful to them. Forsooth, no one is envious of another. They sing a hymn to Love, one to Wisdom, and one each to all the other virtues, and this they do under the direction of the ruler of each virtue. Each one takes the woman he loves most, and they dance for exercise with propriety and stateliness under the peristyles. The women wear their long hair all twisted together and collected into one knot on the crown of the head, but in rolling it they leave one curl. The men, however, have one curl only and the rest of their hair around the head is shaven off. Further, they wear a slight covering, and above this a round hat a little larger than the size of their head. In the fields they use caps, but at home each one wears a biretto white, red, or another color

THE CITY OF THE SUN   39

according to his trade or occupation. Moreover, the magistrates use grander and more imposing-looking coverings for the head.

They hold great festivities when the sun enters the four cardinal points of the heaven, that is when he enters Cancer, Libra, Capricorn, and Aries. On these occasions they have very learned, splendid, and as it were comic performances. They celebrate also every full and every new moon with a festival, as also they do the anniversaries of the founding of the city, and of the days when they have won victories or done any other great achievement. The celebrations take place with the music of female voices, with the noise of trumpets and drums, and the firing of salutations. The poets sing the praises of the most renowned leaders and the victories. Nevertheless, if any of them should deceive even by disparaging a foreign hero, he is punished. No one can exercise the function of a poet who invents that which is not true, and a license like this they think to be a pest of our world, for the reason that it puts a premium upon virtue and often assigns it to unworthy persons, either from fear or flattery, or ambition or avarice. For the praise of no one is a statue erected until after his death; but whilst he is alive, who has found out new arts and very useful secrets, or who has rendered great service to the state either at home or on the battle-field, his name is written in the book of heroes. They do not bury dead bodies, but burn them, so that a plague may not arise from them, and so that they may be converted into fire, a very noble and powerful thing, which has its coming from the sun and returns to it. And for the above reasons no chance is given for idolatry. The statues and pictures of the heroes, however, are there, and the splendid women set apart to become mothers often look at them. Prayers are made from the state to the four horizontal corners of the world. In the morning to the rising sun, then to the setting sun, then to the south, and lastly to the north; and in the contrary order in the evening, first to the setting sun, to the rising sun, to the north, and at length to the south. They repeat but one prayer, which asks for health of body and of mind, and happiness for themselves and all people, and they conclude it with the petition "As it seems best to God." The public prayer for all is long, and it is poured forth to heaven. For this reason the altar is round and is divided crosswise by ways at right angles to one another. By these ways Hoh enters after he has repeated the four prayers, and he prays looking up to heaven. And then a great mystery is seen by them. The priestly vestments are of a beauty and meaning like to those of Aaron. They resemble Nature and they surpass Art.

They divide the seasons according to the revolution of the sun, and not of the stars, and they observe yearly by how much time the one precedes the other. They hold that the sun approaches nearer and nearer, and therefore by ever lessening circles reaches the tropics and the equator every year a little sooner. They measure months by the course of the moon, years by that of the sun. They praise Ptolemy, admire Copernicus, but place Aristarchus and Philolaus before him. They take great pains in endeavoring to understand the construction of the world, and whether or not it will perish, and at what time. They believe that the true oracle of Jesus Christ is by the signs in the sun, in the moon, and in the stars, which signs do not thus appear to many of us foolish ones. Therefore they wait for the renewing of the age, and perchance for its end. They say that is very doubtful whether the world was made from nothing, or from the ruins of other worlds, or from chaos, but they certainly think that it was made, and did not exist from eternity. Therefore they disbelieve in Aristotle, whom they consider a logician and not a philosopher. From analogies, they can draw many arguments against the eternity of the world. The sun and the stars they, so to speak, regard as the living representatives and signs of God, as the temples and holy living altars, and they honor but do not worship them. Beyond all other things they venerate the sun, but they consider no created thing worthy the adoration of worship. This they give to God alone, and thus they serve Him, that they may not come into the power of a tyrant and fall into misery by undergoing punishment by creatures of revenge. They contemplate and know God under the image of the Sun, and they call it the sign of God, His face and living image, by means of which light, heat, life, and the making of all things good and bad proceeds. Therefore they have built an altar like to the Sun in shape, and the priests praise God in the sun and in the stars, as it were His altars, and in the heavens, His temple as it were; and they pray to good angels, who are, so to speak, the intercessors living in the stars, their strong abodes. For God long since set signs of their beauty in heaven, and of His glory in the Sun. They say there is but one heaven, and that the planets move and rise of themselves when they approach the sun or are in conjunction with it.

They assert two principles of the physics of things below, namely, that the Sun is the father, and the Earth the mother; the air is an impure part of the heavens; all fire is derived from the sun. The sea is the sweat of earth, or the fluid of earth combusted, and fused within its bowels; but is the bond of union between air and earth, as the blood is of the spirit and flesh of animals. The world is a great animal, and we live within it as worms live within us. Therefore we do not belong to the system of stars, sun, and earth, but to God only; for in respect to them which seek only to amplify themselves, we are born and live by chance; but in respect to God, whose instruments we are, we are formed by prescience and design, and for a high end. Therefore we are bound to no Father but God, and receive all things from Him. They hold as beyond question the immortality of souls, and that these associate with good angels after death, or with bad angels, according as they have likened themselves in this life to either. For all things seek their like. They differ little from us as to places of reward and punishment. They are in doubt whether there are other worlds beyond ours, and account it madness to say there is nothing. Nonentity is incompatible with the infinite entity of God. They lay down two principles of metaphysics, entity which is the highest God, and nothingness which is the defect of entity. Evil and sin come of the propensity of nothingness; the sin having its cause not efficient, but in deficiency. Deficiency is, they say, of power, wisdom or will. Sin they place in the last of these three, because he who knows and has the power to do good is bound also to have the will, for will arises out of them. They worship God in Trinity, saying God is the supreme Power, whence proceeds the highest Wisdom, which is the same with God, and from these comes Love, which is both Power and Wisdom; but they do not distinguish persons by name, as in our Christian law, which has not been revealed to them. This religion, when its abuses have been removed, will be the future mistress of the world, as great theologians teach and hope. Therefore Spain found the New World (though its first discoverer, Columbus, greatest of heroes, was a Genoese), that all nations should be gathered under one law. We know not what we do, but God knows, whose instruments we are. They sought new regions for lust of gold and riches, but God works to a higher end. The sun strives to burn up the earth, not to produce plants and men, but God guides the battle to great issues. His the praise, to Him the glory!

GRANDMASTER: Oh, if you knew what our astrologers say of the coming age, and of our age, that has in it more history within a hundred years than all the world had in four thousand years before! Of the wonderful invention of printing and guns, and the use of the magnet, and how it all comes of Mercury, Mars, the Moon, and the Scorpion!

CAPTAIN: Ah, Well! God gives all in His good time. They astrologize too much.

Study Questions

1. The prince in charge of breeding is called Love (Mor). Considering his office, what kind of love does he represent? Is self-love, which is criticized as the source of social discontent, the same species of love?
2. What are the problems with the theory that communal property makes everyone rich? Upon what kind of human being is the theory predicated?
3. Construct an argument that would explain why the use of cosmetics by women would be met with the death sentence.
4. What is the principle of organization underlying the discussion of topics in *The City of the Sun*? Consider the connection between the structure of the city and the structure of the discussion.
5. What principle guides the design of the citizens' clothing?
6. Why is deciding issues by vote an uncommon practice in the city?
7. How would you answer the Grandmaster's question about whether the city's government is a monarchy, an aristocracy, or a republic?
8. Are the city's justifications for waging war based upon religious faith or upon reasoned policy? What are the connections between these two positions in such a state?
9. The members of the city may practice the universal religion that Campanella wished to establish. What vestiges of Christianity do you find in it? Compare their ceremonies with Christian rituals.

DENIS DIDEROT (1713–1784)
was born in Langres, a town in eastern France. Son of a cutlery-
maker, he entered the Catholic Church under the tutelage of the
local Jesuits and then went to Paris to further his seminary studies.
But there he began a long rebellion against orthodoxy and custom.
He left the Church to study law but soon abandoned these studies
to live the life of a bohemian. Free to explore whatever he liked—
philosophy, science, or women—Diderot indulged his appetite for
questioning the basic assumptions of any field of knowledge. The
English theorists Bacon, Newton, and Locke and the French philosophers Descartes and Voltaire had prepared the way for such
questioning by establishing the idea that the world was knowable
through human senses, sciences, and logic. Diderot's own scepticism
and curiosity furthered the thinking of the Age of Enlightenment.
He directed and contributed extensively to the famous *Encyclopedia*
(1746–1765), which attempted to redefine the entire universe in
rational, material terms, as if to offer a synthesis of knowledge that
would free men from the fears of religion and its inhibiting morality.

Diderot's translation of the Earl of Shaftesbury's *Inquiry Concerning Merit or Virtue* in 1745 shows his early interest in finding
a purely human morality, free of theological absolutes. His own
position, exemplified in the subtitle of the work reprinted below,
stresses the instinctive goodness of man's character, which can express itself only when liberated from religious and moral laws. This
natural sense of goodness and justice ensures personal and social
happiness for man. Accordingly, man's natural passions are the
source of "virtue," which thus acquires a biological rather than moral
definition. Diderot as a rationalist has a profound faith in man's instinctive and animal nature.

In *A Supplement to Bougainville's "Voyage"* (1772), a Tahitian
native mocks religious rules because they are contrary to human
nature. The subsequent seduction of the Chaplain underlines Diderot's philosophical position: natural man will eventually triumph
over civilized man because of the power of human instincts. But
natural man is also a helpless victim of the disease of civilization the
voyagers bring, which may suggest that the only solution is to return civilized man to his own instinctual life, rather than to actual
primitivism.

The *Supplement* developed from Diderot's review of Louis Bougainville's account of his trip around the world. It reflects the interest of the eighteenth-century intellectuals in primitive societies, an interest held earlier by Shakespeare, Bacon, and Swift, and later by Rousseau and James Boswell. But Diderot's wise savages are not the discovery of scientific exploration; rather they are the result of his philosophical inquiry into the nature of mankind, and we should expect the fictional *Supplement* to modify as well as complement the facts of Bougainville's record.

Reprinted here is the translation by Ralph H. Bowen from *Rameau's Nephew and Other Works of Diderot*.

SUPPLEMENT TO BOUGAINVILLE'S "VOYAGE"

OR, A DIALOGUE BETWEEN A AND B ON THE UNDESIRABILITY OF ATTACHING MORAL VALUES TO CERTAIN PHYSICAL ACTS WHICH CARRY NO SUCH IMPLICATIONS.

> At *quanto meliora monet, pugnantiaque istis,*
> *Dives opis naturae suae: tu si modo recte*
> *Dispensare velis, ac non fugienda petendis*
> *Immiscere; tuo vitio rerumne labores,*
> *Nil referre putas?* [1]
>
> HORACE, *Satires*

CRITIQUE OF BOUGAINVILLE'S "VOYAGE"

A: The weather has played a trick on us. When we returned home yesterday evening the sky was like a splendid vault studded with stars. But evidently its promise of fine weather was false.

B: How can you be so sure?

A: The fog is so thick that you can't see the tops of those trees over there.

B: True enough. But the fog only hangs low because the atmosphere near the ground is already filled with moisture. Perhaps the fog will condense and its moisture fall to the ground.

A: Or, conversely, it may rise higher, past this layer of moist air,

---

[1] How much better it is, and how contrary to certain other precepts, that you, a rich man, should be willing to allot your resources correctly according to their own nature, so as not to mingle desirable things with those that should be avoided! Do you count it as a matter of indifference that you must toil because of your own shortcomings and those of your subject matter?

into the upper levels where the air is less dense. Up there it may not be saturated, as the chemists say.

B: Nothing for it but to wait and see.

A: And what do you plan to do while we are waiting?

B: I have a book to read.

A: Still Bougainville's account of his voyage?

B: Still at it.

A: I can't make head or tail out of that man. When he was young, he went in for mathematics, which implies a sedentary life. And now, suddenly, he deserts his meditations and takes up the active, difficult, wandering, dissipated life of an explorer.

B: Not at all. A ship, after all, is only a floating house, and the sailor who traverses enormous distances is shut up in a narrow little space in which he can scarcely move about. Look at it this way, and you will see how he can go around the globe on a plank, just as you and I can make a tour of the universe on your floor.

A: And another thing that's very odd—the disparity between the man's character and his exploit. Bougainville has a taste for the amusements of polite society; he loves women, the theater, fine meals. He takes as easily to the social whirl as to the inconstancy of the elements that have buffeted him about so much. He is gay and genial; he is a real Frenchman, ballasted on the port side with a treatise on integral and differential calculus, and to starboard with a voyage around the world.

B: He's only doing what everybody does—after a period of strenuous application he looks for distraction, and vice versa.

A: What's your opinion of the "Voyage"?

B: Well, so far as I can judge after a rather superficial reading, I should say that its chief merits are three: it affords us better knowledge of our old globe and its inhabitants, greater safety on the seas, which he sailed with sounding line in hand, and more correct information for the use of our map makers. When he undertook his voyage, Bougainville possessed the necessary scientific preparation and he had the requisite personal qualities—a philosophic attitude, courage and veracity; he had a quick eye for taking things in without having to waste time in making his observations; he had caution, patience, and a real desire to see, to learn and to enlighten himself; he knows the sciences of mathematics, mechanics, geometry, astronomy; he has a sufficient acquaintance with natural history.

A: How is his style?

B: Simple and direct, just right for the subject, unpretentious and clear, especially when one is familiar with the way sailors talk.

A: Was it a long voyage?

B: I've marked his course on this globe. Do you see that line of red dots?

A: Which starts at Nantes?

B: Yes, and runs down to the Straits of Magellan, enters the Pacific Ocean, twists among the islands of the great archipelago extending from the Philippines to New Holland, touches Madagascar, the Cape of Good Hope, continues into the Atlantic, follows the coast of Africa, and finally ends up where it began.

A: Did he have a very hard time of it?

B: All sailors take risks, and accept the need to expose themselves to the hazards of air, fire, earth and water. But the worst hardship is that when he finally makes port somewhere after wandering for months between the sea and the sky, between life and death, after being battered by storms, after risking death from shipwreck, disease, hunger and thirst, after having his ship all but torn apart under his feet—when he falls exhausted and destitute at the feet of a brazen monster of a colonial government he is either refused the most urgent relief or made to wait interminably for it—it is very hard!

A: It's a crime and it ought to be punished.

B: It's one of the disasters our explorer failed to take into account.

A: And he shouldn't have had to. I had thought that the European powers were careful to send out to their overseas possessions only men of upright character and benevolent disposition, humane and sensitive to other people's distress. . . .

B: Oh, yes, you may be sure they worry a lot about that!

A: Have you come across any striking pieces of new information in this book of Bougainville's?

B: A great many.

A: Doesn't he report that wild animals often come right up to a human being, and that birds even fly down and perch on a man's shoulder, wherever they have had no chance to learn the danger of such familiarity?

B: He does, but others have said the same thing before.

A: How does he explain the presence of certain animals on islands that are separated from any continent by stretches of impassable sea? Who could have brought wolves, foxes, dogs, deer or snakes to such places?

B: He doesn't explain it; he only confirms the fact.

A: Well, how do you explain it?

B: Who knows anything about the early history of our planet? How many pieces of land, now isolated, were once pieces of some continent? The general shape of the bodies of water between them is the only clue on which to base some theory of what might have happened.

A: How do you mean?

B: You would have to reason from the shape of the pieces that are missing. Some day we can have a good time working that problem out, if the idea appeals to you. But for the moment, do you see this dot on the map called Lancer's Island? Looking at the position it occupies on the globe, who is there who wouldn't wonder how men came to be there? What means of communication were there between them and the rest of mankind? What will become of them if they go on multiplying on a little spit of land that is less than three miles across?

A: Probably they thin themselves out by eating each other. Perhaps you have there—in the very condition of island life—the origins of a very ancient and very natural form of cannibalism.

B: Or they may limit the growth of population by some superstitious law—perhaps babies are crushed under the feet of a priestess while still in their mothers' wombs.

A: Or perhaps grown men have the edge of a priest's knife put to their throats. Or perhaps some males are castrated. . . .

B: Or some women undergo infibulation, and there you would have the origin of many, many strange customs as cruel as they are necessary, the reasons for which have been lost in the darkness of the past and still torment philosophers. One rule that seems fairly universal is that supernatural and divine institutions seem to grow stronger the longer they remain in effect, and are eventually transformed into national constitutions or civil laws. Similarly, national or civil institutions acquire sanctity and degenerate into supernatural or divine precepts.

A: The worst sort of palingenesis.

B: It is just one more skein woven into the rope with which we are bound hand and foot.

A: Wasn't Bougainville in Paraguay just at the time when the Jesuits were expelled from there?

B: Yes, he was.

A: What does he say about it?

B: Less than he might have said. But he does say enough to make it clear that those cruel sons of Sparta in black robes treated their Indian slaves quite as badly as the ancient Spartans treated their helots. They forced them to work incessantly, grew rich on their sweat, deprived them of all property rights, kept them under the brutalizing influence of superstition, exacted the most profound veneration from them, and strode among them whip in hand, beating them without

regard for age or sex. Another century, and it would have been impossible to get rid of them, or else the attempt would have touched
off a long war between the monks and the sovereign, whose authority they had little by little been undermining.

A: And what about those Patagonian giants about whom Dr.
Maty and La Condamine, the academician, made such a fuss?

B: They are good fellows who come running up to you and shout
"Chaoua!" as they embrace you. They are strong and energetic, but
the tallest of them stands no higher than five feet five or six inches
—there is nothing gigantic about them except their fatness, the
largeness of their heads and the thickness of their limbs. Man is
born with a taste for the marvelous, with a tendency to magnify
everything he sees, so how should one be able to maintain a just
proportion among the things he has seen, especially when one must,
as it were, justify the long trip he has made and the trouble he has
taken to go to some remote place to look at them?

A: Well, what in general is Bougainville's opinion of savages?

B: Apparently they acquire their cruel ways from the daily necessity of defending themselves against wild animals—at least this may
explain what many travelers have observed. Whenever his peace and
safety are not disturbed, the savage is innocent and mild. All warfare originates in conflicting claims to the same bit of property. The
civilized man has a claim which conflicts with the claim of another
civilized man to the possession of a field of which they occupy respectively the two ends, so the field becomes the object of a dispute
between them.

A: And the tiger has a claim, which conflicts with that of the savage, to the possession of a forest. This must be the first instance of
conflicting claims as well as the most ancient cause of war. . . .
Did you happen to see the Tahitian that Bougainville took on board
his vessel and brought back to this country?

B: Yes, I saw him. His name was Aotourou. When they first
sighted land after leaving Tahiti, he mistook it for the voyagers' native country, whether because they had misrepresented the length of
the voyage to him or because, being naturally misled by the small-
ness of the apparent distance from the seashore where he lived to
the point at which the sky seemed to touch the horizon, he had no
idea of the actual size of the earth. The Tahitian custom of having
all women in common was so firmly ingrained in his mind that he
threw himself upon the first European woman who came near him,
and he was getting ready, in all seriousness, to render her one of the
courtesies of Tahiti. He soon got bored, though, living among us.
Because the Tahitian alphabet has no b, c, d, f, g, q, s, y or z, he was

never able to learn to speak our language, which demanded too many strange articulations and new sounds from his inflexible organs of speech. He grew more and more disconsolate from a desire to be back in his own country, and I can understand his feelings. This account of Bougainville of his voyage is the only book that has ever made me hanker after another country than my own. Up to now, I had always thought that a person was never so well off as when at home. Consequently I thought that everyone in the world must feel the same. All this is a natural result of the attraction of the soil, and this is an attraction that is bound up with all the comforts one enjoys at home and is not so sure of finding away from it.

A: What? Don't you find that the average inhabitant of Paris is just as sure that grain grows in the fields of the Roman Campagna as in those of Beauce?

B: Heavens, no! Bougainville finally sent Aotourou back to Tahiti, after having provided for his expenses and made certain that he would arrive safely.

A: Well, friend Aotourou! And weren't you pleased to see your father and mother, your brothers and sisters, your lady loves, your fellow countrymen—and what things you must have had to tell them about us!

B: Precious few things, you may be sure, and they didn't believe a single one of them.

A: Why do you say he had only a few things to tell them?

B: Because he couldn't have taken in very many, and because he wouldn't have been able to find the words in his language to talk about those things he had gained some notion of.

A: And why shouldn't they have believed him?

B: Because when they came to compare their customs with ours they would prefer to think that Aotourou was a liar rather than that we are so crazy.

A: Are you serious?

B: I have no doubt of it. The life of savages is so simple, and our societies are such complicated machines! The Tahitian is close to the origin of the world, while the European is close to its old age. The contrast between them and us is greater than the difference between a newborn baby and a doddering old man. They understand absolutely nothing about our manners or our laws, and they are bound to see in them nothing but shackles disguised in a hundred different ways. Those shackles could only provoke the indignation and scorn of creatures in whom the most profound feeling is a love of liberty.

A: Do you mean to go on and spin out the whole fable about how wonderful life is in Tahiti?

B: It isn't a fable at all. And you would have no doubt about Bougainville's sincerity if you had read the supplement to his account of his voyage.

A: Well, how can one get hold of this supplement?

B: It's right over there, on that table.

A: Will you let me borrow it to read at home?

B: I'd rather not. But if you would like to, we can read it over together.

A: Of course I should like to. Look over there—the fog is starting to settle, and you can see a few patches of blue sky. It seems that it's my fate to be on the wrong side of any argument with you, even when it's over trifles. I must have a very good disposition to be able to forgive you for being so consistently superior!

B: Here, take the manuscript and read it aloud. Skip over the preamble, which doesn't amount to anything, and start with the farewell speech made by one of the island's chiefs to the travelers. That will give you some notion of how eloquent those people can be.

A: But how was Bougainville able to understand this oration if it was spoken in a language he didn't know?

B: You'll find out. The speaker is an old man.

THE OLD MAN'S FAREWELL

He was the father of a numerous family. At the time of the Europeans' arrival, he cast upon them a look that was filled with scorn, though it revealed no surprise, no alarm and no curiosity. They approached him; he turned his back on them and retired into his hut. His thoughts were only too well revealed by his silence and his air of concern, for in the privacy of his thoughts he groaned inwardly over the happy days of his people, now gone forever. At the moment of Bougainville's departure, when all the natives ran swarming onto the beach, tugging at his clothing and throwing their arms around his companions and weeping, the old man stepped forward and solemnly spoke:

"Weep, wretched Tahitians, weep—but rather for the arrival than for the departure of these wicked and grasping men! The day will come when you will know them for what they are. Someday they will return, bearing in one hand that piece of wood you see suspended from this one's belt and in the other the piece of steel that hangs at the side of his companion. They will load you with chains, slit your throats and enslave you to their follies and vices. Someday you will be slaves to them, you will be as corrupt, as vile, as wretched as they are. But I have this consolation—my life is drawing to its close, and I shall not see the calamity that I foretell. Oh Tahitians, Oh my friends! You have the means of warding off a terrible fate, but I would die before I would advise you to make use of it. Let them leave, and let them live."

Then, turning to Bougainville, he went on: "And you, leader of these brigands who obey you, take your vessel swiftly from our shores. We are innocent and happy, and you can only spoil our happiness. We follow the pure instinct of nature, and you have tried to efface her imprint from our hearts. Here all things are for all, and you have preached to us I know not what distinctions between mine and thine. Our women and girls we possess in common; you have shared this privilege with us, and your coming has awakened in them a frenzy they have never known before. They have become mad in your arms; you have become ferocious in theirs. They have begun to hate one another; you have cut one another's throats for them, and they have come home to us stained with your blood.

"We are free—but see where you have driven into our earth the symbol of our future servitude. You are neither a god nor a devil— by what right, then, do you enslave people? Orou! You who understand the speech of these men, tell every one of us, as you have told me, what they have written on that strip of metal—'This land belongs to us.' This land belongs to you! And why? Because you set foot in it? If some day a Tahitian should land on your shores, and if he should engrave on one of your stones or on the bark of one of your trees: 'This land belongs to the people of Tahiti,' what would you think? You are stronger than we are! And what does that signify? When one of our lads carried off some of the miserable trinkets with which your ship is loaded, what an uproar you made, and what revenge you took! And at that very moment you were plotting, in the depths of your hearts, to steal a whole country! You are not slaves; you would suffer death rather than be enslaved, yet you want to make slaves of us! Do you believe, then, that the Tahitian does not know how to die in defense of his liberty? This Tahitian, whom you want to treat as a chattel, as a dumb animal—this Tahitian is your brother. You are both children of Nature—what right do you have over him that he does not have over you?

"You came; did we attack you? Did we plunder your vessel? Did we seize you and expose you to the arrows of our enemies? Did we force you to work in the fields alongside our beasts of burden? We respected our own image in you. Leave us our own customs, which are wiser and more decent than yours. We have no wish to barter what you call our ignorance for your useless knowledge. We possess already all that is good or necessary for our existence. Do we merit your scorn because we have not been able to create superfluous wants for ourselves? When we are hungry, we have something to eat; when we are cold, we have clothing to put on. You have been in our huts—what is lacking there, in your opinion? You are welcome to drive yourselves as hard as you please in pursuit of what you call the comforts of life, but allow sensible people to stop when they see they have nothing to gain but imaginary benefits from the continuation of their painful labors. If you persuade us to go beyond the bounds of strict necessity, when shall we come to the end of our labor? When shall we have time for enjoyment? We have reduced our daily and yearly labors to the least possible amount, because to us nothing seemed more desirable than leisure. Go and bestir yourselves in your own country; there you may torment yourselves as much as you like; but leave us in peace, and do not fill our heads with a hankering after your false needs and imaginary virtues. Look at these men—see how healthy, straight and strong they are. See these women—how straight, healthy, fresh and lovely they are. Take this bow in your hands—it is my own—and call one, two, three, four of your comrades to help you try to bend it. I can bend it myself. I work the soil, I climb mountains, I make my way through the dense forest, and I can run four leagues on the plain in less than an hour. Your young comrades have been hard put to it to keep up with me, and yet I have passed my ninetieth year. . . .

"Woe to this island! Woe to all the Tahitians now living, and to all those yet to be born, woe from the day of your arrival! We used to know but one disease—the one to which all men, all animals and all plants are subject—old age. But you have brought us a new one: you have infected our blood. We shall perhaps be compelled to exterminate with our own hands some of our young girls, some of our women, some of our children, those who have lain with your women, those who have lain with your men. Our fields will be spattered with the foul blood that has passed from your veins into ours. Or else our children, condemned to die, will nourish and perpetuate the evil disease that you have given their fathers and mothers, transmitting it forever to their descendants. Wretched men! You will bear the guilt either of the ravages that will follow your baneful caresses, or of the murders we must commit to arrest the progress of the poison! You speak of crime! Can you conceive of a greater crime than the one you have committed? How do they punish, in your country, the man who has killed his neighbor? Death by the headsman's ax! How do you punish the man who has poisoned his neighbor? Burning at the stake! Compare the second crime with your own, and then tell us, you poisoner of whole nations, what tortures you deserve!

"But a little while ago, the young Tahitian girl blissfully abandoned herself to the embraces of a Tahitian youth and awaited impatiently the day when her mother, authorized to do so by her having reached the age of puberty, would remove her veil and uncover her breasts. She was proud of her ability to excite men's desires, to attract the amorous looks of strangers, of her own relatives, of her own brothers. In our presence, without shame, in the center of a throng of innocent Tahitians who danced and played the flute, she accepted the caresses of the young man whom her young heart and the secret promptings of her senses had marked out for her. The notion of crime and the fear of disease have come among us only with your coming. Now our enjoyments, formerly so sweet, are attended with guilt and terror. That man in black, who stands near to you and listens to me, has spoken to our young men, and I know not what he has said to our young girls, but our youths are hesitant and our girls blush. Creep away into the dark forest, if you wish, with the perverse companion of your pleasures, but allow the good, simple Tahitians to reproduce themselves without shame under the open sky and in broad daylight.

"What more noble or more wholesome feelings could you put in the place of the ones we have nurtured in them and by which they live? When they think the time has come to enrich the nation and the family with a new citizen, they glorify the occasion. They eat in order to live and grow; they grow in order that they may multiply, and in that they see neither vice nor shame. Listen to the consequences of your crimes. Scarcely had you shown yourselves among our people than they became thieves. Scarcely had you set foot upon our soil than it began to reek of blood. You killed the Tahitian who ran to greet you, crying 'Taïo—friend!' And why did you kill him? Because he was tempted by the glitter of your little serpent's eggs. He gave you his fruit; he offered you his wife and daughter; he gave you his hut to live in—and you killed him for taking a handful of those little glass beads without asking your permission. And the others? At the sound of your murderous weapons they fled to the hills. But you should know that had it not been for me they would soon have come down again to destroy you. Oh, why did I appease their anger? Why did I calm their fury? Why do I still restrain them, even at this moment? I do not know, for you surely have no claim to pity. Your own soul is hard and will never feel any.

"You and your men have gone where you pleased, wandered over the whole island; you have been respected; you have enjoyed every-thing: no barrier nor refusal has been placed in your path. You have been invited into our homes; you have sat down at our tables; our people have spread before you the abundance of our land. If you wanted one of our young women, her mother presented her to you all naked, unless she was one of those who are not yet old enough to have the privilege of showing their faces and breasts. Thus you have enjoyed possession of these tender sacrificial victims to the duty of hospitality. For the girl and for you we have strewn the ground with leaves and flowers, the musicians have put their instruments in tune; nothing has troubled the sweetness nor interfered with the freedom of her caresses and yours. We chanted the hymn, the one that urges you to be a man, that urges our child to be a woman; a compliant and voluptuous woman. We danced around your couch. Yet you had hardly left this girl's embrace, having experienced in her arms the sweetest intoxication, than you killed her brother, her friend, or perhaps her father.

"And you have done worse still—look yonder at that enclosure, bristling with arrows, with weapons that heretofore have threatened only our foes—see them now turned against our own children. Look now upon the unhappy companions of your pleasures! See their sor-row! See the distress of their fathers and the despair of their mothers! That is where they are condemned to die at our hands or from the disease you gave them. So leave this place, unless your cruel eyes de-light in the spectacle of death! Go! And may the guilty sea, that spared your lives when you came here, now absolve itself and avenge our wrongs by swallowing you up on your homeward way! And you, Tahitians, go back to your huts, go indoors, all of you, so that these unworthy strangers, as they depart, may hear nothing but the growl-ing of the waves and may see nothing but the white spray dashing in fury on a desert coast!"

He finished speaking, and in an instant the throng of natives dis-appeared. A vast silence reigned over the whole extent of the island, and nothing was to be heard but the dry whistling of the wind and the dull pounding of the waves along the whole length of the coast. It was as though the winds and waters had heard the old man's voice and obeyed him.

B: Well, what do you think of that?

A: The oration strikes me as forceful enough, but in the midst of so much that is unmistakably abrupt and savage I seem to detect a few European ideas and turns of phrase.

B: You must remember that it is a translation from Tahitian into

Spanish and from Spanish into French. The previous night, the old man made a visit to Orou, the one to whom he appealed while speaking, in whose family the knowledge of Spanish had been preserved for several generations. Orou wrote down the old man's harangue in Spanish, and Bougainville had a copy of it in his hand while the old man was speaking.

A: Now I understand only too well why Bougainville suppressed this fragment. But I see there is more, and I have more than a mild curiosity to know what's in the rest.

B: Quite possibly you will find the next part less interesting.

A: Never mind.

B: It is a conversation between the ship's chaplain and a native of the island.

A: Orou?

B: The very same. When Bougainville's ship hove in sight of Tahiti, a great swarm of hollowed-out tree trunks put out from the shore. In an instant his vessel was surrounded by them. In whatever direction he turned his eyes he saw demonstrations of surprise and good will. The natives threw food to the sailors, welcomed them with outstretched arms, clambered up the ship's ropes and clung to its sides. They filled the captain's gig, shouting back and forth between ship and shore. More natives came running down to the beach. As soon as the Europeans had set foot on land, dozens of pairs of friendly arms were thrown around the members of the expedition, who were passed about from group to group and finally led off, each to the hut of a different family. The men kept on embracing their guests around the waist, while the women stroked and patted their hands and cheeks. Imagine what it must have been like to have been there! As a witness of this hospitable scene, at least in thought, tell me what you think of the human race.

A: It's very fine.

B: But I was almost forgetting to tell you about a most peculiar thing. The friendly and generous spectacle I have described was suddenly marred by the cries of a man calling for help. It was the servant of one of Bougainville's officers. Several Tahitian lads had laid hold of him, stretched him out flat on the ground, removed his clothes, and were getting ready to render him the customary politeness of the country.

A: What! Do you mean that those simple people, those good decent savages . . . ?

B: You're jumping to false conclusions. The servant was a woman disguised as a man. Her sex had been kept secret from the crew during the whole voyage, but the Tahitians recognized it at the first glance. She was born in Burgundy and her family name was Barré; she was neither beautiful nor ugly, and twenty-six years old. She had never undressed outside her hammock. She had suddenly got the urge to travel, and her first idea was to circumnavigate the globe. She showed courage and good sense at all times.

A: Those frail constitutions sometimes contain strong characters.

CONVERSATION BETWEEN THE CHAPLAIN AND OROU

B: When the members of Bougainville's expedition were shared out among the native families, the ship's chaplain fell to the lot of Orou. The Tahitian and the chaplain were men of about the same age, that is, about thirty-five years old. At that time, Orou's family consisted of his wife and three daughters, who were called Asto, Palli and Thia. The women undressed their guest, washed his face, hands and feet, and put before him a wholesome though frugal meal. When he was about to go to bed, Orou, who had stepped outside with his family, reappeared and presented to him his wife and three girls—all naked as Eve—and said to him:

"You are young and healthy and you have just had a good supper. He who sleeps alone, sleeps badly; at night a man needs a woman at his side. Here is my wife and here are my daughters. Choose whichever one pleases you most, but if you would like to do me a favor, you will give your preference to my youngest girl, who has not yet had any children."

The mother said: "Poor girl! I don't hold it against her. It's no fault of hers."

The chaplain replied that his religion, his holy orders, his moral standards and his sense of decency all prevented him from accepting Orou's invitation.

Orou answered: "I don't know what this thing is that you call 'religion,' but I can only have a low opinion of it because it forbids you to partake of an innocent pleasure to which Nature, the sovereign mistress of us all, invites everybody. It seems to prevent you from bringing one of your fellow creatures into the world, from doing a favor asked of you by a father, a mother and their children, from repaying the kindness of a host, and from enriching a nation by giving it an additional citizen. I don't know what it is that you call 'holy orders,' but your chief duty is to be a man and to show gratitude. I am not asking you to take my moral standards back with you to your own country, but Orou, your host and your friend, begs you merely to lend yourself to the morality of Tahiti. Is our moral code a better or a worse one than your own? This is an easy question to answer. Does the country you were born in have more people than it can support? If it does, then your morals are neither better nor worse than ours. Or can it feed more people than it now has? Then our morals are better than yours. As for the sense of propriety that leads you to object to my proposal, that I understand, and I freely admit that I am in the wrong. I ask your pardon. I cannot ask you to do anything that might harm your health; if you are too tired, you should by all means go to sleep at once. But I hope that you will not persist in disappointing us. Look at the distress you have caused to appear on the faces of these four women—they are afraid you have noticed some defect in them that arouses your distaste. But even if that were so, would it not be possible for you to do a good deed and have the pleasure of honoring one of my daughters in the sight of her sisters and friends? Come, be generous!"

THE CHAPLAIN: "You don't understand—it's not that. They are all four of them equally beautiful. But there is my religion! My holy orders!"

OROU: "They are mine and I offer them to you; they are all of age and they give themselves to you. However clear a conscience may be demanded of you by this thing, 'religion,' or by those 'holy orders' of yours, you need have no scruples about accepting these women. I am making no abuse of my paternal authority, and you may be sure that I recognize and respect the rights of individuals to their own persons."

At this point in his account, the truthful chaplain has to admit that up to that moment Providence had never exposed him to such strong temptation. He was young, he was excited, he was in torment. He turned his eyes away from the four lovely suppliants, then let his gaze wander back to them again. He lifted his hands and his countenance to Heaven. Thia, the youngest of the three girls, threw her arms around his knees and said to him: "Stranger, do not disappoint my father and mother. Do not disappoint me! Honor me in this hut and among my own family! Raise me to the dignity enjoyed by my sisters, for they make fun of me. Asto, my eldest sister, already has three children; Palli, the second oldest of us, has two; and Thia has none! Stranger, good stranger, do not reject me! Make me a mother! Give me a child whom I can some day lead by the hand as he walks at my side, to be seen by all Tahiti—a little one to nurse at my breast nine months from now, a child of whom I can be proud, and who will be part of my dowry when I go from my father's hut into that of another. Perhaps I shall be more fortunate with you than I have been with our Tahitian young men. If you will only grant me this favor, I will never forget you; I will bless you all my life; I will write your name on my arm and on that of my child; we will always pronounce it with joy; and when you leave this shore, my prayers will go with you across the seas all the way to your own country."

The poor chaplain records that she pressed his hands, that she fastened her eyes on his with the most expressive and touching gaze, that she wept, that her father, mother and sisters went out, leaving him alone with her, and that despite his repetition of "But there is my religion and my holy orders," he awoke the next morning to find the young girl lying at his side. She overwhelmed him with more caresses, and when her father, mother and sisters came in, she called upon them to add their gratitude to hers.

Asto and Palli, who had left the room briefly, soon returned bearing native food, drink and fruits. They embraced their sister and wished her good fortune. They all ate breakfast together; then, when Orou was left alone with the chaplain, he said to him:

"I see that my daughter is pleased with you, and I thank you. But would you be good enough to tell me the meaning of this word, 'religion,' which you have spoken so frequently and so mournfully?"

After considering for a moment what to say, the chaplain replied: "Who made your hut and all the furnishings in it?"

orou: I did.

the chaplain: Well, we believe that this world and everything in it is the work of a maker.

orou: Then he must have hands and feet, and a head.

the chaplain: No.

orou: Where is his dwelling place?

the chaplain: Everywhere.

orou: In this place too?

the chaplain: In this place too.

orou: But we have never seen him.

the chaplain: He cannot be seen.

orou: He sounds to me like a father that doesn't care very much for his children. He must be an old man, because he must be at least as old as the things he made.

the chaplain: No, he never grows old. He spoke to our ancestors and gave them laws; he prescribed to them the way in which he wishes to be honored; he ordained that certain actions are good and others he forbade them to do as being evil.

orou: I see. And one of these evil actions which he has forbidden is that of a man who goes to bed with a woman or girl. But in that case, why did he make two sexes?

THE CHAPLAIN: In order that they might come together—but only when certain conditions are satisfied and only after certain initial ceremonies have been performed. By virtue of these ceremonies one man belongs to one woman and only to her; one woman belongs to one man and only to him.

OROU: For their whole lives?

THE CHAPLAIN: For their whole lives.

OROU: So that if it should happen that a woman should go to bed with some man who was not her husband, or some man should go to bed with a woman that was not his wife . . . but that could never happen because the workman would know what was going on, and since he doesn't like that sort of thing, he wouldn't let it occur.

THE CHAPLAIN: No. He lets them do as they will, and they sin against the law of God (for that is the name by which we call the great workman) and against the law of the country; they commit a crime.

OROU: I should be sorry to give offense by anything I might say, but if you don't mind, I'll tell you what I think.

THE CHAPLAIN: Go ahead.

OROU: I find these strange precepts contrary to nature, and contrary to reason. I think they are admirably calculated to increase the number of crimes and to give endless annoyance to the old workman —who made everything without hands, head or tools, who is everywhere but can be seen nowhere, who exists today and tomorrow but grows not a day older, who gives commands and is not obeyed, who can prevent what he dislikes but fails to do so. His commands are contrary to nature because they assume that a thinking being, one that has feelings and a sense of freedom, can be the property of another being like himself. On what could such a right of ownership be founded? Do you not see that in your country you have confused things that have no feelings, thoughts, desires or wills—things one takes or leaves, keeps or sells, without them suffering or complaining—with things that can neither be bought nor sold, which have freedom, volition, and desires of their own, which have the ability to give or to withhold themselves for a moment or forever, which suffer and complain? These latter things can never be treated like a trader's stock of goods unless one forgets what their true character is and does violence to nature. Furthermore, your laws seem to me to be contrary to the general order of things. For in truth is there anything so senseless as a precept that forbids us to heed the changing impulses that are inherent in our being, or commands that require a degree of constancy which is not possible, that violate the liberty of both male and female by chaining them perpetually to one another? Is there anything more unreasonable than this perfect fidelity that would restrict us, for the enjoyment of pleasures so capricious, to a single partner—than an oath of immutability taken by two individuals made of flesh and blood under a sky that is not the same for a moment, in a cavern that threatens to collapse upon them, at the foot of a cliff that is crumbling into dust, under a tree that is withering, on a bench of stone that is being worn away? Take my word for it, you have reduced human beings to a worse condition than that of the animals. I don't know what your great workman is, but I am very happy that he never spoke to our forefathers, and I hope that he never speaks to our children, for if he does, he may tell them the same foolishness, and they may be foolish enough to believe it. Yesterday, as we were having supper, you told us all about your "magistrates" and "priests." I do not know who these characters are whom you call Magistrates and Priests and who have the authority to govern your conduct—but tell me, are they really masters of good and evil? Can they transform justice into injustice and contrariwise? Is it within their power to attach the name of "good" to harmful actions or the name of "evil" to harmless or useful deeds? One can hardly think so because in that case there would no longer be any difference between true and false, between good and bad, between beautiful and ugly—only such differences as it pleased your great workman, your magistrates or your priests to define as such. You would then have to change your ideas and behavior from one moment to the next. One day you would be told, on behalf of one of your three masters: "Kill," and in all good conscience you would be obliged to kill. Another day they might say: "Steal," and you would be bound to steal. Or: "Do not eat of this fruit," and you would not dare to eat of it; "I forbid you to eat this vegetable or this meat," and you would be careful never to touch them. There is not a single good thing they could not forbid you to enjoy, and no wickedness they could not order you to commit. And where would you be if your three masters, disagreeing among themselves, took it into their heads to permit, enjoin and forbid you to do the same thing, as I am sure must occasionally happen? Then, in order to please your priest, you would have to get yourself into hot water with the magistrate; to satisfy the magistrate, you would have to risk the displeasure of the great workman; and to make yourself agreeable to the great workman, you would have to fly in the face of your own nature. And do you know what will finally happen? You will come to despise all three, and you will be neither man, nor citizen nor pious believer; you will be nothing at all; you will be at odds with all the authorities, at odds with yourself, malicious, disturbed by your own conscience, persecuted by your witless masters, and miserable, as you were yesterday evening when I offered you my wife and daughters and you could only wail: "What about my religion? What about my holy orders?" Would you like to know what is good and what is bad in all times and places? Pay close attention to the nature of things and actions, to your relations with your fellow creatures, to the effect of your behavior on your own well-being and on the general welfare. You are mad if you believe that there is anything in the universe, high or low, that can add or subtract from the laws of nature. Her eternal will is that good shall be chosen rather than evil, and the general welfare rather than the individual's well-being. You may decree the opposite, but you will not be obeyed. By threats, punishment and guilt, you can make more wretches and rascals, make more depraved consciences and more corrupted characters. People will no longer know what they ought or ought not to do. They will feel guilty when they are doing nothing wrong and proud of themselves in the midst of crime; they will have lost the North Star that should guide their course. Give me an honest answer—in spite of the express commands of your three legislators, do the young men in your country never go to bed with a young woman without having received permission?

THE CHAPLAIN: I would be lying if I said they never do.

OROU: And the women, once they have sworn an oath to belong to only one husband, do they never give themselves to another man?

THE CHAPLAIN: Nothing happens more often.

OROU: And are your legislators severe in handing out punishment to such disobedient people, or are they not? If they are, then they are wild animals who make war against nature; if they are not severe, they are fools who risk bringing their authority into contempt by issuing futile prohibitions.

THE CHAPLAIN: The guilty ones, if they escape the rigor of the laws, are punished by public opinion.

OROU: That's like saying that justice is done by means of the whole nation's lack of common sense, and that public folly is the substitute for law.

THE CHAPLAIN: A girl who has lost her honor cannot find a huband.

OROU: Lost her honor! And for what cause?

THE CHAPLAIN: An unfaithful woman is more or less despised.

OROU: Despised! Why should that be?

THE CHAPLAIN: And the young man is called a cowardly seducer.

OROU: Coward? Seducer? Why that?

THE CHAPLAIN: The father and mother and their dishonored child are desolate. An erring husband is called a libertine; a husband who has been betrayed shares the shame of his wife.

OROU: What monstrous foolishness you're talking! And still you must be holding something back, because when people take it upon themselves to rearrange all ideas of justice and propriety to suit their own whims, to apply or remove the names of things in a completely arbitrary manner, to associate the ideas of good and evil with certain actions or to dissociate them for no reason save caprice—then of course people will blame each other, accuse each other, suspect each other, tyrannize, become jealous and envious, deceive and wound one another, conceal, dissimulate, and spy on one another, catch each other out, quarrel and tell lies. Girls will deceive their parents, husbands their wives and wives their husbands. Unmarried girls— yes, I am sure of it—unmarried girls will suffocate their babies; suspicious fathers will neglect or show contempt for their own rightful children; mothers will abandon their infants and leave them to the mercy of fate. Crime and debauchery will appear in every imaginable shape and form. I see all that as plainly as if I had lived among you. These things are so because they must be so, and your society, whose well-ordered ways your chief boasts to you about, can't be anything but a swarm of hypocrites who secretly trample the laws under foot, or a multitude of wretched beings who serve as instruments for inflicting willing torture upon themselves; or imbeciles in whom prejudice has utterly silenced the voice of nature, or ill-fashioned creatures in whom nature cannot claim her rights.

THE CHAPLAIN: That is a close likeness. But do you never marry?

OROU: Oh yes, we marry.

THE CHAPLAIN: Well, how does it work?

OROU: It consists only of an agreement to occupy the same hut and to sleep in the same bed for so long as both partners find the arrangement good.

THE CHAPLAIN: And when they find it bad?

OROU: Then they separate.

THE CHAPLAIN: But what becomes of the children?

OROU: Oh Stranger! That last question of yours finally reveals to me the last depths of your country's wretchedness. Let me tell you, my friend, that the birth of a child is always a happy event, and its death is an occasion for weeping and sorrow. A child is a precious thing because it will grow up to be a man or a woman. Therefore we take infinitely better care of our children than of our plants and animals. The birth of a child is the occasion for public celebration and a source of joy for its entire family. For the hut it means an increase in wealth, while for the nation it signifies additional strength. It means another pair of hands and arms for Tahiti—we see in the newborn baby a future farmer, fisherman, hunter, soldier, husband or father. When a woman goes from her husband's hut back to that of her family, she takes with her all the children she had brought with her as her dowry; those born during the marriage are divided equally between the two spouses, and care is taken to give each an equal number of boys and girls whenever possible.

THE CHAPLAIN: But children are a burden for many years before they are old enough to make themselves useful.

OROU: We set aside for them and for the support of the aged one part in six of all our harvests; wherever the child goes, this support follows him. And so, you see, the larger the family a Tahitian has, the richer he is.

THE CHAPLAIN: One part in six!

OROU: Yes. It's a dependable method for encouraging the growth of population, for promoting respect for our old people and for safeguarding the welfare of our children.

THE CHAPLAIN: And does it ever happen that a couple who have separated decide to live together again?

OROU: Oh, yes. It happens fairly often. Also, the shortest time any marriage can last is one month.

THE CHAPLAIN: Assuming, of course, that the wife is not with child, for in that case, wouldn't the marriage have to last at least nine months?

OROU: Not at all. The child keeps the name of its mother's husband at the time it was conceived, and its paternity, like its means of support, follows it wherever it goes.

THE CHAPLAIN: You spoke about the children that a wife brings to her husband as dowry.

OROU: To be sure. Take my eldest daughter, who has three children. They are able to walk, they are healthy and attractive, and they promise to be strong when they are grown up. If she should take it into her head to get married, she would take them along, for they belong to her, and her husband would be extremely happy to have them in his hut. He would think all the better of his wife if she were carrying still a fourth child at the time of her wedding.

THE CHAPLAIN: *His* child?

OROU: His or another's. The more children our young women

have had, the more desirable they are as wives. The stronger and lustier our young men are, the richer they become. Therefore, careful as we are to protect our young girls from male advances, and our young boys from intercourse with women, before they reach sexual maturity, once they have passed the age of puberty we exhort them all the more strongly to have as many children as possible. You probably haven't fully realized what an important service you will have rendered my daughter Thia if you have succeeded in getting her with child. Her mother will no longer plague her every month by saying, "But Thia, what is the matter with you? You never get pregnant, and here you are nineteen years old. You should have had at least a couple of babies by this time, and you have none. Who is going to look after you in your old age if you throw away your youth in this way? Thia, I begin to think there is something wrong with you, some defect that puts men off. Find out what it is, my child, and correct it if you can. At your age, I was already three times a mother!"

THE CHAPLAIN: What precautions do you take to safeguard your boys and girls before they reach maturity?

OROU: That's the main object of our children's education within the family circle, and it's the most important point in our code of public morality. Our boys, until the age of twenty-two, that is for two to three years after they reach maturity, must wear a long tunic that covers their bodies completely, and they must wear a little chain around their loins. Before they reach nubile age, our girls would not dare to go out without white veils. The two misdeeds of taking off one's chain or of raising one's veil are rarely met with because we teach our children at a very early age what harmful results will ensue. But when the proper time comes—when the male has attained his full strength, when the principal indication of virility lasts for a sufficient time, and when we are confirmed in our judgment by the quality and by the frequent emission of the seminal fluid—and when the young girl seems wilted and suffers from boredom, when she seems mature enough to feel passion, to inspire it and to satisfy it— then the father unfastens his son's chain and cuts the nail on the middle finger of the boy's right hand. The mother removes her daughter's veil. The young man can now ask a woman for her favors or be asked by her to grant his. The girl may walk about freely in public places with her face and breast uncovered; she may accept or reject men's caresses. All we do is to point out in advance to the boy certain girls and to the girl certain boys that they might well choose as partners. The day when a boy or girl is emancipated is a gala holiday. In the case of a girl, the young men assemble the night before around her hut and the air is filled all night long with singing and the sound of musical instruments. When the sun has risen, she is led by her father and mother into an enclosure where dancing is going on and where games of wrestling, running and jumping are in progress. A naked man is paraded in front of her, allowing her to examine his body from all aspects and in all sorts of attitudes. For a young man's initiation, the young girls do the honors of the occasion by letting him look at the nude female body unadorned and unconcealed. The remainder of the ceremony is enacted on a bed of leaves, just as you saw it on your arrival here. At sunset the girl returns to her parents' hut or else moves to the hut of the young man she has chosen and remains there as long as she pleases.

THE CHAPLAIN: But is this celebration a marriage ceremony or is it not?

OROU: Well, as you have said . . .

A: What do I see written there in the margin?

B: It is a note in which the good chaplain says that the parents' advice on how to choose wives and husbands was full of common sense and contained many acute and useful observations, but that he could not bring himself to quote the catechism itself because it would have seemed intolerably licentious to corrupt, superstitious people like us. He adds, nevertheless, that he was sorry to have left out certain details that would have shown, in the first place, what vast progress a nation can make in some important matter without the assistance of physics and anatomy, if it busies itself continually with it, and in the second place, the different ideals of beauty that prevail in a country where one judges forms in the light of momentary pleasures, as contrasted with a nation where they are appreciated for their usefulness over a longer period of time. To be considered beautiful in the former country a woman must have a high color, a wide forehead, a small mouth, large eyes, finely modeled features, a narrow waist, and small hands and feet. . . . With the Tahitians, however, scarcely one of these things is of any account. The woman who attracts the most admirers and the most lovers is the one who seems most likely to bear many children (like the wife of Cardinal d'Ossat) and whose children seem likely to be active, intelligent, brave, healthy and strong. The Athenian Venus has next to nothing in common with the Venus of Tahiti—the former is a flirtatious Venus, the latter a fertile Venus. A woman of Tahiti said scornfully one day to a woman of her acquaintance: "You are beautiful enough, but the children you bear are ugly; I am ugly, but my children are beautiful, so the men prefer me."

Following this note by the chaplain, Orou continues:

OROU: What a happy moment it is for a young girl and her parents when it is discovered that she is with child! She jumps up and runs about, she throws her arms around her father's and mother's necks. She tells them the wonderful news amidst outcries of mutual joy. "Mother! Father! kiss me! I am pregnant!" "Is it really true?" "Really and truly!" "And who got you with child?" "Such-and-such a one."

THE CHAPLAIN: How can she know who the father of her child is?

OROU: How could she not know? With us the same rule that applies to marriage applies also to love affairs—each lasts at least from one moon to the next.

THE CHAPLAIN: And is the rule strictly observed?

OROU: You can judge for yourself. First, the interval between two moons isn't long, but when it appears that two men have well-founded claims to be the father of a child, it no longer belongs to the mother.

THE CHAPLAIN: To whom does it belong?

OROU: To whichever of the two men the mother chooses to give it. This is the only right she has, and since a child is an object of both interest and value, you can understand that among us loose women are rare and that our young men keep away from them.

THE CHAPLAIN: Then you do have a few licentious women? That makes me feel better.

OROU: Yes, we have some, and more than one kind—but that is another subject. When one of our girls gets pregnant, she is twice as pleased with herself if the child's father is a handsome, well-built, brave, intelligent, industrious young man, because she has reason to hope that the child will inherit its father's good qualities. The only thing a girl would be ashamed of would be a bad choice. You have no idea how much store we set by good health, beauty, strength, industry and courage; you have no notion what a tendency there is, even without our having to pay any particular attention to it, for good physical inheritance to be passed on from generation to generation among us. You are a person who has traveled in all sorts of countries—tell me if you have seen anywhere else so many handsome men and beautiful women as in Tahiti. Look at me. What do you think of me? Well, there are ten thousand men on this island who are taller than I am and just as strong; but there is none braver, and for that reason mothers very often point me out to their girls as a good father for their children.

THE CHAPLAIN: And out of all these children you have sired outside your own hut, how many fall to your share?

OROU: Every fourth, be it a boy or a girl. You see, we have developed a kind of circulation of men, women and children—that is, of able-bodied workers of all ages and occupations—which is much more important than trade in foodstuffs (which are only the products of human labor) in your country.

THE CHAPLAIN: I can easily believe it. What is the significance of those black veils that I have seen a few persons wearing?

OROU: They indicate barrenness, either congenital or that which comes with advanced age. Any woman who lays aside such a veil and mingles with men is considered dissolute, and so is any man who raises such a veil and has commerce with a barren woman.

THE CHAPLAIN: And the gray veils?

OROU: That shows that the woman is having her monthly period. Failure to wear this veil when it should be worn also stigmatizes a woman as dissolute if she has relations with men during that time, and likewise the man who has relations with her.

THE CHAPLAIN: Do you punish this libertinism?

OROU: Only with public disapproval.

THE CHAPLAIN: May a father sleep with his daughter, a mother with her son, a brother with his sister, a husband with someone else's wife?

OROU: Why not?

THE CHAPLAIN: Well! To say nothing of the fornication, what of the incest, the adultery?

OROU: What do you mean by those words, *fornication, incest,* and *adultery?*

THE CHAPLAIN: They are crimes, horrible crimes for which people are burned at the stake in my country.

OROU: Well, whether they burn or don't burn in your country is nothing to me. But you cannot condemn the morals of Europe for not being those of Tahiti, nor our morals for not being those of Europe. You need a more dependable rule of judgment than that. And what shall it be? Do you know a better one than general welfare and individual utility? Well, now, tell me in what way your crime of *incest* is contrary to the two aims of our conduct; if you think that everything is settled once and for all because a law has been promulgated, a derogatory word invented, and a punishment established. Why don't you tell me what you mean by *incest.*

THE CHAPLAIN: Why, *incest* . . .

OROU: Yes, incest . . . ? Has it been a long time since your great workman without hands, head or tools made the world?

THE CHAPLAIN: No.

OROU: Did he make the whole human race at one time?

THE CHAPLAIN: No, he made only one man and one woman.

OROU: Had they children?

THE CHAPLAIN: Of course.

OROU: Let's suppose that these two original parents had no sons —only daughters—and that the mother was the first to die. Or that they had only sons and that the wife lost her husband.

THE CHAPLAIN: You embarrass me. But in spite of anything you may say, incest is a horrible crime, so let's talk about something else.

OROU: That's all very well for you to say. But as for me, I won't speak another word until you tell me why incest is such a horrible crime.

THE CHAPLAIN: All right, I'll grant you that perhaps incest does not offend nature, but isn't it objection enough that it threatens the political order? What would happen to the security of the chief of state, and what would become of a nation's tranquillity, if millions of people should come to be under the thumbs of fifty or so fathers of families?

OROU: That would be the lesser of two evils: There would be no single great society but fifty or so little ones, more happiness and one crime the less.

THE CHAPLAIN: I should think, though, that even here, it must not be very common for a son to sleep with his mother.

OROU: No, not unless he has a great deal of respect for her, or a degree of tenderness that makes him forget the disparity in their ages and prefer a woman of forty to a girl of nineteen.

THE CHAPLAIN: What about intercourse between fathers and daughters?

OROU: Hardly more frequent, unless the girl is ugly and little sought after. If her father has a great deal of affection for her, he helps her in getting ready her dowry of children.

THE CHAPLAIN: What you say suggests to me that in Tahiti the women on whom nature has not smiled have a rather hard time of it.

OROU: What you say only shows that you haven't a high opinion of the generosity of our young men.

THE CHAPLAIN: As for unions between brothers and sisters, I imagine they are very common.

OROU: Yes, and very strongly approved of.

THE CHAPLAIN: According to you, the same passion that gives rise to so many evils and crimes in our countries is completely innocent here.

OROU: Stranger, you have poor judgment and a faulty memory. Poor judgment, because whenever something is forbidden, it is inevitable that people should be tempted to do that thing, and do it. Faulty memory, because you have already forgotten what I told you. We do have dissolute old women who sneak out at night without their black veils and offer themselves to men, even though nothing can come of it. If they are recognized or surprised, the punishment is either exile to the northern tip of the island or slavery. There are precocious girls who lift their white veils without their parents' knowledge—for them we have a locked room in the hut. There are young boys who take off their chain before the time established by nature and our laws—in that case the parents get a strong reprimand. There are women who find the nine months of pregnancy a long time; women and girls who are careless about wearing their gray veils—but as a matter of fact we attach little importance to all these lapses. You would find it hard to believe how much our morals have been improved on these points by the fact that we have come to identify in our minds the idea of public and private wealth with the idea of increasing the population.

THE CHAPLAIN: But don't disturbances ever arise when two men have a passion for the same woman, or when two girls desire the same man?

OROU: I haven't seen as many as four instances. The choice of the woman or man settles the matter. If a man should commit any act of violence, that would be a serious misdemeanor, but even then no one would take any notice unless the injured party were to make a public complaint, and it is almost unheard of for a girl or woman to do so. The only thing I have noticed is that our women are a little less considerate of homely men than our young men are of ill-favored women; but no one is worried with this state of affairs.

THE CHAPLAIN: So far as I can see, jealousy is practically unknown here in Tahiti. But tenderness between husband and wife, and maternal love, which are strong, beautiful emotions—if they exist here at all, they must be fairly lukewarm.

OROU: We have put in their place another impulse, which is more universal, powerful and lasting—self-interest. Examine your conscience in all candor, put aside the hypocritical parade of virtue which is always on the lips of your companions, though not in their hearts, and tell me, if there is anywhere on the face of the earth a man who, if he were not held back by shame, would not prefer to lose his child—a husband who would not prefer to lose his wife—rather than lose his fortune and all the amenities of life? You may be sure that if ever a man can be led to care as much about his fellow men as he does about his own bed, his own health, his leisure, his house, his harvests or his fields, he can be depended upon to do his utmost to look out for the well-being of other people. Then you will see him shedding tears over the bed of a sick child or taking care of a mother when she is ill. Then you will find fruitful women, nubile girls and handsome young men highly regarded. Then you will find a great deal of attention paid to the education of the young, because the nation grows stronger with their growth, and suffers a material loss if their well-being is impaired.

THE CHAPLAIN: I am afraid there is some reason in what this savage says. The poor peasant of our European lands wears out his wife in order to spare his horse, lets his child die without help, and calls the veterinary to look after his ox.

OROU: I didn't quite hear what you were just saying. But when you get back to your own country where everything is so well managed, try to teach them how well our method works. Then they will begin to realize how precious a newborn baby is and how important it is to increase the population. Shall I tell you a secret? But take care that you don't let it out. When you came, we let you do what you liked with our women and girls. You were astonished and your gratitude made us laugh. You thanked us, even though we were levying the heaviest of all taxes on you and your companions. We asked no money of you; we didn't loot your ship; we didn't give a hang for any of your stores of food—but our women and girls came to draw the blood out of your veins. When you go away, you will leave with us a brood of children. Do you think we could have extracted a more valuable tribute from you than this tax collected from your own bodies and from your own sub-stance? If you would care to try and estimate its value, imagine that you have yet to sail along two hundred leagues of coastline, and that every twenty miles they collect the same tribute from you! We have vast areas of land yet to be put under the plow; we need workers, and we have tried to get you to give them to us. We have epidemics from time to time, and these losses must be made up; we have sought your aid to fill up the gaps in our population. We have external enemies to deal with, and for this we need soldiers, so we have al-lowed you to give them to us. We have a surplus of women and girls over men, and we have enlisted your services to help us out. Among these women and girls there are some with whom our men have thus far been unable to beget any children, and these were the ones we first assigned to receive your embraces. A neighboring nation holds us in vassalage, and we have to pay an annual tribute to them in men; you and your friends have helped us to pay off this debt, and in five or six years we shall send them your sons if they turn out to be inferior in some way to our own. Although we are stronger and healthier than you, we have observed that you have the edge on us when it comes to intelligence. So we immediately marked out some of our most beautiful women and girls to collect the seed of a race superior to ours. This is an experiment we have tried, and that we hope will succeed. We have taken from you and your fellows the only thing we could get from you. Just because we are savages, don't think we are incapable of calculating where our best advantage lies. Go wherever you will, and you will always find a man as shrewd as you are. He will give you what he has no use for, and he will always ask for something he has need of. If he offers to trade you a piece of gold for a scrap of iron, that is because he doesn't care a hang for gold, and desires iron. By the way, why is it that you are not dressed like the others? What is the significance of the long robe that covers you from head to foot, and what is that pointed bag that you let hang over your shoulders and sometimes draw up around your ears?

THE CHAPLAIN: The reason I dress as I do is that I am a member of a society of men who are called monks in my country. The most sacred of their vows is never to have intercourse with any woman and never to beget any children.

OROU: Then what kind of work do you do?

THE CHAPLAIN: None.

OROU: And your magistrates allow that sort of idleness—the worst of all?

THE CHAPLAIN: They more than allow it: they honor it and make others do the same.

OROU: My first thought was that nature, or some accident, or some cruel form of sorcery, had deprived you of the ability to reproduce your kind, and that out of pity they had let you go on living instead of killing you. But my daughter tells me that you are a man as robust as any Tahitian and that she has high hopes of getting good results from your repeated caresses. Well, at last I know why you kept mumbling yesterday evening, "But there's my religion, my holy orders!" Could you explain to me why it is that your magistrates show you such favor and treat you with so much respect?

THE CHAPLAIN: I don't know.

OROU: Still, you must know why it was that, although you are a man, you have condemned yourself of your own free will to be one no longer?

THE CHAPLAIN: That's hard to explain, and it would take too long.

OROU: Are monks faithful to their vows of sterility?

THE CHAPLAIN: No.

OROU: I was sure of it. Do you also have female monks?

THE CHAPLAIN: Yes.

OROU: As well behaved as the male monks?

THE CHAPLAIN: They are kept more strictly in seclusion, they dry up from unhappiness and die of boredom.

OROU: So nature is avenged for the injury done to her! Ugh! What a country! If everything is managed the way you say, you are more barbarous than we are.

The good chaplain tells us that he spent the rest of the day wandering about the island, visiting a number of huts, and that in the evening, after supper, the father and mother begged him to go to bed with Palli, the second eldest daughter. She offered herself in the same undress as Thia's, and he tells us that several times during the night he cried out, "My religion! My holy orders!" The third night he suffered the same guilty torments in the arms of Asto, the eldest, and the fourth night, not to be unfair, he devoted to his hostess.

A: Before you go on with his remarks, I have a favor to ask of you, which is to remind me of what happened in New England.[2]

B: This is the story. A prostitute, Miss Polly Baker, upon becoming pregnant for the fifth time, was brought before the high court of Connecticut, near Boston. The law condemns all women of loose life who become mothers when they are unable to pay a fine. Miss Polly, on coming up before her judges for a hearing, delivered herself of the following speech:

"Allow me, gentlemen, to address you briefly. I am a girl who is both wretched and poor and I lack the means to pay lawyers for my defense. But I shall not detain you long. I do not flatter myself that in handing down your sentence upon me you will deviate from the law. What I dare to hope is that you will deign to petition the government on my behalf and relieve me of the fine. This is the fifth time, gentlemen, that I appear before you for the same cause. Twice I have paid heavy fines, twice I have suffered the shame of punishment in public because I was unable to pay. This may be in conformity with the law—I do not argue the point. But there may some-

---

[2] The story that follows has of course no basis in fact. It has been shown to be an invention of Benjamin Franklin's and is reprinted in the 1905 edition of his *Writings* (vol. I, 172 and II, 463–67). In Franklin's day it was reproduced in two British periodicals and translated, with some variations, by both Diderot and Abbé Raynal. It does not occur in any of the printed versions of Diderot's *Supplément* before that edited in 1935 by Gilbert Chinard, who supplied these bibliographical details. The wording here given is not Franklin's but a translation of Diderot's French, which departs in important ways from the original.

times be unjust laws which should be abrogated. There may be some that are too severe, and the legislative power should suspend the sentences rendered. I say that the law which condemns me is at once unjust in itself and too severe upon me.

"I have never offended anybody in the place where I live and I defy my enemies—if I have any—to prove that I have ever done the slightest injury to man, woman, or child. Allow me to forget for a moment that the law exists, in which case I cannot imagine what my crime may be. I have, at the peril of my life, brought five handsome children into the world; I have nourished them at my breast, I have reared them by my toil, and I would have done even more for them had I not had to pay the fines that deprived me of the means.

"Is it a crime to increase the number of His Majesty's subjects in a new country which is short of inhabitants? I took away no woman's husband; I seduced no young man; never have I been accused of any evil deed. If any man can complain of me, it can only be the minister who has been deprived of the fee paid him for marriages. But even that is not my fault. I appeal to you, gentlemen, and ask whether you do not think me sensible enough to prefer the honorable status of wife to the shameful condition in which I have lived hitherto.

"I have always wanted, and still want, to get married, and I make bold to say that I would give as strong evidence of the good conduct, industry, and economy, which befit a woman, as I have so far given of fertility. I defy anybody to say that I have refused to enter that state. The first and only offer of it that was made me, I accepted while still a virgin. I was simple enough to entrust my honor to a man who had none. He gave me my first child and left me. That man is one known to you all; he is actually a judge like yourselves and sits on the same bench. I had hoped that he would appear to-day in court and that he would have enlisted your interest and pity in my favor, that is, in favor of a poor wretch whom he has made such.

"I should have been incapable of exposing him and making him blush for what passed between us. Am I then wrong to complain of the injustice of the law? The first cause of my error, my seducer, is raised to power and honors by the same government which punishes my distress with whips and infamy. I shall be told that I have transgressed the precepts of religion. If I have offended God, leave Him the task of punishing me. You have already excommunicated me from His church: is that not enough? Why add to the torments of Hell which you think are awaiting me in the next world the pain of a fine and a whipping in this one?

"Forgive these remarks, gentlmen. I am no theologian, but I find it hard to believe that it is a great crime to have brought into the world some handsome children to whom God has given a soul and who adore Him. If you make laws to change the nature of human actions, make some against bachelors, whose numbers grow larger every day. They seduce and bring dishonor into family life, deceive young girls like me and then compel them to live in the shameful state in which I find myself, in the midst of a society that rejects and despises them. It is they who break the public peace; theirs are the crimes that deserve reprobation far greater than mine."

This strange speech had the effect hoped for by Miss Baker. The judges remitted the fine and the punishment that replaces it. Her seducer, informed of what had occurred, felt remorse for his behavior and sought to make amends. Two days later he married Miss Baker and made an honest woman of her whom five years earlier he had made a prostitute.

A: And all this is no invention of yours?

B: No.

A: I am very glad to hear it.

B: I am not sure whether the Abbé Raynal does not also report the facts in his *History of Trade in the Two Indies.*

A: An excellent work and so different in tone from his previous ones that the Abbé has been suspected of having pressed other hands into service.

B: That is unfair to him.

A: Malicious gossip, rather.[3] People will pluck at the laurel leaves that bind a great man's brow and the plucking goes so far that he is left without a single leaf.

B: But time gathers them up again and restores the crown.

A: Yes, but the man is dead then. He has suffered from his contemporaries' buffetings, and he is insensible to his rehabilitation by posterity.

CONTINUATION OF THE DIALOGUE

A: I like this courteous chaplain.

B: And I have formed a high opinion of the manners and customs of Tahiti, and of Orou's speeches.

A: Yes, even though they are cast somewhat in a European mold.

[3] This is a handsome compliment of Diderot's, who had himself been one of Raynal's collaborators in that large work.

B: I suppose they are. But now, to continue, the good chaplain complains that his visit to Tahiti was too short. He says that it is very difficult to form a just estimate of the customs of a people that is wise enough to stop when it has attained a golden mean, happy enough to inhabit a part of the world where the fertility of the soil guarantees a long and languid life, industrious enough to provide for the most pressing needs, and indolent enough so that their innocence, repose and felicity are not endangered by a too rapid advance of knowledge. They have no laws and hold no opinions that would stigmatize as evil something that is not by its nature evil. Their plowing and their harvesting are done in common. Their sense of property is very limited. The passion of love, reduced to simple physical appetites, produces none of the disturbances that we connect with it. The whole island lives like one large family, in which each hut is like a single apartment in one of our big houses. The chaplain ends by assuring us that he will never forget the Tahitians, and confesses that he was tempted to throw his vestments into the ship and spend the rest of his days with them. And he fears that he will have more than one occasion to be sorry he didn't.

A: But despite this eulogy, what practical conclusions can you draw from the strange morals and picturesque customs of an uncivilized people?

B: As I see it, human progress began when certain physical causes —for example, the necessity of winning a livelihood from stony soil —brought man's cunning into play. This first push was enough to carry him forward some distance beyond his original goal. When once the aim of satisfying his elementary needs was achieved, he was swept on into the boundless ocean of imagination, with no means of returning. May the happy Tahitians stop where they are now! I see that except in that remote corner of the earth, there has never been any morality and that perhaps in no other part of the world will there ever be any.

A: What do you mean by morality?

B: I mean a general obedience to, and a conduct arising from, the laws, whether they be good or bad. If the laws are good, morals are good; if the laws are bad, morals are bad. If the laws, good or bad, are not observed, the worst possible condition for a society, there are no morals. Now what chance is there of getting people to observe the laws when the laws are contradictory? Read the history of centuries and nations, ancient and modern, and you will find that there are three codes of law under which men have lived—the code of nature, the civil code, and the laws of religion. They have been obliged to violate each of these codes in turn because they have never been in harmony. The result has been that nowhere do we find anyone (as Orou suspected in speaking of our own country) who can be called at once a man, a citizen, and a believer.

A: From which you conclude that if morality were to be based on the eternal, universal relations of men with one another, the religious law would perhaps become superfluous, and the civil law should become nothing more than an explicit statement of the laws of nature.

B: Exactly; otherwise the penalty will be that we shall increase the numbers of the wicked instead of multiplying the good.

A: Or else, if it is considered necessary to preserve all three sets of laws, civil and religious law should be strictly patterned on the law of nature, which we carry with us, graven on our hearts, wherever we go, and which will always be the strongest.

B: What you say is not wholly true. When we are born we bring nothing into the world with us except a constitution similar to that of other human beings—the same needs, an impulsion toward the same pleasures, a common dislike for the same pains: that is what makes man what he is, and the code of morality appropriate to men should rest on no other foundations than these.

A: Yes, but it's not easy to work out in detail.

B: Nothing could be more difficult. Indeed, I believe that the most backward nation in the world, the Tahitians, who have simply held fast to the law of nature, are nearer to having a good code of law than is any civilized nation.

A: For the reason that it would be easier for them to get rid of some of their rustic ways than for us to turn the clock back and reform our abuses.

B: Especially those connected with the relations between men and women.

A: You may be right. But let's begin at the beginning. Let us put nature resolutely to the question and see, without prejudice, what answers she will give on this question.

B: A good idea.

A: Is marriage part of the natural order?

B: If, by marriage, you mean the preference the female has for one male over all others, or that a male has for one female as over against other females—in other words, a mutual preference, leading to the formation of a more or less durable union that perpetuates the species by reproducing individuals—if you mean no more than that, then yes, marriage is part of the natural order.

A: I think so, and for the same reason, because the preference you speak of can be observed not only among human beings but also in various other animal species. You have only to think of the large number of stallions that go chasing after the same mare in our pastures every spring. Only one of them finally gets himself accepted as her mate. But how about courtship?

B: If, by courtship, you mean the vast and varied assortment of expedients, both subtle and forceful, that passion inspires in both male and female when one of them is trying to obtain that preference which leads to the sweetest, most important and most universal of enjoyments—then yes, courtship is part of the natural order.

A: I think so too. Witness the whole variety of small attentions the male renders the female in order to please her, and the countless ways females of all species have of stirring up the passion and attracting the preference of the male. But what about flirtation?

B: That is nothing but deception, for it consists of simulating a passion that one doesn't feel at all and promising favors that one has no intention of conferring. The male flirt is making sport of the female, and vice versa. It's a perfidious game that often ends in the most deplorable fiasco imaginable; a ridiculous sort of jumping through the hoop, in the course of which both the deceiver and the deceived are punished alike by the waste of the most precious part of their lives.

A: So you would say that flirtation is not a part of nature?

B: I wouldn't say that.

A: What about constancy in love?

B: Nothing I could say on that subject would equal what Orou told the chaplain; it is a vain delusion that two children may have at the age when they know nothing about themselves, or when they are blinded by a moment of ecstasy to the transitory character of everything in nature.

A: And that rare phenomenon, marital fidelity?

B: In our part of the world it is the punishment for stubborness which an honest man and an honest woman must suffer. In Tahiti it is a will-o'-the-wisp.

A: And jealousy?

B: It's the passion of a starved, miserly creature who is afraid of being deprived. In man it is an unjust attitude produced by our false moral standards and the extension of property rights to a free, conscious, thinking being that has a will of its own.

A: Then, according to you, jealousy has no place in nature?

B: I didn't say that. Nature includes both vices and virtues along with everything else.

A: A jealous man is gloomy.

B: For the same reason that tyrants are gloomy—they know what they are up to.

A: And modesty?

B: Now you're asking me to give a course on the principles of love-making. A man does not want to be disturbed or distracted while he is taking his pleasure. The delights of love are followed by a condition of lassitude that would put a man at the mercy of his enemy if the latter attacked him at such a moment. Apart from this there is nothing natural in modesty—all the rest is social convention. The chaplain himself, in a third fragment that I haven't yet read to you, notes that the Tahitians are not embarrassed by certain involuntary actions that the nearness of a woman excites in them; and the women and girls are never flustered—though they are sometimes stirred—by the sight of such things. As soon as a woman came to belong to a certain man, and as soon as another man's furtive enjoyment of that girl's favors came to be considered robbery, then the words *modesty, demureness,* and *propriety* were born, along with a whole retinue of imaginary vices. In a word, people tried to build up between the sexes a barrier that would hinder them from tempting one another to violate the laws imposed upon them—but these barriers often produce the contrary effect, since they serve to heat up the imagination, and provoke desires. I have sometimes thought of all the trees planted around our kings' palaces—the sight of a bodice that both reveals and conceals a woman's breasts suggests the same idea—and in both instances I seem to detect a secret wish to escape into the forest, a suppressed impulse to recapture the freedom of our old habitat. The Tahitians would say, "Why do you hide your body? What are you ashamed of? Is it wrong to yield to the noblest urges of one's nature? Man, show yourself frankly if you are well-liked. Woman, if this man is attractive to you welcome his advances with the same frankness."

A: Don't get angry. Though we may begin by acting like civilized people, it is seldom that we don't wind up acting like the Tahitians.

B: Yes, but the preliminaries required by convention waste half the lifetime of a man of genius.

A: True enough, but what's the harm in it? It merely slows down by that much the pernicious impetuosity of the human spirit against which you were inveighing not so long ago. Someone once asked one of our most eminent living philosophers why it is that men court women and not the other way around, to which he replied that it is logical, when you want something, to ask someone who is always in a position to give it.

B: That explanation has always struck me as more ingenious than correct. Nature—indecently, if you like—impels both sexes toward each other with equal force, and in the dreary wild state of nature, which one may imagine, although it probably doesn't exist any-where . . .

A: Not even in Tahiti?

B: No . . . the gap which divides a man from a woman would be crossed first by the more amorously inclined of the two. If one of them hesitates or runs away or pursues or avoids the other or attacks him or puts up a defense against him, the reason is simply that pas-sion, which flares up more abruptly in the one than in the other, does not impel them with equal force. Hence it happens that sexual desire is aroused, consummated and extinguished on one side while it is scarcely developed on the other, and both are disappointed. This is a realistic account of what might happen between two young peo-ple who were perfectly free and innocent of sophistication. But after women have learned through experience and education what more or less painful consequences can follow a blissful interlude, their hearts tremble at a man's approach. The man's heart is far from trembling; he is urged on by his senses and he obeys. The woman's senses cry out for gratification, but she is afraid to listen to them. It's up to the man to find ways of putting her fears to rest, to sweep her off her feet and overwhelm her with ecstasy. Men have kept all of their natural desire for women, whereas, as a geometrician might say, the natural attraction that women feel toward men is di-rectly proportional to the passion they feel and inversely proportional to their fears. This ratio is complicated by a multitude of elements which reflect the usages of our society, and these elements work to-gether to augment the timidity of one sex and the length of time the other sex spends in pursuit. It is a kind of problem in tactics, as when the means of defense and the power of the offense have kept exactly abreast. We have consecrated the woman's resistance, we at-tach blame to the man's violence—violence that would be only a slight injury in Tahiti, but becomes a crime in our cities.

A: But how did it come about that an act so solemn in its purpose, an act to which nature invites us by so powerful a summons—how did it come about that this act, the greatest, the sweetest and the most innocent of pleasures, has become the chief source of our de-pravity and bad conduct?

B: Orou explained it ten times over to the chaplain. Listen once more to what he said, and try to remember it:

It is owing to the tyranny of men, who have converted the posses-sion of a woman into a right of property.

It is owing to the development of morality and custom, which have burdened the conjugal state with too many conditions.

It is owing to our civil laws, which have subjected the institution of marriage to endless formalities.

It is owing to our form of society, in which the disparity of rank and of wealth has given rise to notions of propriety and impropriety.

It is owing to a strange contradiction that is found in all existing societies—the birth of a child, although it is always considered an increase in the national wealth, is usually even more certain to mean more abject poverty for the family into which it is born.

It is owing to our rulers' political philosophy which teaches them to subordinate everything to their own interests and their own security.

It is owing to religious institutions, because their teachings have attached the labels "vice" and "virtue" to actions that are completely independent of morality.

How far we have departed from nature and happiness! Yet nature's sovereignty cannot be destroyed; it will persist in spite of all the obstacles raised in its way. Men may write as much as they like on tablets of bronze—to borrow the saying of Marcus Aurelius—that it is criminal to rub two intestines together voluptuously—the human heart will only be torn between the threats contained in the inscription and the violence of its own impulses. But the untamed heart will not cease to cry out against its oppressors, and in the course of a lifetime the terrible inscription will be ignored a hundred times by the average person. You may engrave on marble: Thou shalt not eat of the ixion nor of the wild vulture; thou shalt have carnal knowledge of no woman save only thy wife; thou shalt not take thy sister in marriage—but you must not forget to increase the severity of the penalties in proportion as your prohibitions become more arbitrary. Indeed, you may make them as ferocious as you please; still you will never be able to root out my natural impulses.

A: How concise the legal codes of nations would be if they only conformed strictly to the law of nature! How many errors and vices would be spared to man!

B: Shall I outline for you the historical origin of nearly all our unhappiness? It is simply this: Once upon a time there was a natural man; then an artificial man was built up inside him. Since then a civil war has been raging continuously within his breast. Sometimes the natural man proves stronger; at other times he is laid low by the artificial, moral man. But whichever gains the upper hand, the poor freak is racked and torn, tortured, stretched on the wheel, continually suffering, continually wretched, whether because he is out of his senses with some misplaced passion for glory or because imaginary shame curbs and bows him down. But in spite of all this, there are occasions when man recovers his original simplicity under the pressure of extreme necessity:

A: Poverty and sickness are two great exorcists.

B: Yes, you've put your finger on it. What, in fact, becomes of all our conventional virtues under such circumstances? A man in dire need is without scruples, and grave illness makes a woman forget her modesty.

A: So I have noticed.

B: And there's another thing that has probably not escaped you —the gradual reappearance of the moral, artificial man follows step by step during one's progress from illness to convalescence and from convalescence to full recovery. The internal warfare breaks out again as soon as the illness is cured, although the invader is almost always at a temporary disadvantage.

A: That's very true. I have had occasion to learn from my own experience that during a period of convalescence the natural man seems to manifest a vigor that is downright damaging to the artificial, moral man. But tell me, in a word, is it better to civilize man or allow him to follow his instincts?

B: Must I be frank?

A: Certainly.

B: If you want to become a tyrant, civilize him; poison him as best you can with a system of morality that is contrary to nature. Devise all sorts of hobbles for him, contrive a thousand obstacles for him to trip over, saddle him with phantoms which terrify him, stir up an eternal conflict inside him, and arrange things so that the natural man will always have the artificial, moral man's foot upon his neck. Do you want men to be happy and free? Then keep your nose out of his affairs—then he will be drawn toward enlightenment and depravity, depending on all sorts of unforeseeable circumstances. But as for our celebrated lawgivers, who have cast us in our present rigid and awkward mold, you may be sure that they have acted to serve their interests and not ours. I call to witness all our political, civil and religious institutions—examine them thoroughly: unless I am very much mistaken, you will see how, through the ages, the human race has been broken to the halter that a handful of rascals were itching to slip over its head. Watch out for the fellow who talks about putting things in order! Putting things in order always means getting other people under your control. The Calabrians are just about the only ones who have refused to be taken in by the flattery of lawgivers.

A: You are an admirer of the state of anarchy in Calabria?

B: I am only appealing to experience, and I'll wager that their barbarous society is less vicious than our "polite society." You hear a great deal about their spectacular crimes, but how many of our everyday rascalities do you suppose it would take to even up the score? I look upon uncivilized people as a number of separate, isolated springs. Naturally these springs occasionally slip loose and snap against each other, and then one or two of them may get broken. In order to prevent this, some sublime genius endowed with profound wisdom fitted all the little springs together into a complicated machine called society. All the springs are wound up in such a way that they are always pushing against each other, and more get broken in a single day in the state of civilization than would have in a whole year if they had been left in their natural anarchy. What a mess! What wreckage! And what wholesale destruction of little springs when two, three or four of these gigantic machines happen to run smack into each other!

A: So you would prefer to live in the raw, wild state of nature?

B: In truth, it's a difficult choice to make. Still, I have heard that on more than one occasion city people have set to plundering each other and then taken to the woods to live, and I've never heard that any forest dwellers ever put on proper clothes and went to live in the city.

A: I have often thought that for every individual the sum total of good and bad was different, but that for any species of animals there was a definite aggregate of happiness and unhappiness that was not subject to change. So perhaps, for all our striving, we do ourselves as much harm as good. Perhaps we have only tormented ourselves in order to make both sides of the equation a little larger without disturbing in the least the eternally necessary balance between its two sides. On the other hand, it isn't to be doubted that the average civilized man lives longer than the average uncivilized native.

B: Well, but what conclusion can you draw from that, seeing that the length of time a machine lasts is no true measure of the stresses and strains that are put on it?

A: I see that you are inclined, on the whole, to believe that men become more wicked and unhappy the more civilized they become.

B: Without going through the list of all the countries in the world, I can only assure you that you won't find the human condition perfectly happy anywhere but in Tahiti. And in only one little spot on the map of Europe will you find it even tolerable—there a set of haughty rulers, anxious about their own safety, have found ways and means of reducing man to what you would have to call a state of bestiality.

A: Are you talking about Venice?

B: Possibly. At least you won't deny that there's no place where enlightenment has made so little headway, where there is less artificial morality, or where there are fewer imaginary vices and virtues.

A: I didn't expect you to sing the praises of the Venetian Republic.

B: No, I'm not singing its praises. I am only pointing out to you one of the ways slavery can be compensated for, a way that all visitors to Venice have noticed and commented on.

A: A poor compensation!

B: Perhaps so. The Greeks proscribed the man who added one string to Mercury's lyre.

A: And that prohibition in itself is the most biting satire on their early lawgivers. They should have cut the first string instead of adding a new one.

B: You see what I'm driving at. Wherever there is a lyre you may be sure it has strings. Wherever natural appetites are brought under regulation you can be sure there will be loose women.

A: Just like La Reymer.

B: And abominable men.

A: Just like Gardeil.

B: And people who get into trouble through no fault of their own.

A: Like Tanié, Mademoiselle de la Chaux, the Chevalier Desroches and Madame de La Carlière.[4] There's no doubt that in Tahiti you would search in vain for a parallel to the depravity of the first two or to the misfortunes of the last three. So what should we do— go back to the state of nature or obey the laws?

B: We should speak out against foolish laws until they get reformed, and meanwhile we should obey them as they are. Anyone who takes it upon himself, on his private authority, to break a bad law, thereby authorizes everyone else to break the good ones. There is less harm to be suffered in being mad among madmen than in being sane all by oneself. We should say to ourselves—and shout incessantly too—that shame, dishonor and penalties have been erroneously attached to actions that are in themselves perfectly harmless. But let us not do those things, because shame, dishonor and penalties are the greatest evils of all. Let us follow the good chaplain's example—be monks in France and savages in Tahiti.

A: Put on the costume of the country you visit, but keep the suit of clothes you will need to go home in.

B: But especially, be scrupulously honorable and truthful in our

[4] All the persons referred to are characters in Diderot's short story, "Ceci n'est pas un conte."

dealings with those frail creatures who can only gratify our desires by putting in jeopardy the most precious advantages of society.

. . . Well, what has become of that thick fog?

A: It seems to have settled.

B: So when we've had our dinner, we'll have a choice between staying inside and going for a stroll?

A: I suppose that will depend more on the ladies' inclination than ours.

B: The women again! You can't take a step in any direction without running straight into them.

A: What do you say, shall we read them the chaplain's account of his talk with Orou?

B: What do you suppose they would say if we did?

A: I haven't the faintest notion.

B: Well, what would they think of it?

A: Probably the opposite of what they would say.

Study Questions

1. The comments of A and B frame the Tahitian story. What is the purpose of this rhetorical frame? Discuss the thematic connection between the Frenchmen's attitude toward women and the Tahitians' attitude. How does the discussion of the formation of civil and religious laws from the survival instinct prepare us for the account of the Tahitian society? What is the relevance of the Polly Baker story? How should we interpret B's remark that we should "be monks in France and savages in Tahiti"? Is it meant to be sarcastic or serious?

2. The Chaplain believes he must talk to Orou as one would speak to a simple child, but Orou is a skilled debater. Trace the logic in Orou's refutation of the Chaplain's argument for the existence of the "Great Workman."

3. The Tahitians have no private property and consider human life itself the only value. Does this make people economic commodities? Discuss the nature of wealth in Tahiti.

4. What is the purpose of the Tahitian wedding ceremony? What real requirements of Tahitian society does the ritual fulfill? Analyze the modern wedding ceremony in the same way for comparison.

5. The Tahitians forbid sexual relations if children are not the intended result. (The Chaplain's religious doctrine might declare

the same thing.) Is sex in Tahiti simply a biological f₁
devoid of love?

6. In what way does "self-interest" in Tahiti become in¹
   ers?

7. Discuss the merits of this statement: "The Tahitians are no more
   pure or innocent than the Europeans; they just define their vices
   as virtues."

8. Is Tahiti anarchic? What guides the course of behavior there?

$\mathcal{W}$ILLIAM MORRIS (1834–1896)
was born in a rural suburb of London, and through his father's wise
investment became heir to a substantial fortune. His early interest
in the Middle Ages and love of ritual drew him to the Church, and
he entered Oxford to prepare to receive orders. After visiting the
continental cathedrals and becoming acquainted with John Ruskin's
writing on architecture, his interest turned to the art of the Church.
Finishing at Oxford, he found support for his view of art in the Pre-
Raphaelite Brotherhood, a group dedicated to the revival of the style
of Italian art predating Raphael. With the encouragement of the
brotherhood, and especially of its foremost member, Dante Gabriel
Rossetti, Morris discovered his talent for design and decorative work.
In 1861 Morris, Marshall, Faulkner and Company began taking
orders for finely crafted furniture, stained glass, wood carvings, and
jewelry. Morris went on to create highly ornamental wallpaper de-
signs and to renovate the art of printing decorative books at his
Kelmscott Press, which published many of his own literary works.

Morris' investment in craftsmanship was not just a business venture. As a defender of the Marxian view that mass production and the
division of labor in modern industry reduce man to an expendable
machine part, Morris felt that the only way to combat commerciali-
zation was to reinstill the pride of artistic creation in the ordinary
laborer. Politically a Socialist, Morris was influenced mainly by John
Ruskin, who asserted that the only real value was life itself. They
both believed that without creativity, imagination, and individuality,
human life loses its value, and man becomes an inert fragment of
his total creative being. For Morris and Ruskin, the creative life had
been lost since medieval times; then, each laborer, unhampered by
exacting standardization and repetition of effort, could stamp his
own personality onto his work, which was a complete and unique
product, at once useful and beautiful. Morris' early attraction to the
Middle Ages, then, finally expressed itself not only in a vogue-set-
ting artistic style but also in an aesthetic doctrine that served as a
revolutionary ideology for reforming nineteenth-century society.

News From Nowhere (1888), originally published by Kelmscott,
was written in response to Edward Bellamy's Looking Backward.
According to Bellamy, twenty-first-century America would rely almost completely upon advanced machinery to do its work. Appro-
priately, Morris' society is postindustrial, molded on the medieval

model, and retains only the most indispensable mechanical hardware for difficult projects. Training in crafts and domestic skills is almost the only formal education received by the members of this class-free society, thus enabling them to exchange jobs for diversion. Work as art brings its own reward in the form of personal pleasure; the common good is served without the need for monetary incentive. This simple formulation may be overly wishful, but we should note that Morris' thesis resolves the two antagonistic forces that Freud theorizes are the source of society's inevitable discontent—the social requirement for work and the personal drive to indulge in the pleasures of the self.

News from Nowhere is reprinted here in a very slightly abridged form.

NEWS FROM NOWHERE; OR, AN EPOCH OF UNREST: BEING SOME CHAPTERS FROM A UTOPIAN ROMANCE

CHAPTER I

DISCUSSION AND BED

Up at the League, says a friend, there had been one night a brisk conversational discussion, as to what would happen on the Morrow of the Revolution, finally shading off into a vigorous statement by various friends of their views on the future of the fully-developed new society.

Says our friend: Considering the subject, the discussion was good-tempered; for those present being used to public meetings and after-lecture debates, if they did not listen to each other's opinions (which could scarcely be expected of them), at all events did not always attempt to speak all together, as is the custom of people in ordinary polite society when conversing on a subject which interests them. For the rest, there were six persons present, and consequently six sections of the party were represented, four of which had strong but divergent Anarchist opinions. One of the sections, says our friend, a man whom he knows very well indeed, sat almost silent at the beginning of the discussion, but at last got drawn into it, and finished by roaring out very loud, and damning all the rest for fools; after which befell a period of noise, and then a lull, during which the aforesaid section, having said good-night very amicably, took his way home by himself to a western suburb, using the means of travelling which civilisation has forced upon us like a habit. As he sat in that vapour-bath of hurried and discontented humanity, a carriage of the underground railway, he, like others, stewed discontentedly, while in self-reproachful mood he turned over the many excellent and conclusive arguments which, though they lay at his fingers' ends, he had forgotten in the just past discussion. But this frame of mind he was so used to, that it didn't last him long, and after a brief discomfort, caused by disgust with himself for having lost his temper (which he was also well used to), he found himself musing on the subject-matter of discussion, but still discontentedly and unhappily. "If I could but see a day of it," he said to himself; "if I could but see it!"

As he formed the words, the train stopped at his station, five minutes' walk from his own house, which stood on the banks of the Thames, a little way above an ugly suspension bridge. He went out of the station, still discontented and unhappy, muttering "If I could but see it! if I could but see it!" but had not gone many steps towards the river before (says our friend who tells the story) all that discontent and trouble seemed to slip off him.

It was a beautiful night of early winter, the air just sharp enough to be refreshing after the hot room and the stinking railway carriage. The wind, which had lately turned a point or two north of west, had blown the sky clear of all cloud save a light fleck or two which went swiftly down the heavens. There was a young moon halfway up the sky, and as the home-farer caught sight of it, tangled in the branches of a tall old elm, he could scarce bring to his mind the shabby London suburb where he was, and he felt as if he were in a pleasant country place—pleasanter, indeed, than the deep country was as he had known it.

He came right down to the river-side, and lingered a little, looking over the low wall to note the moonlit river, near upon high water, go swirling and glittering up to Chiswick Eyot: as for the ugly bridge below, he did not notice it or think of it, except when for a moment (says our friend) it struck him that he missed the row of lights downstream. Then he turned to his house door and let himself in; and even as he shut the door to, disappeared all remembrance of that brilliant logic and foresight which had so illuminated the recent discussion; and of the discussion itself there remained no trace, save a vague hope, that was now become a pleasure, for days of peace and rest, and cleanness and smiling goodwill.

In this mood he tumbled into bed, and fell asleep after his wont, in two minutes' time; but (contrary to his wont) woke up again not long after in that curiously wide-awake condition which sometimes surprises even good sleepers; a condition, under which we feel all our wits preternaturally sharpened, while all the miserable muddles we have ever got into, all the disgraces and losses of our lives, will insist on thrusting themselves forward for the consideration of those sharpened wits.

In this state he lay (says our friend) till he had almost begun to enjoy it: till the tale of his stupidities amused him, and the entanglements before him, which he saw so clearly, began to shape themselves into an amusing story for him.

He heard one o'clock strike, then two and then three; after which he fell asleep again. Our friend says that from that sleep he awoke once more, and afterwards went through such surprising adventures that he thinks that they should be told to our comrades, and indeed the public in general, and therefore proposes to tell them now. But, says he, I think it would be better if I told them in the first person, as if it were myself who had gone through them; which, indeed, will be the easier and more natural to me, since I understand the feelings and desires of the comrade of whom I am telling better than any one else in the world does.

CHAPTER II

A MORNING BATH

Well, I awoke, and found that I had kicked my bed-clothes off; and no wonder, for it was hot and the sun shining brightly. I jumped up and washed and hurried on my clothes, but in a hazy and half-awake condition, as if I had slept for a long, long while, and could not shake off the weight of slumber. In fact, I rather took it for granted that I was at home in my own room than saw that it was so.

When I was dressed, I felt the place so hot that I made haste to get out of the room and out of the house; and my first feeling was a delicious relief caused by the fresh air and pleasant breeze; my second, as I began to gather my wits together, mere measureless wonder: for it was winter when I went to bed the last night, and now, by witness of the river-side trees, it was summer, a beautiful bright morning seemingly of early June. However, there was still the Thames sparkling under the sun, and near high water, as last night I had seen it gleaming under the moon.

I had by no means shaken off the feeling of oppression, and where-ever I might have been should scarce have been quite conscious of the place; so it was no wonder that I felt rather puzzled in despite of the familiar face of the Thames. Withal I felt dizzy and queer; and remembering that people often got a boat and had a swim in mid-stream, I thought I would do no less. It seems very early, quoth I to myself, but I daresay I shall find someone at Biffin's to take me. However, I didn't get as far as Biffin's, or even turn to my left thitherward, because just then I began to see that there was a landing-stage right before me in front of my house: in fact, on the place where my next-door neighbor had rigged one up, though somehow it didn't look like that either. Down I went on to it, and sure enough among the empty boats moored to it lay a man on his sculls in a solid-looking tub of a boat clearly meant for bathers. He nodded to me, and bade me good-morning as if he expected me, so I jumped in without any words, and he paddled away quietly as I peeled for my swim. As we went, I looked down on the water, and couldn't help saying:

"How clear the water is this morning!"

"Is it?" said he; "I didn't notice it. You know the floodtide always thickens it a bit."

"H'm," said I, "I have seen it pretty muddy even at half-ebb."

He said nothing in answer, but seemed rather astonished; and as he now lay just stemming the tide, and I had my clothes off, I jumped in without more ado. Of course when I had my head above water again I turned towards the tide, and my eyes naturally sought for the bridge, and so utterly astonished was I by what I saw, that I forgot to strike out, and went spluttering under water again, and when I came up made straight for the boat; for I felt that I must ask some questions of my waterman, so bewildering had been the half-sight I had seen from the face of the river with the water hardly out of my eyes; though by this time I was quit of the slumbrous and dizzy feeling, and was wide-awake and clear-headed.

As I got in up the steps which he had lowered, and he held out his hand to help me, we went drifting speedily up towards Chiswick; but now he caught up the sculls and brought her head round again, and said:

"A short swim, neighbour; but perhaps you find the water cold this morning, after your journey. Shall I put you ashore at once, or would you like to go down to Putney before breakfast?"

He spoke in a way so unlike what I should have expected from a Hammersmith waterman, that I stared at him, as I answered, "Please to hold her a little; I want to look about me a bit."

"All right," he said; "it's no less pretty in its way here than it is off Barn Elms; it's jolly everywhere this time in the morning. I'm glad you got up early; it's barely five o'clock yet."

If I was astonished with my sight of the river banks, I was no less astonished at my waterman, now that I had time to look at him and see him with my head and eyes clear.

He was a handsome young fellow, with a peculiarly pleasant and friendly look about his eyes,—an expression which was quite new to me, though I soon became familiar with it. For the rest, he was dark-haired and berry-brown of skin, well-knit and strong, and obviously used to exercising his muscles, but with nothing rough or coarse about him, and clean as might be. His dress was not like any modern work-a-day clothes I had seen, but would have served very well as a costume for a picture of fourteenth century life: it was of dark blue cloth, simple enough, but of fine web, and without a stain on it. He had a brown leather belt round his waist, and I noticed that its clasp was of damascened steel beautifully wrought. In short, he seemed to be like some specially manly and refined young gentle-man, playing waterman for a spree, and I concluded that this was the case.

I felt that I must make some conversation; so I pointed to the Surrey bank, where I noticed some light plank stages running down the foreshore, with windlasses at the landward end of them, and said, "What are they doing with those things here? If we were on the Tay, I should have said that they were for drawing the salmon nets; but here—"

"Well," said he, smiling, "of course that is what they *are* for. Where there are salmon, there are likely to be salmon-nets, Tay or Thames; but of course they are not always in use; we don't want salmon *every* day of the season."

I was going to say, "But is this the Thames?" but held my peace in my wonder, and turned my bewildered eyes eastward to look at the bridge again, and thence to the shores of the London river; and surely there was enough to astonish me. For though there was a bridge across the stream and houses on its banks, how all was changed from last night! The soap-works with their smoke-vom-iting chimneys were gone; the engineer's works gone; the lead-works gone; and no sound of rivetting and hammering came down the west wind from Thorneycroft's. Then the bridge! I had perhaps dreamed of such a bridge, but never seen such an one out of an illuminated manuscript; for not even the Ponte Vecchio at Florence came any-where near it. It was of stone arches, splendidly solid, and as grace-ful as they were strong; high enough also to let ordinary river traffic through easily. Over the parapet showed quaint and fanciful little buildings, which I supposed to be booths or shops, beset with painted and gilded vanes and spirelets. The stone was a little weathered, but showed no marks of the grimy sootiness which I was used to on every London building more than a year old. In short, to me a wonder of a bridge.

The sculler noted my eager astonished look, and said, as if in answer to my thoughts:

"Yes, it *is* a pretty bridge, isn't it? Even the up-stream bridges, which are so much smaller, are scarcely daintier, and the down-stream ones are scarcely more dignified and stately."

I found myself saying, almost against my will, "How old is it?"

"Oh, not very old," he said; "it was built or at least opened, in 2003. There used to be a rather plain timber bridge before then."

The date shut my mouth as if a key had been turned in a padlock fixed to my lips; for I saw that something inexplicable had happened, and that if I said much, I should be mixed up in a game of cross questions and crooked answers. So I tried to look unconcerned, and to glance in a matter-of-course way at the banks of the river, though this is what I saw up to the bridge and a little beyond; say as far as the site of the soap-works. Both shores had a line of very pretty houses, low and not large, standing back a little way from the river; they were mostly built of red brick and roofed with tiles, and looked, above all, comfortable, and as if they were, so to say, alive, and sympathetic with the life of the dwellers in them. There was a continuous garden in front of them, going down to the water's edge, in which the flowers were now blooming luxuriantly, and sending delicious waves of summer scent over the eddying stream. Behind the houses, I could see great trees rising, mostly planes, and looking down the water there were the reaches towards Putney almost as if they were a lake with a forest shore, so thick were the big trees; and I said aloud, but as if to myself:

"Well, I'm glad that they have not built over Barn Elms."

I blushed for my fatuity as the words slipped out of my mouth, and my companion looked at me with a half smile which I thought I understood; so to hide my confusion I said, "Please take me ashore now: I want to get my breakfast."

He nodded, and brought her head round with a sharp stroke, and in a trice we were at the landing-stage again. He jumped out and I followed him; and of course I was not surprised to see him wait, as if for the inevitable after-piece that follows the doing of a service to a fellow-citizen. So I put my hand into my waistcoat-pocket, and said, "How much?" though still with the uncomfortable feeling that perhaps I was offering money to a gentleman.

He looked puzzled, and said, "How much? I don't quite understand what you are asking about. Do you mean the tide? If so, it is close on the turn now."

I blushed, and said, stammering, "Please don't take it amiss if I ask you; I mean no offence: but what ought I to pay you? You see I am a stranger, and don't know your customs—or your coins."

And therewith I took a handful of money out of my pocket, as one does in a foreign country. And by the way, I saw that the silver had oxydised, and was like a blackleaded stove in colour.

He still seemed puzzled, but not at all offended; and he looked at the coins with some curiosity. I thought, Well after all, he *is* a waterman, and is considering what he may venture to take. He seems such a nice fellow that I'm sure I don't grudge him a little over-payment. I wonder, by the way, whether I couldn't hire him as a guide for a day or two, since he is so intelligent.

Therewith my new friend said thoughtfully:

"I think I know what you mean. You think that I have done you a service; so you feel yourself bound to give me something which I am not to give to a neighbour, unless he had done something special for me. I have heard of this kind of thing; but pardon me for saying, that it seems to us a troublesome and roundabout custom; and we don't know how to manage it. And you see this ferrying and giving people casts about the water is my *business,* which I would do for anybody; so to take gifts in connection with it would look very queer. Besides, if one person gave me something, then another might, and another, and so on; and I hope you won't think me rude if I say that I shouldn't know where to stow away so many mementos of friendship."

And he laughed loud and merrily, as if the idea of being paid for his work was a very funny joke. I confess I began to be afraid that the man was mad, though he looked sane enough; and I was rather glad to think that I was a good swimmer, since we were so close to a deep swift stream. However, he went on by no means like a madman:

"As to your coins, they are curious, but not very old; they seem to be all of the reign of Victoria; you might give them to some scantily-furnished museum. Ours has enough of such coins, besides a fair number of earlier ones, many of which are beautiful, whereas these nineteenth century ones are so beastly ugly, ain't they? We have a piece of Edward III, with the king in a ship, and little leopards and fleurs-de-lys all along the gunwale, so delicately worked. You see," he said, with something of a smirk, "I am fond of working in gold and fine metals; this buckle here is an early piece of mine."

No doubt I looked a little shy of him under the influence of that doubt as to his sanity. So he broke off short, and said in a kind voice:

"But I see that I am boring you, and I ask your pardon. For, not to mince matters, I can tell you that you *are* a stranger, and must come from a place very unlike England. But also it is clear that it won't do to overdose you with information about this place, and that you had best suck it in little by little. Further, I should take it as very kind in you if you would allow me to be the showman of our new world to you, since you have stumbled on me first. Though indeed it will be a mere kindness on your part, for almost anybody would make as good a guide, and many much better."

There certainly seemed no flavour in him of Colney Hatch; and besides I thought I could easily shake him off if it turned out that he really was mad; so I said:

"It is a very kind offer, but it is difficult for me to accept it, unless—" I was going to say, Unless you will let me pay you properly; but fearing to stir up Colney Hatch again, I changed the sentence into, "I fear I shall be taking you away from your work—or your amusement."

"O," he said, "don't trouble about that, because it will give me an opportunity of doing a good turn to a friend of mine, who wants to take my work here. He is a weaver from Yorkshire, who has rather overdone himself between his weaving and his mathematics, both indoor work, you see; and being a great friend of mine, he naturally came to me to get him some outdoor work. If you think you can put up with me, pray take me as your guide."

He added presently: "It is true that I have promised to go upstream to some special friends of mine, for the hay-harvest; but they won't be ready for us for more than a week: and besides, you might go with me, you know, and see some very nice people, besides making notes of our ways in Oxfordshire. You could hardly do better if you want to see the country."

I felt myself obliged to thank him, whatever might come of it; and he added eagerly:

"Well, then, that's settled. I will give my friend a call; he is living in the Guest House like you, and if he isn't up yet, he ought to be this fine summer morning."

Therewith he took a little silver bugle-horn from his girdle and blew two or three sharp but agreeable notes on it; and presently from the house which stood on the site of my old dwelling (of which more hereafter) another young man came sauntering towards us. He was not so well-looking or so strongly made as my sculler friend, being sandy-haired, rather pale, and not stout-built; but his face was not wanting in that happy and friendly expression which I had noticed in his friend. As he came up smiling towards us, I saw with pleasure that I must give up the Colney Hatch theory as to the waterman, for no two madmen ever behaved as they did before a sane man. His dress also was of the same cut as the first man's, though somewhat gayer, the surcoat being light green with a golden spray embroidered on the breast, and his belt being of filagree silver-work.

He gave me good-day very civilly, and greeting his friend joyously, said:

"Well, Dick, what is it this morning? Am I to have my work, or rather your work? I dreamed last night that we were off up the river fishing."

"All right, Bob," said my sculler; "you will drop into my place, and if you find it too much, there is George Brightling on the look out for a stroke of work, and he lives close handy to you. But see, here is a stranger who is willing to amuse me to-day by taking me as his guide about our country-side, and you may imagine I don't want to lose the opportunity; so you had better take to the boat at once. But in any case I shouldn't have kept you out of it for long, since I am due in the hayfields in a few days."

The newcomer rubbed his hands with glee, but turning to me, said in a friendly voice:

"Neighbour, both you and friend Dick are lucky, and will have a good time to-day, as indeed I shall too. But you had better both come in with me at once and get something to eat, lest you should forget your dinner in your amusement. I suppose you came into the Guest House after I had gone to bed last night?"

I nodded, not caring to enter into a long explanation which would have led to nothing, and which in truth by this time I should have begun to doubt myself. And we all three turned toward the door of the Guest House.

CHAPTER III

THE GUEST HOUSE & BREAKFAST THEREIN

I lingered a little behind the others to have a stare at this house, which, as I have told you, stood on the site of my old dwelling.

It was a longish building with its gable ends turned away from the road, and long traceried windows coming rather low down set in the wall that faced us. It was very handsomely built of red brick with a lead roof; and high up above the windows there ran a frieze of figure subjects in baked clay, very well executed, and designed with a force and directness which I had never noticed in modern work before. The subjects I recognised at once, and indeed was very particularly familiar with them.

However, all this I took in in a minute; for we were presently within doors, and standing in a hall with a floor of marble mosaic and an open timber roof. There were no windows on the side opposite to the river, but arches below leading into chambers, one of which showed a glimpse of a garden beyond, and above them a long space of wall gaily painted (in fresco, I thought) with similar subjects to those of the frieze outside; everything about the place was handsome and generously solid as to material; and though it was not very large (somewhat smaller than Crosby Hall perhaps), one felt in it that exhilarating sense of space and freedom which satisfactory architecture always gives to an unanxious man who is in the habit of using his eyes.

In this pleasant place, which of course I knew to be the hall of the Guest House, three young women were flitting to and fro. As they were the first of the sex I had seen on this eventful morning, I naturally looked at them very attentively, and found them at least as good as the gardens, the architecture, and the male men. As to their dress, which of course I took note of, I should say that they were decently veiled with drapery, and not bundled up with millinery; that they were clothed like women, not upholstered like armchairs, as most women of our time are. In short, their dress was somewhat between that of the ancient classical costume and the simpler forms of the fourteenth century garments, though it was clearly not an imitation of either: the materials were light and gay to suit the season. As to the women themselves, it was pleasant indeed to see them, they were so kind and happy-looking in expression of face, so shapely and well-knit of body, and thoroughly healthy-looking and strong. All were at least comely, and one of them very handsome and regular of feature. They came up to us at once merrily and without the least affectation of shyness, and all three shook hands with me as if I were a friend newly come back from a long journey: though I could not help noticing that they looked askance at my garments; for I had on my clothes of last night, and at the best was never a dressy person.

A word or two from Robert the weaver, and they bustled about on our behoof, and presently came and took us by the hands and led us to a table in the pleasantest corner of the hall, where our breakfast was spread for us; and, as we sat down, one of them hurried out by the chambers aforesaid, and came back again in a little while with a great bunch of roses, very different in size and quality to what Hammersmith had been wont to grow, but very like the produce of an old country garden. She hurried back thence into the buttery, and came back once more with a delicately made glass, into which she put the flowers and set them down in the midst of our table. One of the others, who had run off also, then came back with a big cabbage-leaf filled with strawberries, some of them barely ripe, and said as she set them on the table, "There, now; I thought of that before I got up this morning; but looking at the stranger here getting into your boat, Dick, put it out of my head; so that I was not before *all* the blackbirds: however, there are a few about as good as you will get them anywhere in Hammersmith this morning."

Robert patted her on the head in a friendly manner; and we fell to on our breakfast, which was simple enough, but most delicately cooked, and set on the table with much daintiness. The bread was particularly good, and was of several different kinds, from the big, rather close, dark-coloured, sweet-tasting farmhouse loaf, which was most to my liking, to the thin pipe-stems of wheaten crust, such as I have eaten in Turin.

As I was putting the first mouthfuls into my mouth, my eye caught a carved and gilded inscription on the panelling, behind what we should have called the High Table in an Oxford college hall, and a familiar name in it forced me to read it through. Thus it ran:

"*Guests and neighbours, on the site of this Guest-hall once stood the lecture-room of the Hammersmith Socialists. Drink a glass to the memory! May 1962.*"

It is difficult to tell you how I felt as I read these words, and I suppose my face showed how much I was moved, for both my friends looked curiously at me, and there was silence between us for a little while.

Presently the weaver, who was scarcely so well mannered a man as the ferryman, said to me rather awkwardly:

"Guest, we don't know what to call you: is there any indiscretion in asking you your name?"

"Well," said I, "I have some doubts about it myself; so suppose you call me Guest, which is a family name, you know, and add William to it if you please."

Dick nodded kindly to me; but a shade of anxiousness passed over the weaver's face, and he said:

"I hope you don't mind my asking, but would you tell me where you come from? I am curious about such things for good reasons, literary reasons."

Dick was clearly kicking him underneath the table; but he was not much abashed, and awaited my answer somewhat eagerly. As for me, I was just going to blurt out "Hammersmith," when I bethought me what an entanglement of cross purposes that would lead us into; so I took time to invent a lie with circumstance, guarded by a little truth, and said:

"You see, I have been such a long time away from Europe that things seem strange to me now; but I was born and bred on the edge of Epping Forest; Walthamstow and Woodford, to wit."

"A pretty place, too," broke in Dick; "a very jolly place, now that the trees have had time to grow again since the great clearing of houses in 1955."

William and Dick talk with Boffin, the Golden Dustman of Hammersmith, a nickname for Henry Johnson, who is viewed as an eccentric for writing novels and for laboring over the local colour of earlier times in them.

William and Dick then set off in a carriage.

CHAPTER IV
A MARKET BY THE WAY

We turned away from the river at once, and were soon in the main road that runs through Hammersmith. But I should have had no guess as to where I was, if I had not started from the waterside; for King Street was gone, and the highway ran through wide sunny meadows and garden-like tillage. The Creek, which we crossed at once, had been rescued from its culvert, and as we went over its pretty bridge we saw its waters, yet swollen by the tide, covered with gay boats of different sizes. There were houses about, some on the road, some amongst the fields with pleasant lanes leading down to them, and each surrounded by a teeming garden. They were all pretty in design, and as solid as might be, but countryfied in appearance, like yeomen's dwellings; some of them of red brick like those by the river, but more of timber and plaster, which were by the necessity of their construction so like mediæval houses of the same materials that I fairly felt as if I were alive in the fourteenth century; a sensation helped out by the costume of the people that we met or passed, in whose dress there was nothing "modern." Almost everybody was gaily dressed, but especially the women, who were so well-looking, or even so handsome, that I could scarcely refrain my tongue from calling my companion's attention to the fact. Some faces I saw that were thoughtful, and in these I noticed great nobility of expression, but none that had a glimmer of unhappiness, and the greater part (we came upon a good many people) were frankly and openly joyous.

I thought I knew the Broadway by the lie of the roads that still met there. On the north side of the road was a range of buildings and courts, low, but very handsomely built and ornamented, and in that way forming a great contrast to the unpretentiousness of the houses round about; while above this lower building rose the steep lead-covered roof and the buttresses and higher part of the wall of a great hall, of a splendid and exuberant style of architecture, of which one can say little more than that it seemed to me to embrace the best qualities of the Gothic of northern Europe with those of the Saracenic and Byzantine, though there was no copying of any one of these styles. On the other, the south side, of the road was an octagonal building with a high roof, not unlike the Bapistry at Florence in outline, except that it was surrounded by a lean-to that clearly made an arcade or cloisters to it: it also was most delicately ornamented.

This whole mass of architecture which we had come upon so suddenly from amidst the pleasant fields was not only exquisitely beautiful in itself, but it bore upon it the expression of such generosity and abundance of life that I was exhilarated to a pitch that I had never yet reached. I fairly chuckled for pleasure. My friend seemed to understand it, and sat looking on me with a pleased and affectionate interest. We had pulled up amongst a crowd of carts, wherein sat handsome, healthy-looking people, men, women, and children very gaily dressed, and which were clearly market carts, as they were full of very tempting-looking country produce.

I said, "I need not ask if this is a market, for I see clearly that it is; but what market is it that it is so splendid? And what is the glorious hall there, and what is the building on the south side?"

"O," said he, "it is just our Hammersmith market; and I am glad you like it so much, for we are really proud of it. Of course the hall inside is our winter Mote-House; for in summer we mostly meet in the fields down by the river opposite Barn Elms. The building on our right hand is our theatre: I hope you like it."

"I should be a fool if I didn't," said I.

He blushed a little as he said: "I am glad of that, too, because I had a hand in it; I made the great doors, which are of damascened bronze. We will look at them later in the day, perhaps: but we ought to be getting on now. As to the market, this is not one of our busy days; so we shall do better with it another time, because you will see more people."

I thanked him, and said: "Are these the regular country people? What very pretty girls there are amongst them!"

As I spoke, my eye caught the face of a beautiful woman, tall, dark-haired, and white-skinned, dressed in a pretty light-green dress in honour of the season and the hot day, who smiled kindly on me, and more kindly still, I thought on Dick; so I stopped a minute, but presently went on:

"I ask because I do not see any of the country-looking people I should have expected to see at a market—I mean selling things there."

"I don't understand," said he, "what kind of people you would expect to see; nor quite what you mean by 'country' people. These are the neighbours, and that like they run in the Thames valley. There are parts of these islands which are rougher and rainier than we are here, and there people are rougher in their dress; and they themselves are tougher and more hard-bitten than we are to look at. But some people like their looks better than ours; they say they have more character in them—that's the word. Well, it's a matter of taste. — Anyhow, the cross between us and them generally turns out well," added he, thoughtfully.

I heard him, though my eyes were turned away from him, for that pretty girl was just disappearing through the gate with her big basket of early peas, and I felt that disappointed kind of feeling which overtakes one when one has seen an interesting or lovely face in the streets which one is never likely to see again; and I was silent a little. At last I said: "What I mean is, that I haven't seen any poor people about—not one."

He knit his brows, looked puzzled, and said: "No, naturally; if anybody is poorly, he is likely to be within doors, or at best crawling about the garden: but I don't know of any one sick at present. Why should you expect to see poorly people on the road?"

"No, no," I said; "I don't mean sick people. I mean poor people, you know; rough people."

"No," said he, smiling merrily, "I really do not know. The fact is, you must come along quick to my great-grandfather, who will understand you better than I do. Come on, Greylocks!" Therewith he shook the reins, and we jogged along merrily eastward.

CHAPTER V
CHILDREN ON THE ROAD

We came on many groups both coming and going, or wandering in the edges of the wood. Amongst these were many children from six or eight years old up to sixteen or seventeen. They seemed to me to be especially fine specimens of their race, and were clearly enjoying themselves to the utmost; some of them were hanging about little tents pitched on the greensward, and by some of these fires were burning, with pots hanging over them gipsy fashion. Dick explained to me that there were scattered houses in the forest, and indeed we caught a glimpse of one or two. He said they were mostly quite small, such as used to be called cottages when there were slaves in the land, but they were pleasant enough and fitting for the wood.

"They must be pretty well stocked with children," said I, pointing to the many youngsters about the way.

"O," said he, "these children do not all come from the near houses, the woodland houses, but from the countryside generally. They often make up parties, and come to play in the woods for weeks together in summer-time, living in tents, as you see. We rather encourage them to it; they learn to do things for themselves, and get to notice the wild creatures; and, you see, the less they stew inside houses the better for them. Indeed, I must tell you that many grown people will go to live in the forests through the summer; though they for the most part go to the bigger ones, like Windsor, or the Forest of Dean, or the northern wastes. Apart from the other pleasures of it, it gives them a little rough work, which I am sorry to say is getting somewhat scarce for these last fifty years."

He broke off, and then said, "I tell you all this, because I see that if I talk I must be answering questions, which you are thinking, even if you are not speaking them out; but my kinsman will tell you more about it."

I saw that I was likely to get out of my depth again, and so merely for the sake of tiding over an awkwardness and to say something, I said:

"Well, the youngsters here will be all the fresher for school when the summer gets over and they have to go back again."

"School?" he said; "yes, what do you mean by that word? I don't see how it can have anything to do with children. We talk, indeed, of a school of herring and a school of painting, and in the former sense we might talk of a school of children—but otherwise," said he, laughing, "I must own myself beaten."

Hang it! thought I, I can't open my mouth without digging up some new complexity. I wouldn't try to set my friend right in his etymology; and I thought I had best say nothing about the boy-farms which I had been used to call schools, as I saw pretty clearly that they had disappeared; and so I said after a little fumbling, "I was using the word in the sense of a system of education."

"Education?" said he, meditatively, "I know enough Latin to know that the word must come from *educere,* to lead out; and I have heard it used; but I have never met anybody who could give me a clear explanation of what it means."

You may imagine how my new friends fell in my esteem when I heard this frank avowal; and I said, rather contemptuously, "Well, education means a system of teaching young people."

"Why not old people also?" said he with a twinkle in his eye. "But," he went on, "I can assure you our children learn, whether they go through a 'system of teaching' or not. Why, you will not find one of these children about here, boy or girl, who cannot swim; and every one of them has been used to tumbling about the little forest ponies—there's one of them now! They all of them know how to cook; the bigger lads can mow; many can thatch and do odd jobs at carpentering; or they know how to keep shop. I can tell you they know plenty of things."

"Yes, but their mental education, the teaching of their minds," said I, kindly translating my phrase.

"Guest," said he, "perhaps you have not learned to do these things I have been speaking about; and if that's the case, don't you run away with the idea that it doesn't take some skill to do them, and doesn't give plenty of work for one's mind: you would change your opinion if you saw a Dorsetshire lad thatching, for instance. But, however, I understand you to be speaking of book-learning; and as to that, it is a simple affair. Most children, seeing books lying about, manage to read by the time they are four years old; though I am told it has not always been so. As to writing, we do not encourage them to scrawl too early (though scrawl a little they will), because it gets them into a habit of ugly writing; and what's the use of a lot of ugly writing being done, when rough printing can be done so easily. You understand that handsome writing we like, and many people will write their books out when they make them, or get them written; I mean books of which only a few copies are needed—poems, and such like, you know. However, I am wandering from my lambs; but you must excuse me, for I am interested in this matter of writing, being myself a fair-writer."

"Well," said I, "about the children; when they know how to read and write, don't they learn something else—languages, for instance?"

"Of course," he said; "sometimes even before they can read, they can talk French, which is the nearest language talked on the other side of the water; and they soon get to know German also, which is talked by a huge number of communes and colleges on the mainland. These are the principal languages we speak in these islands, along with English or Welsh, or Irish, which is another form of Welsh; and children pick them up very quickly, because their elders all know them; and besides our guests from over sea often bring their children with them, and the little ones get together, and rub their speech into one another."

"And the older languages?" said I.

"O, yes," said he, "they mostly learn Latin and Greek along with the modern ones, when they do anything more than merely pick up the latter."

"And history?" said I; "how do you teach history?"

"Well," said he, "when a person can read, of course he reads what he likes to; and he can easily get someone to tell him what are the best books to read on such or such a subject, or to explain what he doesn't understand in the books when he is reading them."

"Well," said I, "what else do they learn? I suppose they don't all learn history?"

"No, no," said he; "some don't care about it; in fact, I don't think many do. I have heard my great-grandfather say that it is mostly in periods of turmoil and strife and confusion that people care much about history; and you know," said my friend, with an amiable smile, "we are not like that now. No; many people study facts about the make of things and the matters of cause and effect, so that knowledge increases on us, if that be good; and some, as you heard about friend Bob yonder, will spend time over mathematics. 'Tis no use forcing people's tastes."

Said I: "But you don't mean that children learn all these things?"

Said he: "That depends on what you mean by children; and also you must remember how much they differ. As a rule, they don't do much reading, except for a few storybooks, till they are about fifteen years old; we don't encourage early bookishness: though you will find some children who *will* take to books very early; which perhaps is not good for them; but it's no use thwarting them; and very often it doesn't last long with them, and they find their level before they are twenty years old. You see, children are mostly given to imitating their elders, and when they see most people about them engaged in genuinely amusing work, like house-building and street-paving, and gardening, and the like, that is what they want to be doing; so I don't think we need fear having too many book-learned men."

What could I say? I sat and held my peace, for fear of fresh entanglements. Besides, I was using my eyes with all my might, wondering as the old horse jogged on, when I should come into London proper, and what it would be like now.

But my companion couldn't let his subject quite drop, and went on meditatively:

"After all, I don't know that it does them much harm, even if they do grow up book-students. Such people as that, 'tis a great pleasure seeing them so happy over work which is not much sought for. And besides, these students are generally such pleasant people; so kind and sweet tempered; so humble, and at the same time so anxious to teach everybody all that they know. Really, I like those that I have met prodigiously."

CHAPTER VI

A LITTLE SHOPPING

As he spoke, we came suddenly out of the woodland into a short street of handsomely built houses, which my companion named to me at once as Piccadilly: the lower part of these I should have called shops, if it had not been that, as far as I could see, the people were ignorant of the arts of buying and selling. Wares were displayed in their finely designed fronts, as if to tempt people in, and people stood and looked at them, or went in and came out with parcels under their arms, just like the real thing. On each side of the street ran an elegant arcade to protect foot-passengers, as in some of the old Italian cities. About half-way down, a huge building of the kind I was now prepared to expect told me that this also was a centre of some kind, and had its special public buildings.

Said Dick: "Here, you see, is another market on a different plan from most others: the upper stories of these houses are used for guest-houses; for people from all about the country are apt to drift up hither from time to time, as folk are very thick upon the ground, which you will see evidence of presently, and there are people who are fond of crowds, though I can't say that I am."

I couldn't help smiling to see how long a tradition would last.

Here was the ghost of London still asserting itself as a center,—an intellectual centre, for aught I knew. However, I said nothing, except that I asked him to drive very slowly, as the things in the booths looked exceedingly pretty.

"Yes," said he, "this is a very good market for pretty things, and is mostly kept for the handsomer goods, as the Houses-of-Parliament market, where they set out cabbages and turnips and such like things, along with beer and the rougher kind of wine, is so near."

Then he looked at me curiously, and said, "Perhaps you would like to do a little shopping, as 'tis called."

I looked at what I could see of my rough blue duds, which I had plenty of opportunity of contrasting with the gay attire of the citizens we had come across; and I thought that if, as seemed likely, I should presently be shown about as a curiosity for the amusement of this most unbusinesslike people, I should like to look a little less like a discharged ship's purser. But in spite of all that had happened, my hand went down into my pocket again, where to my dismay it met nothing metallic except two rusty old keys, and I remembered that amidst our talk in the guest-hall at Hammersmith I had taken the cash out of my pocket to show to the pretty Annie, and had left it lying there. My face fell fifty per cent., and Dick, beholding me, said rather sharply:

"Hilloa, Guest! what's the matter now? Is it a wasp?"

"No," said I, "but I've left it behind."

"Well," said he, "whatever you have left behind, you can get in this market again, so don't trouble yourself about it."

I had come to my senses by this time, and remembering the astounding customs of this country, had no mind for another lecture on social economy and the Edwardian coinage; so I said only:

"My clothes— Couldn't I? You see— What do you think could be done about them?"

He didn't seem in the least inclined to laugh, but said quite gravely:

"O don't get new clothes yet. You see, my great-grandfather is an antiquarian, and he will want to see you just as you are. And, you know, I mustn't preach to you, but surely it wouldn't be right for you to take away people's pleasure of studying your attire, by just going and making yourself like everybody else. You feel that, don't you?" said he, earnestly.

I did *not* feel it my duty to set myself up for a scarecrow amidst this beauty-loving people, but I saw I had got across some ineradicable prejudice, and that it wouldn't do to quarrel with my new friend. So I merely said, "O certainly, certainly."

"Well," said he, pleasantly, "you may as well see what the inside of these booths is like: think of something you want."

Said I: "Could I get some tobacco and a pipe?"

"Of course," said he; "what was I thinking of, not asking you before? Well, Bob is always telling me that we nonsmokers are a selfish lot, and I'm afraid he is right. But come along; here is a place just handy."

Therewith he drew rein and jumped down, and I followed. A very handsome woman, splendidly clad in figured silk, was slowly passing by, looking into the windows as she went. To her quoth Dick: "Maiden, would you kindly hold our horse while we go in for a little?" She nodded to us with a kind smile, and fell to patting the horse with her pretty hand.

"What a beautiful creature!" said I to Dick as we entered.

"What, old Greylocks?" said he, with a sly grin.

"No, no," said I; "Goldylocks,—the lady."

"Well, so she is," said he. " 'Tis a good job there are so many of them that every Jack may have his Jill: else I fear that we should get fighting for them. Indeed," said he, becoming very grave, "I don't say that it does not happen even now, sometimes. For you know love is not a very reasonable thing, and perversity and self-will are commoner than some of our moralists think." He added, in a still more sombre tone: "Yes, only a month ago there was a mishap down by us, that in the end cost the lives of two men and a woman, and, as it were, put out the sunlight for us for a while. Don't ask me about it just now; I may tell you about it later on."

By this time we were within the shop or booth, which had a counter, and shelves on the walls, all very neat, though without any pretence of showiness, but otherwise not very different to what I had been used to. Within were a couple of children—a brown-skinned boy of about twelve, who sat reading a book, and a pretty little girl of about a year older, who was sitting also reading behind the counter; they were obviously brother and sister.

"Good morning, little neighbours," said Dick. "My friend here wants tobacco and a pipe; can you help him?"

"O yes, certainly," said the girl with a sort of demure alertness which was somewhat amusing. The boy looked up, and fell to staring at my outlandish attire, but presently reddened and turned his head, as if he knew that he was not behaving prettily.

"Dear neighbour," said the girl, with the most solemn countenance of a child playing at keeping a shop, "what tobacco is it you would like?"

"Latakia," quoth I, feeling as if I were assisting at a child's game, and wondering whether I should get anything but make-believe.

But the girl took a dainty little basket from a shelf beside her, went to a jar, and took out a lot of tobacco and put the filled basket down on the counter before me, where I could both smell and see that it was excellent Latakia.

"But you haven't weighed it," said I, "and—how much am I to take?"

"Why," she said, "I advise you to cram your bag, because you may be going where you can't get Latakia. Where is your bag?"

I fumbled about, and at last pulled out my piece of cotton print which does duty with me for a tobacco pouch. But the girl looked at it with some disdain, and said:

"Dear neighbour, I can give you something much better than that cotton rag." And she tripped up the shop and came back presently, and as she passed the boy whispered something in his ear, and he nodded and got up and went out. The girl held up in her finger and thumb a red morocco bag, gaily embroidered, and said, "There, I have chosen one for you, and you are to have it: it is pretty, and will hold a lot."

Therewith she fell to cramming it with the tobacco, and laid it down by me and said, "Now for the pipe: that also you must let me choose for you; there are three pretty ones just come in."

She disappeared again, and came back with a big-bowled pipe in her hand, carved out of some hard wood very elaborately, and mounted in gold sprinkled with little gems. It was, in short, as pretty and gay a toy as I had ever seen; something like the best kind of Japanese work, but better.

"Dear me!" said I, when I set eyes on it, "this is altogether too grand for me, or for anybody but the Emperor of the World. Besides, I shall lose it: I always lose my pipes."

The child seemed rather dashed, and said, "Don't you like it, neighbour?"

"O yes," I said, "of course I like it."

"Well, then, take it," said she, "and don't trouble about losing it. What will it matter if you do? Somebody is sure to find it, and he will use it, and you can get another."

I took it out of her hand to look at it, and while I did so, forgot my caution, and said, "But however am I to pay for such a thing as this?"

Dick laid his hand on my shoulder as I spoke, and turning I met his eyes with a comical expression in them, which warned me against another exhibition of extinct commercial morality; so I reddened and held my tongue, while the girl simply looked at me with the deepest gravity, as if I were a foreigner blundering in my speech, for she clearly didn't understand me a bit.

"Thank you so very much," I said at last, effusively, as I put the pipe in my pocket, not without a qualm of doubt as to whether I shouldn't find myself before a magistrate presently.

"O, you are so very welcome," said the little lass, with an affectation of grown-up manners at their best which was very quaint. "It is such a pleasure to serve dear old gentlemen like you; specially when one can see at once that you have come from far over sea."

"Yes, my dear," quoth I, "I have been a great traveller."

As I told this lie from pure politeness, in came the lad again, with a tray in his hands, on which I saw a long flask and two beautiful glasses. "Neighbours," said the girl (who did all the talking, her brother being very shy, clearly) "please to drink a glass to us before you go, since we do not have guests like this every day."

Therewith the boy put the tray on the counter and solemnly poured out a straw-coloured wine into the long bowls. Nothing loth, I drank, for I was thirsty with the hot day; and thinks I, I am yet in the world, and the grapes of the Rhine have not yet lost their flavour; for if ever I drank good Steinberg, I drank it that morning; and I made a mental note to ask Dick how they managed to make fine wine when there were no longer labourers compelled to drink rot-gut instead of the fine wine which they themselves made.

"Don't you drink a glass to us, dear little neighbours?" said I.

"I don't drink wine," said the lass; "I like lemonade better: but I wish your health!"

"And I like ginger-beer better," said the little lad.

Well, well, thought I, neither have children's tastes changed much. And therewith we gave them good day and went out of the booth.

To my disappointment, like a change in a dream, a tall old man was holding our horse instead of the beautiful woman. He explained to us that the maiden could not wait, and that he had taken her place; and he winked at us and laughed when he saw how our faces fell, so that we had nothing for it but to laugh also.

"Where are you going?" said he to Dick.

"To Bloomsbury," said Dick.

"If you two don't want to be alone, I'll come with you," said the old man.

"All right," said Dick, "tell me when you want to get down and I'll stop for you. Let's get on."

So we got under way again; and I asked if children generally waited on people in the markets. "Often enough," said he, "when it isn't a matter of dealing with heavy weights, but by no means always. The children like to amuse themselves with it, and it is good for them, because they handle a lot of diverse wares and get to learn about them, how they are made, and where they come from, and so on. Besides, it is such very easy work that anybody can do it. It is said that in the early days of our epoch there were a good many people who were hereditarily afflicted with a disease called Idleness, because they were the direct descendants of those who in the bad times used to force other people to work for them—the people, you know, who are called slave-holders or employers of labour in the history books. Well, these Idleness-stricken people used to serve booths *all* their time, because they were fit for so little. Indeed, I believe that at one time they were actually *compelled* to do some such work, because they, especially the women, got so ugly and produced such ugly children if their disease was not treated sharply, that the neighbours couldn't stand it. However, I am happy to say that all that is gone by now; the disease is either extinct, or exists in such a mild form that a short course of aperient medicine carries it off. It is sometimes called the Blue-devils now, or the Mulleygrubs. Queer names, ain't they?"

"Yes," said I, pondering much. But the old man broke in:

"Yes, all that is true, neighbour; and I have seen some of those poor women grown old. But my father used to know some of them when they were young; and he said that they were as little like young women as might be: they had hands like bunches of skewers, and wretched little arms like sticks; and waists like hour-glasses, and thin lips and peaked noses and pale cheeks; and they were always pretending to be offended at anything you said or did to them. No wonder they bore ugly children, for no one except men like them could be in love with them—poor things!"

He stopped, and seemed to be musing on his past life, and then said:

"And do you know, neighbours, that once on a time people were still anxious about that disease of Idleness: at one time we gave ourselves a great deal of trouble in trying to cure people of it. Have you not read any of the medical books on the subject?"

"No," said I; for the old man was speaking to me.

"Well," said he, "it was thought at the time that it was the survival of the old mediæval disease of leprosy: it seems it was very catching, for many of the people afflicted by it were much secluded, and were waited upon by a special class of diseased persons queerly dressed up, so that they might be known. They wore amongst other garments, breeches made of worsted velvet, that stuff which used to be called plush some years ago."

All this seemed very interesting to me, and I should like to have made the old man talk more. But Dick got rather restive under so much ancient history: besides, I suspect he wanted to keep me as fresh as he could for his great-grandfather. So he burst out laughing at last, and said: "Excuse me, neighbours, but I can't help it. Fancy people not liking to work!—it's too ridiculous. Why, even you like to work, old fellow—sometimes," said he, affectionately patting the old horse with the whip. "What a queer disease! it may well be called Mulleygrubs!"

And he laughed out again most boisterously; rather too much so, I thought, for his usual good manners; and I laughed with him for company's sake, but from the teeth outward only; for I saw nothing funny in people not liking to work, as you may well imagine.

CHAPTER VII

TRAFALGAR SQUARE

I pulled out my magnificent pipe and fell a-smoking, and the old horse jogged on again. As we went, I said:

"This pipe is a very elaborate toy, and you seem so reasonable in this country, and your architecture is so good, that I rather wonder at your turning out such trivialities."

It struck me as I spoke that this was rather ungrateful of me, after having received such a fine present; but Dick didn't seem to notice my bad manners, but said:

"Well, I don't know; it *is* a pretty thing, and since nobody need make such things unless they like, I don't see why they shouldn't make them, *if* they like. Of course, if carvers were scarce they would all be busy on the architecture, as you call it, and then these 'toys' (a good word) would not be made; but since there are plenty of people who can carve—in fact, almost everybody, and as work is somewhat scarce, or we are afraid it may be, folk do not discourage this kind of petty work."

He mused a little, and seemed somewhat perturbed; but presently his face cleared, and he said: "After all, you must admit that the pipe is a very pretty thing, with the little people under the trees all cut so clean and sweet;—too elaborate for a pipe, perhaps, but— well, it is very pretty."

"Too valuable for its use, perhaps," said I.

"What's that?" said he; "I don't understand."

I was just going in a helpless way to try to make him understand, when we came by the gates of a big rambling building, in which work of some sort seemed going on. "What building is that?" said I, eagerly; for it was a pleasure amidst all these strange things to see something a little like what I was used to: "it seems to be a factory."

"Yes," he said, "I think I know what you mean, and that's what it is; but we don't call them factories now, but Banded-workshops: that is, places were people collect who want to work together."

"I suppose," said I, "power of some sort is used there?"

"No, no," said he. "Why should people collect together to use power, when they can have it at the places where they live, or hard by, any two or three of them; or any one, for the matter of that? No; folk collect in these Banded-workshops to do hand-work in which working together is necessary or convenient; such work is often very pleasant. In there, for instance, they make pottery and glass,—there, you can see the tops of the furnaces. Well, of course it's handy to have fair-sized ovens and kilns and glass-pots, and a good lot of things to use them for: though of course there are a good many such places, as it would be ridiculous if a man had a liking for pot-making or glass-blowing that he should have to live in one place or be obliged to forego the work he liked."

"I see no smoke coming from the furnaces," said I.

"Smoke?" said Dick; "why should you see smoke?"

I held my tongue, and he went on: "It's a nice place inside, though as plain as you see outside. As to the crafts, throwing the clay must be jolly work: the glass-blowing is rather a sweltering job; but some folk like it very much indeed; and I don't much wonder: there is such a sense of power, when you have got deft in it, in dealing with the hot metal. It makes a lot of pleasant work," said he, smiling, "for however much care you take of such goods, break they will, one day or another, so there is always plenty to do."

I held my tongue and pondered.

We came just here on a gang of men road-mending, which delayed us a little; but I was not sorry for it; for all I had seen hitherto seemed a mere part of a summer holiday; and I wanted to see how this folk would set to on a piece of real necessary work. They had been resting, and had only just begun work again as we came up; so that the rattle of the picks was what woke me from my musing. There were about a dozen of them, strong young men, looking much like a boating party at Oxford would have looked in the days I remembered, and not more troubled with their work: their outer raiment lay on the road-side in an orderly pile under the guardianship

of a six-year-old boy, who had his arm thrown over the neck of a
big mastiff, who was as happily lazy as if the summer-day had been
made for him alone. As I eyed the pile of clothes, I could see the
gleam of gold and silk embroidery on it, and judged that some of
these workmen had tastes akin to those of the Golden Dustman of
Hammersmith. Beside them lay a good big basket that had hints
about it of cold pie and wine: a half dozen of young women stood
by watching the work or the workers, both of which were worth
watching, for the latter smote great strokes and were very deft in
their labour, and as handsome clean-built fellows as you might find
a dozen of in a summer day. They were laughing and talking merrily with each other and the women, but presently their foreman
looked up and saw our way stopped. So he stayed his pick and
sang out, "Spell ho, mates! here are neighbours want to get past."
Whereon the others stopped also, and drawing around us, helped
the old horse by easing our wheels over the half undone road, and
then, like men with a pleasant task on hand, hurried back to their
work, only stopping to give us a smiling good-day; so that the sound
of the picks broke out again before Greylocks had taken to his jog-
trot. Dick looked back over his shoulder at them and said:

"They are in luck to-day: it's right down good sport trying how
much pick-work one can get into an hour; and I can see those neighbours know their business well. It is not a mere matter of strength
getting on quickly with such work; is it, Guest?"

"I should think not," said I, "but to tell you the truth, I have
never tried my hand at it."

"Really?" said he gravely, "that seems a pity; it is good work for
hardening the muscles, and I like it; though I admit it is pleasanter
the second week than the first. Not that I am a good hand at it: the
fellows used to chaff me at one job where I was working, I remember, and sing out to me, 'Well rowed, stroke!' 'Put your back into it,
bow!' "

"Not much of a joke," quoth I.

"Well," said Dick, "everything seems like a joke when we have a
pleasant spell of work on, and good fellows merry about us; we feel
so happy, you know." Again I pondered silently.

*The old man traveling with Dick and William bids them fare-
well. Dick introduces William to his great-grandfather, who is "over
a hundred and five," and who lives near the British Museum. Dick
is surprised to find a woman named Clara there and talks with her
in another room, while William and Dick's kinsman converse.*

CHAPTER IX

CONCERNING LOVE

The old man, whose name, by the bye, like his kinsman's, was Hammond, smiled and nodded, and wheeling his seat round to me, bade me sit in a heavy oak chair, and said, as he saw my eyes fix on its curious carving:

"Yes, I am much tied to the past, *my* past, you understand. These very pieces of furniture belong to a time before my early days; it was my father who got them made; if they had been done within the last fifty years they would have been much cleverer in execution; but I don't think I should have liked them the better. We were almost beginning again in those days: and they were brisk, hot-headed times. But you hear how garrulous I am: ask me questions, ask me questions about anything, dear guest; since I *must* talk, make my talk profitable to you."

I was silent for a minute, and then I said, somewhat nervously: "Excuse me if I am rude; but I am so much interested in Richard, since he has been so kind to me, a perfect stranger, that I should like to ask a question about him."

"Well," said old Hammond, "if he were not 'kind,' as you call it, to a perfect stranger he would be thought a strange person, and people would be apt to shun him. But ask on, ask on! don't be shy of asking."

Said I: "That beautiful girl, is he going to be married to her?"

"Well," said he, "yes, he is. He has been married to her once already, and now I should say it is pretty clear that he will be married to her again."

"Indeed," quoth I, wondering what that meant.

"Here is the whole tale," said old Hammond; "a short one enough; and now I hope a happy one: they lived together two years the first time; were both very young; and then she got it into her head that she was in love with somebody else. So she left poor Dick; I say *poor* Dick, because he had not found any one else. But it did not last long, only about a year. Then she came to me, as she was in the habit of bringing her troubles to the old carle, and asked me how Dick was, and whether he was happy, and all the rest of it. So I saw how the land lay, and said he was very unhappy, and not at all well; which last at any rate was a lie. There, you can guess the rest. Clara came to have a long talk with me to-day, but Dick will serve her turn much better. Indeed, if he hadn't chanced in upon me to-day I should have had to have sent for him to-morrow."

"Dear me," said I. "Have they any children?"

"Yes," said he, "two; they are staying with one of my daughters at present, where, indeed, Clara has mostly been. I wouldn't lose sight of her, as I felt sure they would come together again: and Dick, who is the best of good fellows, really took the matter to heart. You see, he had no other love to run to, as she had. So I managed it all; as I have done with such-like matters before."

"Ah," said I, "no doubt you wanted to keep them out of the Divorce Court: but I suppose it often has to settle such matters."

"Then you suppose nonsense," said he. "I know that there used to be such lunatic affairs as divorce-courts: but just consider; all the cases that came into them were matters of property quarrels: and I think, dear guest," said he, smiling, "that though you do come from another planet, you can see from the mere outside look of our world that quarrels about private property could not go on amongst us in our days."

Indeed, my drive from Hammersmith to Bloomsbury, and all the quiet happy life I had seen so many hints of, even apart from my shopping, would have been enough to tell me that "the sacred rights of property," as we used to think of them, were now no more. So I sat silent while the old man took up the thread of the discourse again, and said:

"Well, then, property quarrels being no longer possible, what remains in these matters that a court of law could deal with? Fancy a court for enforcing a contract of passion or sentiment! If such a thing were needed as a *reductio ad absurdum* of the enforcement of contract, such a folly would do that for us."

He was silent again a little, and then said: "You must understand once for all that we have changed these matters; or rather, that our way of looking at them has changed, as we have changed within the last two hundred years. We do not deceive ourselves, indeed, or believe that we can get rid of all the trouble that besets the dealings between the sexes. We know that we must face the unhappiness that comes of man and woman confusing the relations between natural passion, and sentiment, and the friendship which, when things go well, softens the awakening from passing illusions: but we are not so mad as to pile up degradation on that unhappiness by engaging in sordid squabbles about livelihood and position, and the power of tyrannising over the children who have been the results of love or lust."

Again he paused awhile, and again went on: "Calf love, mistaken

for a heroism that shall be life-long, yet early waning into disappointment; the inexplicable desire that comes on a man of riper years to
be the all-in-all to some one woman, whose ordinary human kindness and human beauty he has idealised into superhuman perfection, and made the one object of his desire; or lastly the reasonable
longing of a strong and thoughtful man to become the most intimate
friend of some beautiful and wise woman, the very type of the
beauty and glory of the world which we love so well,—as we exult
in all the pleasure and exaltation of spirit which goes with these
things, so we set ourselves to bear the sorrow which not unseldom
goes with them also; remembering those lines of the ancient poet (I
quote roughly from memory one of the many translations of the
nineteenth century):

> 'For this the Gods have fashioned man's grief and evil day
> That still for man hereafter might be the tale and the lay.

"Well, well, 'tis little likely anyhow that all tales shall be lacking,
or all sorrow cured."

He was silent for some time, and I would not interrupt him. At
last he began again: "But you must know that we of these generations are strong and healthy of body, and live easily; we pass our
lives in reasonable strife with nature, exercising not one side of ourselves only, but all sides, taking the keenest pleasure in all the life
of the world. So it is a point of honour with us not to be self-centred;
not to suppose that the world must cease because one man is sorry;
therefore we should think it foolish, or if you will, criminal, to exaggerate these matters of sentiment and sensibility: we are no more
inclined to eke out our sentimental sorrows than to cherish our
bodily pains; and we recognise that there are other pleasures besides
love-making. You must remember, also, that we are long-lived, and
that therefore beauty both in man and woman is not so fleeting as it
was in the days when we were burdened so heavily by self-inflicted
diseases. So we shake off these griefs in a way which perhaps the
sentimentalists of other times would think contemptible and un-
heroic, but which we think necessary and manlike. As on the other
hand, therefore, we have ceased to be commercial in our love-matters,
so also we have ceased to be *artificially* foolish. The folly which
comes by nature, the unwisdom of the immature man, or the older
man caught in a trap, we must put up with that, nor are we much
ashamed of it; but to be conventionally sensitive or sentimental—my
friend, I am old and perhaps disappointed, but at least I think we
have cast off *some* of the follies of the older world."

He paused, as if for some words of mine; but I held my peace:

then he went on: "At least, if we suffer from the tyranny and fickle-ness of nature or our own want of experience, we neither grimace about it, nor lie. If there must be sundering betwixt those who meant never to sunder, so it must be: but there need be no pretext of unity when the reality of it is gone: nor do we drive those who well know that they are incapable of it to profess an undying sentiment which they cannot really feel: thus it is that as that monstrosity of venal lust is no longer possible, so also it is no longer needed. Don't mis-understand me. You did not seem shocked when I told you that there were no law-courts to enforce contracts of sentiment or passion; but so curiously are men made, that perhaps you will be shocked when I tell you that there is no code of public opinion which takes the place of such courts, and which might be as tyrannical and unreason-able as they were. I do not say that people don't judge their neigh-bours' conduct, sometimes, doubtless, unfairly. But I do say that there is no unvarying conventional set of rules by which people are judged; no bed of Procrustes to stretch or cramp their minds and lives; no hypocritical excommunication which people are *forced* to pronounce, either by unconsidered habit, or by the unexpressed threat of the lesser interdict if they are lax in their hypocrisy. Are you shocked now?"

"No–o—no," said I, with some hesitation. "It is all so different."

"At any rate," said he, "one thing I think I can answer for: what-ever sentiment there is, it is real—and general; it is not confined to people very specially refined. I am also pretty sure, as I hinted to you just now, that there is not by a great way as much suffering involved in these matters either to men or to women as there used to be. But excuse me for being so prolix on this question! You know you asked to be treated like a being from another planet."

"Indeed I thank you very much," said I. "Now may I ask you about the position of women in your society?"

He laughed very heartily for a man of his years, and said: "It is not without reason that I have got a reputation as a careful student of history. I believe I really do understand 'the Emancipation of Women movement' of the nineteenth century. I doubt if any other man now alive does."

"Well?" said I, a little bit nettled by his merriment.

"Well," said he, "of course you will see that all that is a dead con-troversy now. The men have no longer any opportunity of tyrannis-ing over the women, or the women over the men; both of which things took place in those old times. The women do what they can do best, and what they like best, and the men are neither jealous of it or injured by it. This is such a commonplace that I am almost ashamed to state it."

I said, "O; and legislation? do they take any part in that?"

Hammond smiled and said: "I think you may wait for an answer to that question till we get on to the subject of legislation. There may be novelties to you in that subject also."

"Very well," I said; "but about this woman question? I saw at the Guest House that the women were waiting on the men: that seems a little like reaction, doesn't it?"

"Does it?" said the old man; "perhaps you think housekeeping an unimportant occupation, not deserving of respect. I believe that was the opinion of the 'advanced' women of the nineteenth century, and their male backers. If it is yours, I recommend to your notice an old Norwegian folk-lore tale called How the Man minded the House, or some such title; the result of which minding was that, after various tribulations, the man and the family cow balanced each other at the end of a rope, the man hanging half-way up the chimney, the cow dangling from the roof, which, after the fashion of the country, was of turf and sloping down low to the ground. Hard on the cow, I think. Of course no such mishap could happen to such a superior person as yourself," he added, chuckling.

I sat somewhat uneasy under this dry gibe. Indeed, his manner of treating this latter part of the question seemed to me a little disrespectful.

"Come, now, my friend," quoth he, "don't you know that it is a great pleasure to a clever woman to manage a house skilfully, and to do it so that all the house-mates about her look pleased, and are grateful to her? And then, you know, everybody likes to be ordered about by a pretty woman: why, it is one of the pleasantest forms of flirtation. You are not so old that you cannot remember that. Why, I remember it well."

And the old fellow chuckled again, and at last fairly burst out laughing.

"Excuse me," said he, after a while; "I am not laughing at anything you could be thinking of, but at that silly nineteenth-century fashion, current amongst rich so-called cultivated people, of ignoring all the steps by which their daily dinner was reached, as matters too low for their lofty intelligence. Useless idiots! Come, now, I am a 'literary man,' as we queer animals used to be called, yet I am a pretty good cook myself."

"So am I," said I.

"Well, then," said he, "I really think you can understand me better than you would seem to do, judging by your words and your silence."

Said I: "Perhaps that is so; but people putting in practice commonly this sense of interest in the ordinary occupations of life rather startles me. I will ask you a question or two presently about that. But I want to return to the position of women amongst you. You have studied the 'emancipation of women' business of the nineteenth century: don't you remember that some of the 'superior' women wanted to emancipate the more intelligent part of their sex from the bearing of children?"

The old man grew quite serious again. Said he: "I *do* remember about that strange piece of baseless folly, the result, like all other follies of the period, of the hideous class tyranny which then obtained. What do we think of it now? you would say. My friend, that is a question easy to answer. How could it possibly be but that maternity should be highly honoured amongst us? Surely it is a matter of course that the natural and necessary pains which the mother must go through form a bond of union between man and woman, an extra stimulus to love and affection between them, and that this is universally recognised. For the rest, remember that all the *artificial* burdens of motherhood are now done away with. A mother has no longer any mere sordid anxieties for the future of her children. They may indeed turn out better or worse; they may disappoint her highest hopes; such anxieties as these are a part of the mingled pleasure and pain which goes to make up the life of mankind. But at least she is spared the fear (it was most commonly the certainty) that artificial disabilities would make her children something less than men and women: she knows that they will live and act according to the measure of their own faculties. In times past, it is clear that the 'Society' of the day helped its Judaic god, and the 'Man of Science' of the time, in visiting the sins of the fathers upon the children. How to reverse this process, how to take the sting out of heredity, has for long been one of the most constant cares of the thoughtful men amongst us. So that, you see, the ordinarily healthy woman (and almost all our women are both healthy and at least comely), respected as a child-bearer and rearer of children, desired as a woman, loved as a companion, unanxious for the future of her children, has far more instinct for maternity than the poor drudge and mother of drudges of past days could ever have had; or than her sister of the upper classes, brought up in affected ignorance of natural facts, reared in an atmosphere of mingled prudery and prurience."

"You speak warmly," I said, "but I can see that you are right."

"Yes," he said, "and I will point out to you a token of all the benefits which we have gained by our freedom. What did you think of the looks of the people whom you have come across to-day?"

Said I: "I could hardly have believed that there could be so many good-looking people in any civilised country."

He crowed a little, like the old bird he was. "What! are we still civilised?" said he. "Well, as to our looks, the English and Jutish blood, which on the whole is predominant here, used not to produce much beauty. But I think we have improved it. I know a man who has a large collection of portraits printed from photographs of the nineteenth century, and going over those and comparing them with the everyday faces in these times, puts the improvement in our good looks beyond a doubt. Now, there are some people who think it not too fantastic to connect this increase of beauty directly with our freedom and good sense in the matters we have been speaking of: they believe that a child born from the natural and healthy love between a man and a woman, even if that be transient, is likely to turn out better in all ways, and especially in bodily beauty, than the birth of the respectable commercial marriage bed, or of the dull despair of the drudge of that system. They say, Pleasure begets pleasure. What do you think?"

"I am much of that mind," said I.

CHAPTER X

QUESTIONS AND ANSWERS

"Well," said the old man, shifting in his chair, "you must get on with your questions, Guest; I have been some time answering this first one."

Said I: "I want an extra word or two about your ideas of education; although I gathered from Dick that you let your children run wild and didn't teach them anything; and in short, that you have so refined your education, that now you have none."

"Then you gathered left-handed," quoth he. "But of course I understand your point of view about education, which is that of times past, when 'the struggle for life,' as men used to phrase it (i.e., the struggle for a slave's rations on one side, and for a bouncing share of the slaveholders' privilege on the other), pinched 'education' for most people into a niggardly dole of not very accurate information; something to be swallowed by the beginner in the art of living whether he liked it or not, and was hungry for it or not: and which had been chewed and digested over and over again by people who didn't care about it in order to serve it out to other people who didn't care about it."

I stopped the old man's rising wrath by a laugh, and said: "Well, *you* were not taught that way, at any rate, so you may let your anger run off you a little."

"True, true," said he, smiling. "I thank you for correcting my ill-temper: I always fancy myself as living in any period of which we may be speaking. But, however, to put it in a cooler way: you expected to see children thrust into schools when they had reached an age conventionally supposed to be the due age, whatever their varying faculties and dispositions might be, and when there, with like disregard to facts to be subjected to a certain conventional course of 'learning.' My friend, can't you see that such a proceeding means ignoring the fact of *growth,* bodily and mental? No one could come out of such a mill uninjured; and those only would avoid being crushed by it who would have the spirit of rebellion strong in them. Fortunately most children have had that at all times, or I do not know that we should ever have reached our present position. Now you see what it all comes to. In the old times all this was the result of *poverty.* In the nineteenth century, society was so miserably poor, owing to the systematised robbery on which it was founded, that real education was impossible for anybody. The whole theory of their so-called education was that it was necessary to shove a little information into a child, even if it were by means of torture, and accompanied by twaddle which it was well known was of no use, or else he would lack information lifelong: the hurry of poverty forbade anything else. All that is past; we are no longer hurried, and the information lies ready to each one's hand when his own inclinations impel him to seek it. In this as in other matters we have become wealthy: we can afford to give ourselves time to grow."

"Yes," said I, "but suppose the child, youth, man, never wants the information, never grows in the direction you might hope him to do: suppose, for instance, he objects to learning arithmetic or mathematics; you can't force him when he *is* grown; can't you force him while he is growing, and oughtn't you to do so?"

"Well," said he, "were you forced to learn arithmetic and mathematics?"

"A little," said I.

"And how old are you now?"

"Say fifty-six," said I.

"And how much arithmetic and mathematics do you know now?" quoth the old man, smiling rather mockingly.

Said I: "None whatever, I am sorry to say."

Hammond laughed quietly, but made no other comment on my admission, and I dropped the subject of education, perceiving him to be hopeless on that side.

They discuss the renovation of London and other large cities, where slums and manufacturing districts have been replaced by pleasant houses and meadows.

I confess I was not sorry to cut short with a question his glorifications of the age he lived in. Said I: "How about the smaller towns? I suppose you have swept those away entirely?"

"No, no," said he, "it hasn't gone that way. On the contrary, there has been but little clearance, though much rebuilding, in the smaller towns. Their suburbs, indeed, when they had any, have melted away into the general country, and space and elbow-room has been got in their centres: but there are the towns still with their streets and squares and market-places; so that it is by means of these smaller towns that we of to-day can get some kind of idea of what the towns of the older world were like;—I mean to say at their best."

"Take Oxford, for instance," said I.

"Yes," said he, "I suppose Oxford was beautiful even in the nineteenth century. At present it has the great interest of still preserving a great mass of precommercial building, and is a very beautiful place, yet there are many towns which have become scarcely less beautiful."

Said I: "In passing, may I ask if it is still a place of learning?"

"Still?" said he, smiling. "Well, it has reverted to some of its best traditions; so you may imagine how far it is from its nineteenth-century position. It is real learning, knowledge cultivated for its own sake—the Art of Knowledge, in short—which is followed there, not the Commercial learning of the past. Though perhaps you do not know that in the nineteenth century Oxford and its less interesting sister Cambridge became definitely commercial. They (and especially Oxford) were the breeding places of a peculiar class of parasites, who called themselves cultivated people; they were indeed cynical enough, as the so-called educated classes of the day generally were; but they affected an exaggeration of cynicism in order that they might be thought knowing and worldly-wise. The rich middle classes (they had no relation with the working classes) treated them with the kind of contemptuous toleration with which a mediæval baron treated his jester; though it must be said that they were by no means so pleasant as the old jesters were, being, in fact, *the* bores of society. They were laughed at, despised—and paid. Which last was what they aimed at."

Dear me! thought I, how apt history is to reverse contemporary judgments. Surely only the worst of them were as bad as that. But I must admit that they were mostly prigs, and that they *were* commercial. I said aloud, though more to myself than to Hammond, "Well, how could they be better than the age that made them?"

"True," he said, "but their pretensions were higher."

"Were they?" said I, smiling.

"You drive me from corner to corner," said he, smiling in turn. "Let me say at least that they were a poor sequence to the aspirations of Oxford of 'the barbarous Middle Ages.' "

"Yes, that will do," said I.

"Also," said Hammond, "what I have been saying of them is true in the main. But ask on!"

I said: "We have heard about London and the manufacturing districts and the ordinary towns: how about the villages?"

Said Hammond: "You must know that toward the end of the nineteenth century the villages were almost destroyed, unless where they became mere adjuncts to the manufacturing districts, or formed a sort of minor manufacturing district themselves. Houses were allowed to fall into decay and actual ruin; trees were cut down for the sake of the few shillings which the poor sticks would fetch; the building became inexpressibly mean and hideous. Labour was scarce; but wages fell nevertheless. All the small country arts of life which once added to the little pleasures of country people were lost. The country produce which passed through the hands of the husbandmen never got so far as their mouths. Incredible shabbiness and niggardly pinching reigned over the fields and acres which, in spite of the rude and careless husbandry of the times, were so kind and bountiful. Had you any inkling of all this?"

"I have heard that it was so," said I; "but what followed?"

"The change," said Hammond, "which in these matters took place very early in our epoch, was most strangely rapid. People flocked into the country villages, and, so to say, flung themselves upon the freed land like a wild beast upon his prey; and in a very little time the villages of England were more populous than they had been since the fourteenth century, and were still growing fast. Of course, this invasion of the country was awkward to deal with, and would have created much misery, if the folk had still been under the bondage of class monopoly. But as it was, things soon righted themselves. People found out what they were fit for, and gave up attempting to push themselves into occupations in which they must needs fail. The town invaded the country; but the invaders, like the warlike invaders of early days, yielded to the influence of their surroundings, and became country people; and in their turn, as they became more numerous than the townsmen, influenced them also; so that the difference between town and country grew less and less; and it was indeed this world of the country vivified by the thought and briskness of town-bred folk which has produced that happy and leisurely but eager life of which you have had a first taste. Again I say, many blunders were made, but we have had time to set them right. Much was left for the men of my earlier life to deal with. The crude ideas of the first half of the twentieth century, when men were still oppressed by the fear of poverty, and did not look enough to the present pleasure of ordinary daily life, spoilt a great deal of what the commercial age had left us of external beauty: and I admit that it was but slowly that men recovered from the injuries they had inflicted on themselves even after they became free. But slowly as the recovery came, it *did* come; and the more you see of us, the clearer it will be to you that we are happy. That we live amidst beauty without any fear of becoming effeminate; that we have plenty to do, and on the whole enjoy doing it. What more can we ask of life?"

He paused, as if he were seeking for words with which to express his thought. Then he said:

"This is how we stand. England was once a country of clearings amongst the woods and wastes, with a few towns interspersed, which were fortresses for the feudal army, markets for the folk, gathering places for the craftsmen. It then became a country of huge and foul workshops and fouler gambling-dens, surrounded by an ill-kept, poverty-stricken farm, pillaged by the masters of the workshops. It is now a garden, where nothing is wasted and nothing is spoilt, with the necessary dwellings, sheds, and workshops scattered up and down the country, all trim and neat and pretty. For, indeed, we should be too much ashamed of ourselves if we allowed the making of goods, even on a large scale, to carry with it the appearance, even, of desolation and misery. Why, my friend, those housewives we were talking of just now would teach us better than that."

Said I: "This side of your change is certainly for the better. But though I shall soon see some of these villages, tell me in a word or two what they are like, just to prepare me."

"Perhaps," said he, "you have seen a tolerable picture of these villages as they were before the end of the nineteenth century. Such things exist."

"I have seen several of such pictures," said I.

"Well," said Hammond, "our villages are something like the best of such places, with the church or mote-house of the neighbours for their chief building. Only note that there are no tokens of poverty about them; no tumble-down picturesque; which, to tell you the truth, the artist usually availed himself of to veil his incapacity for drawing architecture. Such things do not please us, even when they indicate no misery. Like the mediævals, we like everything trim and clean, and orderly and bright; as people always do when they have any sense of architectural power; because then they know that they can have what they want, and they won't stand any nonsense from Nature in their dealings with her."

"Besides the villages, are there any scattered country houses?" said I.

"Yes, plenty," said Hammond; "in fact, except in the wastes and forests and amongst the sand-hills (like Hindhead in Surrey), it is not easy to be out of sight of a house; and where the houses are thinly scattered they run large, and are more like the old colleges than ordinary houses as they used to be. That is done for the sake of society, for a good many people can dwell in such houses, as the country dwellers are not necessarily husbandmen; though they almost all help in such work at times. The life that goes on in these big dwellings in the country is very pleasant, especially as some of the most studious men of our time live in them, and altogether there is a great variety of mind and mood to be found in them which brightens and quickens the society there."

"I am rather surprised," said I, "by all this, for it seems to me that after all the country must be tolerably populous."

"Certainly," said he; "the population is pretty much the same as it was at the end of the nineteenth century; we have spread it, that is all. Of course, also, we have helped to populate other countries—where we were wanted and were called for."

Said I: "One thing, it seems to me, does not go with your word of 'garden' for the country. You have spoken of wastes and forests, and I myself have seen the beginning of your Middlesex and Essex forest. Why do you keep such things in a garden? and isn't it very wasteful to do so?"

"My friend," he said, "we like these pieces of wild nature, and can afford them, so we have them; let alone that as to the forests, we need a great deal of timber, and suppose that our sons and sons' sons will do the like. As to the land being a garden, I have heard that they used to have shrubberies and rockeries in gardens once; and though I might not like the artificial ones, I assure you that some of the natural rockeries of our garden are worth seeing. Go north this summer and look at the Cumberland and Westmoreland ones,—where, by the way, you will see some sheep-feeding, so that they are not so wasteful as you think; not so wasteful as forcing grounds for fruit out of season, *I* think. Go and have a look at the sheep-walks high up the slopes between Ingleborough and Pen-y-gwent, and tell me if you think we *waste* the land there by not covering it with factories for making things that nobody wants, which was the chief business of the nineteenth century."

"I will try to go there," said I.

"It won't take much trying," said he.

CHAPTER XI

CONCERNING GOVERNMENT

"Now," said I, "I have come to the point of asking questions which I suppose will be dry for you to answer and difficult for you to explain; but I have foreseen for some time past that I must ask them, will I 'nill I. What kind of a government have you? Has republicanism finally triumphed? or have you come to a mere dictatorship, which some persons in the nineteenth century used to prophesy as the ultimate outcome of democracy? Indeed, this last question does not seem so very unreasonable, since you have turned your Parliament House into a dung-market. Or where do you house your present Parliament?"

The old man answered my smile with a hearty laugh, and said: "Well, well, dung is not the worst kind of corruption; fertility may come of that, whereas mere dearth came from the other kind, of which those walls once held the great supporters. Now, dear guest, let me tell you that our present parliament would be hard to house in one place, because the whole people is our parliament."

"I don't understand," said I.

"No, I suppose not," said he. "I must now shock you by telling you that we have no longer anything which you, a native of another planet, would call a government."

"I am not so much shocked as you might think," said I, "as I know something about governments. But tell me, how do you manage, and how have you come to this state of things?"

Said he: "It is true that we have to make some arrangements about our affairs, concerning which you can ask presently; and it is also true that everybody does not always agree with the details of these arrangements; but, further, it is true that a man no more needs an elaborate system of government, with its army, navy, and police, to force him to give way to the will of the majority of his *equals*, than he wants a similar machinery to make him understand that his head and a stone wall cannot occupy the same space at the same moment. Do you want further explanation?"

"Well, yes, I do," quoth I.

Old Hammond settled himself in his chair with a look of enjoyment which rather alarmed me, and made me dread a scientific disquisition: so I sighed and abided. He said:

"I suppose you know pretty well what the process of government was in the bad old times?"

"I am supposed to know," said I.

HAMMOND: What was the government of those days? Was it really the Parliament or any part of it?

I: No.

HAMMOND: Was not the Parliament on the one side a kind of watch-committee sitting to see that the interests of the Upper Classes took no hurt; and on the other side a sort of blind to delude the people into supposing that they had some share in the management of their own affairs?

I: History seems to show us this.

HAMMOND: To what extent did the people manage their own affairs?

I: I judge from what I have heard that sometimes they forced the Parliament to make a law to legalise some alteration which had already taken place.

HAMMOND: Anything else?

I: I think not. As I am informed, if the people made any attempt to deal with the *cause* of their grievances, the law stepped in and said, this is sedition, revolt, or what not, and slew or tortured the ringleaders of such attempts.

HAMMOND: If Parliament was not the government then, nor the people either, what was the government?

I: Can you tell me?

HAMMOND: I think we shall not be far wrong if we say that government was the Law-Courts, backed up by the executive, which handled the brute force that the deluded people allowed them to use for their own purposes; I mean the army, navy, and police.

I: Reasonable men must needs think you are right.

HAMMOND: Now as to those Law-Courts. Were they places of fair dealing according to the ideas of the day? Had a poor man a good chance of defending his property and person in them?

I: It is a commonplace that even rich men looked upon a law-suit as a dire misfortune, even if they gained the case; and as for a poor one—why, it was considered a miracle of justice and beneficence if a poor man who had once got into the clutches of the law escaped prison or utter ruin.

HAMMOND: It seems, then, my son, that the government by Law-Courts and police, which was the real government of the nineteenth century, was not a great success even to the people of that day, living under a class system which proclaimed inequality and poverty as the law of God and the bond which held the world together.

1: So it seems, indeed.

HAMMOND: And now that all this is changed, and the "rights of property," which mean the clenching the fist on a piece of goods and crying out to the neighbours, You shan't have this!—now that all this has disappeared so utterly that it is no longer possible even to jest upon its absurdity, is such a Government possible?

1: It is impossible.

HAMMOND: Yes, happily. But for what other purpose than the protection of the rich from the poor, the strong from the weak, did this Government exist?

1: I have heard that it was said that their office was to defend their own citizens against attack from other countries.

HAMMOND: It was said; but was anyone expected to believe this? For instance, did the English Government defend the English citizen against the French?

1: So it was said.

HAMMOND: Then if the French had invaded England and conquered it, they would not have allowed the English workmen to live well?

1, laughing: As far as I can make out, the English masters of the English workmen saw to that: they took from their workmen as much of their livelihood as they dared, because they wanted it for themselves.

HAMMOND: But if the French had conquered, would they not have taken more still from the English workmen?

1: I do not think so; for in that case the English workmen would have died of starvation; and then the French conquest would have ruined the French, just as if the English horses and cattle had died of under-feeding. So that after all, the English *workmen* would have been no worse off for the conquest: their French masters could have got no more from them than their English masters did.

HAMMOND: This is true; and we may admit that the pretensions of the government to defend the poor (i.e., the useful) people against other countries come to nothing. But that is but natural; for we have seen already that it was the function of government to protect the rich against the poor. But did not the government defend its rich men against other nations?

1: I do not remember to have heard that the rich needed defence; because it is said that even when two nations were at war, the rich men of each nation gambled with each other pretty much as usual, and even sold each other weapons wherewith to kill their own countrymen.

HAMMOND: In short, it comes to this, that whereas the so-called government of protection of property by means of the law-courts meant destruction of wealth, this defence of the citizens of one country against those of another country by means of war or the threat of war meant pretty much the same thing.

1: I cannot deny it.

HAMMOND: Therefore the government really existed for the destruction of wealth?

1: So it seems. And yet—

HAMMOND: Yet what?

1: There were many rich people in those times.

HAMMOND: You see the consequences of that fact?

1: I think I do. But tell me out what they were.

HAMMOND: If the government habitually destroyed wealth, the country must have been poor?

1: Yes, certainly.

HAMMOND: Yet amidst this poverty the persons for the sake of whom the government existed insisted on being rich whatever might happen?

1: So it was.

HAMMOND: What *must* happen if in a poor country some people insist on being rich at the expense of the others?

1: Unutterable poverty for the others. All this misery, then, was caused by the destructive government of which we have been speaking?

HAMMOND: Nay, it would be incorrect to say so. The government itself was but the necessary result of the careless, aimless tyranny of the times; it was but the machinery of tyranny. Now tyranny has come to an end, and we no longer need such machinery; we could not possibly use it since we are free. Therefore in your sense of the word we have no government. Do you understand this now?

1: Yes, I do. But I will ask you some more questions as to how you as free men manage your affairs.

HAMMOND: With all my heart. Ask away.

CHAPTER XII

CONCERNING THE ARRANGEMENT OF LIFE

"Well," I said, "about those 'arrangements' which you spoke of as taking the place of government, could you give me any account of them?"

"Neighbour," he said, "although we have simplified our lives a great deal from what they were, and have got rid of many conventionalities and many sham wants, which used to give our forefathers much trouble, yet our life is too complex for me to tell you in detail by means of words how it is arranged; you must find that out by living amongst us. It is true that I can better tell you what we don't do, than what we do do."

"Well?" said I.

"This is the way to put it," said he: "We have been living for a hundred and fifty years, at least, more or less in our present manner, and a tradition or habit of life has been growing on us; and that habit has become a habit of acting on the whole for the best. It is easy for us to live without robbing each other. It would be possible for us to contend with and rob each other, but it would be harder for us than refraining from strife and robbery. That is in short the foundation of our life and our happiness."

"Whereas in the old days," said I, "it was very hard to live without strife and robbery. That's what you mean, isn't it, by giving me the negative side of your good conditions?"

"Yes," he said, "it was so hard, that those who habitually acted fairly to their neighbours were celebrated as saints and heroes, and were looked up to with the greatest reverence."

"While they were alive?" said I.

"No," said he, "after they were dead."

"But as to these days," I said; "you don't mean to tell me that no one ever transgresses this habit of good fellowship?"

"Certainly not," said Hammond, "but when the transgressions occur, everybody, transgressors and all, know them for what they are; the errors of friends, not the habitual actions of persons driven into enmity against society."

"I see," said I; "you mean that you have no 'criminal' classes."

"How could we have them," said he, "since there is no rich class to breed enemies against the state by means of the injustice of the state?"

Said I: "I thought that I understood from something that fell from you a little while ago that you had abolished civil law. Is that so, literally?"

"It abolished itself, my friend," said he. "As I said before, the civil Law-Courts were upheld for the defence of private property; for nobody ever pretended that it was possible to make people act fairly to each other by means of brute force. Well, private property being abolished, all the laws and all the legal 'crimes' which it had manufactured of course came to an end. Thou shalt not steal, had to be translated into, Thou shalt work in order to live happily. Is there any need to enforce that commandment by violence?"

"Well," said I, "that is understood, and I agree with it; but how about the crimes of violence? would not their occurrence (and you admit that they occur) make criminal law necessary?"

Said he: "In your sense of the word, we have no criminal law either. Let us look at the matter closer, and see whence crimes of violence spring. By far the greater part of these in past days were the result of the laws of private property, which forbade the satisfaction of their natural desires to all but a privileged few, and of the general visible coercion which came of those laws. All *that* cause of violent crime is gone. Again, many violent acts came from the artificial perversion of the sexual passions, which caused overweening jealousy and the like miseries. Now, when you look carefully into these, you will find that what lay at the bottom of them was mostly the idea (a law-made idea) of the woman being the property of the man, whether he were husband, father, brother, or what not. *That* idea has of course vanished with private property, as well as certain follies about the 'ruin' of women for following their natural desires in an illegal way, which of course was a convention caused by the laws of private property.

"Another cognate cause of crimes of violence was the family tyranny, which was the subject of so many novels and stories of the past, and which once more was the result of private property. Of course that is all ended, since families are held together by no bond of coercion, legal or social, but by mutual liking and affection, and everybody is free to come or go as he or she pleases. Furthermore, our standards of honour and public estimation are very different from the old ones; success in besting our neighbours is a road to renown now closed, let us hope for ever. Each man is free to exercise his special faculty to the utmost, and every one encourages him in so doing. So that we have got rid of the scowling envy, coupled by the poets with hatred, and surely with good reason; heaps of unhappiness and ill-blood were caused by it, which with irritable and passionate men—i.e., energetic and active men—often led to violence."

I laughed, and said: "So that you now withdraw your admission, and say that there is no violence amongst you?"

"No," said he, "I withdraw nothing; as I told you, such things will happen. Hot blood will err sometimes. A man may strike another, and the stricken strike back again, and the result be a homicide, to put it at the worst. But what then? Shall we the neighbours make it worse still? Shall we think so poorly of each other as to suppose that the slain man calls on us to revenge him, when we *know* that if he had been maimed, he would, when in cold blood and able to weigh all the circumstances, have forgiven his maimer? Or will the death of the slayer bring the slain man to life again and cure the unhappiness his loss has caused?"

"Yes," I said, "but consider, must not the safety of society be safeguarded by some punishment?"

"There, neighbour!" said the old man, with some exultation. "You have hit the mark. That *punishment* of which men used to talk so wisely and act so foolishly, what was it but the expression of their fear? And they had need to fear, since *they*—i.e., the rulers of society—were dwelling like an armed band in a hostile country. But we who live amongst our friends need neither fear nor punish. Surely if we, in dread of an occasional rare homicide, an occasional rough blow, were solemnly and legally to commit homicide and violence, we could only be a society of ferocious cowards. Don't you think so, neighbour?"

"Yes, I do, when I come to think of it from that side," said I.

"Yet you must understand," said the old man, "that when any violence is committed, we expect the transgressor to make any atonement possible to him, and he himself expects it. But again, think if the destruction or serious injury of a man momentarily overcome by wrath or folly can be any atonement to the commonwealth? Surely it can only be an additional injury to it."

Said I: "But suppose the man has a habit of violence,—kills a man a year, for instance?"

"Such a thing is unknown," said he. "In a society where there is no punishment to evade, no law to triumph over, remorse will certainly follow transgression."

"And lesser outbreaks of violence," said I, "how do you deal with them? for hitherto we have been talking of great tragedies, I suppose?"

Said Hammond: "If the ill-doer is not sick or mad (in which case he must be restrained till his sickness or madness is cured) it is clear that grief and humiliation must follow the ill-deed; and society in general will make that pretty clear to the ill-doer if he should chance to be dull to it; and again, some kind of atonement will follow,—at the least, an open acknowledgement of the grief and humiliation. Is it so hard to say, I ask your pardon, neighbour?—Well, sometimes it is hard—and let it be."

"You think that enough?" said I.

"Yes," said he, "and moreover it is all that we *can* do. If in addition we torture the man, we turn his grief into anger, and the humiliation he would otherwise feel for *his* wrongdoing is swallowed up by a hope of revenge for *our* wrongdoing to him. He has paid the legal penalty, and can 'go and sin again' with comfort. Shall we commit such a folly, then? Remember Jesus had got the legal penalty remitted before he said Go and sin no more.' Let alone that in a society of equals you will not find any one to play the part of torturer or jailer, though many to act as nurse or doctor."

"So," said I, "you consider crime a mere spasmodic disease, which requires no body of criminal law to deal with it?"

"Pretty much so," said he; "and since, as I have told you, we are a healthy people generally, so we are not likely to be much troubled with *this* disease."

"Well, you have no civil law, and no criminal law. But have you no laws of the market, so to say—no regulation for the exchange of wares? for you must exchange, even if you have no property."

Said he: "We have no obvious individual exchange, as you saw this morning when you went a-shopping; but of course there are regulations of the markets, varying according to the circumstances and guided by general custom. But as these are matters of general assent, which nobody dreams of objecting to, so also we have made no provision for enforcing them: therefore I don't call them laws. In law, whether it be criminal or civil, execution always follows judgment, and someone must suffer. When you see the judge on his bench, you see through him, as clearly as if he were made of glass, the policeman to emprison, and the soldier to slay some actual living person. Such follies would make an agreeable market, wouldn't they?"

"Certainly," said I, "that means turning the market into a mere battle-field, in which many people must suffer as much as in the battle-field of bullet and bayonet. And from what I have seen I should suppose that your marketing, great and little, is carried on in a way that makes it a pleasant occupation."

"You are right, neighbour," said he. "Although there are so many, indeed by far the greater number amongst us, who would be unhappy if they were not engaged in actually making things, and things which turn out beautiful under their hands,—there are many, like the housekeepers I was speaking of, whose delight is in administration and organisation, to use long-tailed words; I mean people who like keeping things together, avoiding waste, seeing that nothing sticks fast uselessly. Such people are thoroughly happy in their business, all the more as they are dealing with actual facts, and not merely passing counters round to see what share they shall have in the privileged taxation of useful people, which was the business of the commercial folk in past days. Well, what are you going to ask me next?"

CHAPTER XIII
CONCERNING POLITICS

Said I: "How do you manage with politics?"

Said Hammond, smiling: "I am glad that it is of *me* that you ask that question; I do believe that anybody else would make you explain yourself, or try to do so, till you were sickened of asking questions. Indeed, I believe I am the only man in England who would know what you mean; and since I know, I will answer your question briefly by saying that we are very well off as to politics,—because we have none. If ever you make a book out of this conversation, put this in a chapter by itself, after the model of old Horrebow's Snakes in Iceland."

"I will," said I.

CHAPTER XIV
HOW MATTERS ARE MANAGED

Said I: "How about your relations with foreign nations?"

"I will not affect not to know what you mean," said he, "but I will tell you at once that the whole system of rival and contending nations which played so great a part in the 'government' of the world of civilisation has disappeared along with the inequality betwixt man and man in society."

"Does not that make the world duller?" said I.

"Why?" said the old man.

"The obliteration of national variety," said I.

"Nonsense," he said, somewhat snappishly. "Cross the water and see. You will find plenty of variety: the landscape, the building, the diet, the amusements, all various. The men and women varying in looks as well as in habits of thought; the costume far more various than in the commercial period. How should it add to the variety or dispel the dulness, to coerce certain families or tribes, often heterogeneous and jarring with one another, into certain artificial and mechancial groups, and call them nations, and stimulate their patriotism—i.e., their foolish and envious prejudices?"

"Well—I don't know how," said I.

"That's right," said Hammond cheerily; "you can easily understand that now we are freed from this folly it is obvious to us that by means of this very diversity the different strains of blood in the world can be serviceable and pleasant to each other, without in the least wanting to rob each other: we are all bent on the same enterprise, making the most of our lives. And I must tell you whatever quarrels or misunderstandings arise, they very seldom take place between people of different race; and consequently since there is less unreason in them, they are the more readily appeased."

"Good," said I, "but as to those matters of politics; as to general differences of opinion in one and the same community. Do you assert that there are none?"

"No, not at all," said he, somewhat snappishly; "but I do say that differences of opinion about real solid things need not, and with us do not, crystallise people into parties permanently hostile to one another, with different theories as to the build of the universe and the progress of time. Isn't that what politics used to mean?"

"H'm, well," said I, "I am not so sure of that."

Said he: "I take you, neighbour; they only *pretended* to this serious difference of opinion; for if it had existed they could not have dealt together in the ordinary business of life; couldn't have eaten together, bought and sold together, gambled together, cheated other people together, but must have fought whenever they met: which would not have suited them at all. The game of the masters of politics was to cajole or force the public to pay the expense of a luxurious life and exciting amusement for a few cliques of ambitious persons: and the *pretence* of serious difference of opinion, belied by every action of their lives, was quite good enough for that. What has all that got to do with us?"

Said I: "Why, nothing, I should hope. But I fear— In short, I have been told that political strife was a necessary result of human nature."

"Human nature!" cried the old boy, impetuously; "what human nature? The human nature of paupers, of slaves, of slave-holders, or the human nature of wealthy freemen? Which? Come, tell me that!"

"Well," said I, "I suppose there would be a difference according to circumstances in people's action about these matters."

"I should think so, indeed," said he. "At all events, experience shows that it is so. Amongst us, our differences concern matters of business, and passing events as to them, and could not divide men permanently. As a rule, the immediate outcome shows which opinion on a given subject is the right one; it is a matter of fact, not of speculation. For instance, it is clearly not easy to knock up a political party on the question as to whether haymaking in such and such a countryside shall begin this week or next, when all men agree that it must at latest begin the week after next, and when any man can go down into the fields himself and see whether the seeds are ripe enough for the cutting."

Said I: "And you settle these differences, great and small, by the will of the majority, I suppose?"

"Certainly," said he; "how else could we settle them? You see in matters which are merely personal which do not affect the welfare of the community—how a man shall dress, what he shall eat and drink, what he shall write and read, and so forth—there can be no difference of opinion, and everybody does as he pleases. But when the matter is of common interest to the whole community, and the doing or not doing something affects everybody, the majority must have their way; unless the minority were to take up arms and show by force that they were the effective or real majority; which, however, in a society of men who are free and equal is little likely to happen; because in such a community the apparent majority *is* the real majority, and the others, as I have hinted before, know that too well to obstruct from mere pigheadedness; especially as they have had plenty of opportunity of putting forward their side of the question."

"How is that managed?" said I.

"Well," said he, "let us take one of our units of management, a commune, or a ward, or a parish (for we have all three names, indicating little real distinction between them now, though time was there was a good deal). In such a district, as you would call it, some neighbours think that something ought to be done or undone: a new town-hall built; a clearance of inconvenient houses; or say a stone bridge substituted for some ugly old iron one,—there you have undoing and doing in one. Well, at the next ordinary meeting of the neighbours, or Mote, as we call it, according to the ancient tongue of the times before bureaucracy, a neighbour proposes the change, and of course, if everybody agrees, there is an end of discussion, except about details. Equally, if no one backs the proposer, —'seconds him,' it used to be called—the matter drops for the time being; a thing not likely to happen amongst reasonable men, however, as the proposer is sure to have talked it over with others before the Mote. But supposing the affair proposed and seconded, if a few of the neighbours disagree to it, if they think that the beastly iron bridge will serve a little longer and they don't want to be bothered with building a new one just then, they don't count heads that time, but put off the formal discussion to the next Mote; and meantime arguments *pro* and *con* are flying about, and some get printed, so that everybody knows what is going on; and when the Mote comes together again there is a regular discussion and at last a vote by show of hands. If the division is a close one, the question is again put off for further discussion; if the division is a wide one, the minority are asked if they will yield to the more general opinion, which they often, nay, most commonly do. If they refuse, the question is debated a third time, when, if the minority has not perceptibly grown, they always give way; though I believe there is some half-forgotten rule by which they might still carry it on further; but I say, what always happens is that they are convinced, not perhaps that their view is the wrong one, but they cannot persuade or force the community to adopt it."

"Very good," said I; "but what happens if the divisions are still narrow?"

Said he: "As a matter of principle and according to the rule of such cases, the question must then lapse, and the majority, if so narrow, has to submit to sitting down under the *status quo*. But I must tell you that in point of fact the minority very seldom enforces this rule, but generally yields in a friendly manner."

"But do you know," said I, "that there is something in all this very like democracy; and I thought that democracy was considered to be in a moribund condition many, many years ago."

The old boy's eyes twinkled. "I grant you that our methods have that drawback. But what is to be done? We can't get *anyone* amongst us to complain of his not always having his own way in the teeth of the community, when it is clear that *everybody* cannot have that indulgence. What *is* to be done?"

"Well," said I, "I don't know."

Said he: "The only alternatives to our method that I can conceive of are these. First, that we should choose out, or breed, a class of superior persons capable of judging on all matters without consulting the neighbours; that, in short, we should get for ourselves what used to be called an aristocracy of intellect; or, secondly, that for the purpose of safe-guarding the freedom of the individual will, we should revert to a system of private property again, and have slaves and slave-holders once more. What do you think of those two expedients?"

"Well," said I, "there is a third possibility—to wit, that every man should be quite independent of every other, and that thus the tyranny of society should be abolished."

He looked hard at me for a second or two, and then burst out laughing very heartily; and I confess that I joined him. When he recovered himself he nodded at me, and said: "Yes, yes, I quite agree with you—and so we all do."

"Yes," I said, "and besides, it does not press hardly on the minority: for, take this matter of the bridge, no man is obliged to work on it if he doesn't agree to its building. At least, I suppose not."

He smiled and said: "Shrewdly put; and yet from the point of view of the native of another planet. If the man of the minority does find his feelings hurt, doubtless he may relieve them by refusing to help in building the bridge. But, dear neighbour, that is not a very effective salve for the wound caused by the 'tyranny of a majority' in our society; because all work that is done is either beneficial or hurtful to every member of society. The man is benefited by the bridge-building if it turns out a good thing, and hurt by it if it turns out a bad one, whether he puts a hand to it or not; and meanwhile he is benefiting the bridge-builders by his work, whatever that may be. In fact, I see no help for him except the pleasure of saying 'I told you so' if the bridge-building turns out to be a mistake and hurts him; if it benefits him he must suffer in silence. A terrible tyranny our Communism, is it not? Folk used often to be warned against this very unhappiness in times past, when for every well-fed, contented person you saw a thousand miserable starvelings. Whereas for us, we grow fat and well-liking on the tyranny; a tyranny, to say the truth, not to be made visible by any microscope I know. Don't be afraid, my friend; we are not going to seek for troubles by calling our peace and plenty and happiness by ill names whose very meaning we have forgotten!"

He sat musing for a little, and then started and said: "Are there any more questions, dear guest? The morning is waning fast amidst my garrulity."

CHAPTER XV

ON THE LACK OF INCENTIVE TO LABOUR IN A COMMUNIST SOCIETY

"Yes," said I. "I was expecting Dick and Clara to make their appearance any moment: but is there time to ask just one or two questions before they come?"

"Try it, dear neighbour—try it," said old Hammond. "For the more you ask me the better I am pleased; and at any rate if they do come and find me in the middle of an answer, they must sit quiet and pretend to listen till I come to an end. It won't hurt them; they will find it quite amusing enough to sit side by side, conscious of their proximity to each other."

I smiled, as I was bound to, and said: "Good; I will go on talking without noticing them when they come in. Now, this is what I want to ask you about—to wit, how you get people to work when there is no reward of labour, and especially how you get them to work strenuously?"

"No reward of labour?" said Hammond, gravely. "The reward of labour is *life*. Is that not enough?"

"But no reward for especially good work," quoth I.

"Plenty of reward," said he—"the reward of creation. The wages which God gets, as people might have said time agone. If you are going to ask to be paid for the pleasure of creation, which is what excellence in work means, the next thing we shall hear of will be a bill sent in for the begetting of children."

"Well, but," said I, "the man of the nineteenth century would say there is a natural desire towards the procreation of children, and a natural desire not to work."

"Yes, yes," said he, "I know the ancient platitude,—wholly untrue; indeed, to us quite meaningless. Fourier, whom all men laughed at, understood the matter better."

"Why is it meaningless to you?" said I.

He said: "Because it imples that all work is suffering, and we are so far from thinking that, that, as you may have noticed, whereas we are not short of wealth, there is a kind of fear growing up amongst us that we shall one day be short of work. It is a pleasure which we are afraid of losing, not a pain."

"Yes," said I, "I have noticed that, and I was going to ask you about that also. But in the meantime, what do you positively mean to assert about the pleasurableness of work amongst you?"

"This, that *all* work is now pleasurable; either because of the hope of gain in honour and wealth with which the work is done, which causes pleasurable excitement, even when the actual work is not pleasant; or else because it has grown into a pleasurable *habit,* as in the case with what you may call mechanical work; and lastly (and most of our work is of this kind) because there is conscious sensuous pleasure in the work itself; it is done, that is, by artists."

"I see," said I. "Can you now tell me how you have come to this happy condition? For, to speak plainly, this change from the conditions of the older world seems to me far greater and more important than all the other changes you have told me about as to crime, politics, property, marriage."

"You are right there," said he. "Indeed, you may say rather that it is this change which makes all the others possible. What is the object of Revolution? Surely to make people happy. Revolution having brought its foredoomed change about, how can you prevent the counter-revolution from setting in except by making people happy? What! shall we expect peace and stability from unhappiness? The gathering of grapes from thorns and figs from thistles is a reasonable expectation compared with that! And happiness without happy daily work is impossible."

"Most obviously true," said I: for I thought the old boy was preaching a little. "But answer my question, as to how you gained this happiness."

"Briefly," said he, "by the absence of artificial coercion, and the freedom for every man to do what he can do best, joined to the knowledge of what productions of labour we really want. I must admit that this knowledge we reached slowly and painfully."

"Go on," said I, "give me more detail; explain more fully. For this subject interests me intensely."

"Yes, I will," said he; "but in order to do so I must weary you by talking a little about the past. Contrast is necessary for this explanation. Do you mind?"

"No, no," said I.

Said he, settling himself in his chair again for a long talk: "It is clear from all that we hear and read, that in the last age of civilisation men had got into a vicious circle in the matter of production of wares. They had reached a wonderful facility of production, and in order to make the most of that facility they had gradually created (or allowed to grow, rather) a most elaborate system of buying and selling, which has been called the World-Market; and that World-Market, once set a-going, forced them to go on making more and more of these wares, whether they needed them or not. So that while (of course) they could not free themselves from the toil of making real necessaries, they created in a never-ending series sham or artificial necessaries, which became, under the iron rule of the aforesaid World-Market, of equal importance to them with the real necessaries which supported life. By all this they burdened themselves with a prodigious mass of work merely for the sake of keeping their wretched system going."

"Yes—and then?" said I.

"Why, then, since they had forced themselves to stagger along under this horrible burden of unnecessary production, it became impossible for them to look upon labour and its results from any other point of view than one—to wit, the ceaseless endeavour to expend the least possible amount of labour on any article made, and yet at the same time to make as many articles as possible. To this 'cheapening of production,' as it was called, everything was sacrificed: the happiness of the workman at his work, nay, his most elementary comfort and bare health, his food, his clothes, his dwelling, his leisure, his amusement, his education—his life, in short—did not weigh a grain of sand in the balance against this dire necessity of 'cheap production' of things, a great part of which were not worth producing at all. Nay, we are told, and we must believe it, so overwhelming is the evidence, though many of our people scarcely *can* believe it, that even rich and powerful men, the masters of the poor devils aforesaid, submitted to live amidst sights and sounds and smells which it is in the very nature of man to abhor and flee from, in order that their riches might bolster up this supreme folly. The whole community, in fact, was cast into the jaws of this ravening monster, 'the cheap production' forced upon it by the World-Market."

"Dear me!" said I. "But what happened? Did not their cleverness and facility in production master this chaos of misery at last? Couldn't they catch up with the World-Market, and then set to work to devise means for relieving themselves from this fearful task of extra labour?"

He smiled bitterly. "Did they even try to?" said he. "I am not sure. You know that according to the old saw the beetle gets used to living in dung; and these people, whether they found the dung sweet or not, certainly lived in it."

His estimate of the life of the nineteenth century made me catch my breath a little; and I said feebly, "But the labour-saving machines?"

"Heyday!" quoth he. "What's that you are saying? the labour-saving machines? Yes, they were made to 'save labour' (or, to speak more plainly, the lives of men) on one piece of work in order that it might be expended—I will say wasted—on another, probably useless, piece of work. Friend, all their devices for cheapening labour simply resulted in increasing the burden of labour. The appetite of the World-Market grew with what it fed on: the countries within the ring of 'civilisation' (that is, organised misery) were glutted with the abortions of the market, and force and fraud were used unsparingly to 'open up' countries *outside* that pale. This process of 'opening up' is a strange one to those who have read the professions of the men of that period and do not understand their practice; and perhaps shows us at its worst the great vice of the nineteenth century, the use of hypocrisy and cant to evade the responsibility of vicarious ferocity. When the civilised World-Market coveted a country not yet in its clutches, some transparent pretext was found—the suppression of a slavery different from, and not so cruel as that of commerce; the pushing of a religion no longer believed in by its promoters; the 'rescue' of some desperado or homicidal madman whose misdeeds had got him into trouble amongst the natives of the 'barbarous' country—any stick, in short, which would beat the dog at all. Then some bold, unprincipled, ignorant adventurer was found (no difficult task in the days of competition), and he was bribed to 'create a market' by breaking up whatever traditional society there might be in the doomed country, and by destroying whatever leisure or pleasure he found there. He forced wares on the natives which they did not want, and took their natural products in 'exchange,' as this form of robbery was called, and thereby he 'created new wants,' to supply which (that is, to be allowed to live by their new masters) the hapless, helpless people had to sell themselves into the slavery of hopeless toil so that they might have something wherewith to purchase the nullities of 'civilisation.' Ah," said the old man, pointing to the Museum, "I have read books and papers in there, telling strange stories indeed of the dealings of civilisation (or organised misery) with 'non-civilisation;' from the time when the British Government deliberately sent blankets infected with small-pox as choice gifts to inconvenient tribes of Red-skins, to the time when Africa was infested by a man named Stanley, who—"

"Excuse me," said I, "but as you know, time presses; and I want to keep our question on the straightest line possible; and I want at once to ask this about these wares made for the World-Market—how about their quality; these people who were so clever about making goods, I suppose they made them well?"

"Quality!" said the old man crustily, for he was rather peevish at being cut short in his story; "how could they possibly attend to such trifles as the quality of the wares they sold? The best of them were of a lowish average, the worst were transparent make-shifts for the things asked for, which nobody would have put up with if they could have got anything else. It was a current jest of the time that the wares were made to sell and not to use; a jest which you, as coming from another planet, may understand, but which our folk could not."

Said I: "What! did they make nothing well?"

"Why, yes," said he, "there was one class of goods which they did make thoroughly well, and that was the class of machines which were used for making things. These were usually quite perfect pieces of workmanship, admirably adapted to the end in view. So that it may be fairly said that the great achievement of the nineteenth century was the making of machines which were wonders of invention, skill, and patience, and which were used for the production of measureless quantities of worthless make-shifts. In truth, the owners of the machines did not consider anything which they made as wares, but simply as means for the enrichment of themselves. Of course, the only admitted test of utility in wares was the finding of buyers for them—wise men or fools, as it might chance."

"And people put up with this?" said I.

"For a time," said he.

"And then?"

"And then the overturn," said the old man, smiling, "and the nineteenth century saw itself as a man who has lost his clothes whilst bathing, and has to walk naked through the town."

"You are very bitter about that unlucky nineteenth century," said I.

"Naturally," said he, "since I know so much about it."

He was silent a little, and then said: "There are traditions—nay, real histories—in our family about it: my grandfather was one of its victims. If you know something about it, you will understand what he suffered when I tell you that he was in those days a genuine artist, a man of genius, and a revolutionist."

"I think I do understand," said I: "but now, as it seems, you have reversed all this?"

"Pretty much so," said he. "The wares which we make are made because they are needed: men make for their neighbours' use as if they were making for themselves, not for a vague market of which they know nothing, and over which they have no control: as there is no buying and selling, it would be mere insanity to make goods on the chance of their being wanted; for there is no longer anyone who can be *compelled* to buy them. So that whatever is made is good, and thoroughly fit for its purpose. Nothing *can* be made except for genuine use; therefore no inferior goods are made. Moreover, as aforesaid, we have now found out what we want, so we make no more than we want; and as we are not driven to make a vast quantity of useless things, we have time and resources enough to consider our pleasure in making them. All work which would be irksome to do by hand is done by immensely improved machinery; and in all work which it is a pleasure to do by hand machinery is done without. There is no difficulty in finding work which suits the special turn of mind of everybody; so that no man is sacrificed to the wants of another. From time to time, when we have found out that some piece of work was too disagreeable or troublesome, we have given it up and done altogether without the thing produced by it. Now, surely you can see that under these circumstances all the work that we do is an exercise of the mind and body more or less pleasant to be done: so that instead of avoiding work everybody seeks it: and, since people have got defter in doing the work generation after generation, it has become so easy to do, that it seems as if there were less done, though probably more is produced. I suppose this explains that fear, which I hinted at just now, of a possible scarcity in work, which perhaps you have already noticed, and which is a feeling on the increase, and has been for a score of years."

"But do you think," said I, "that there is any fear of a work-famine amongst you?"

"No, I do not," said he, "and I will tell why; it is each man's business to make his own work pleasanter and pleasanter, which of course tends towards raising the standard of excellence, as no man enjoys turning out work which is not a credit to him, and also to greater deliberation in turning it out; and there is such a vast number of things which can be treated as works of art, that this alone gives employment to a host of deft people. Again, if art be inexhaustible, so is science also; and though it is no longer the only innocent occupation which is thought worth an intelligent man spending his time upon, as it once was, yet there are, and I suppose will be, many people who are excited by its conquest of difficulties, and care for it more than for anything else. Again, as more and more of pleasure is imported into work, I think we shall take up kinds of work which produce desirable wares, but which we gave up because we could not carry them on pleasantly. Moreover, I think that it is only in parts of Europe which are more advanced than the rest of the world that you will hear this talk of the fear of a work-famine. Those lands which were once the colonies of Great Britain, for instance, and especially America—that part of it, above all, which was once the United States—are now and will be for a long while a great resource to us. For these lands, and, I say especially the northern parts of America, suffered so terribly from the full force of the last days of civilisation, and became such horrible places to live in, that they are now very backward in all that makes life pleasant. Indeed, one may say that for nearly a hundred years the people of the northern parts of America have been engaged in gradually making a dwelling-place out of a stinking dust-heap; and there is still a great deal to do, especially as the country is so big."

"Well," said I, "I am exceedingly glad to think that you have such a prospect of happiness before you. But I should like to ask a few more questions, and then I have done for to-day."

CHAPTER XVI

DINNER IN THE HALL OF THE BLOOMSBURY MARKET

As I spoke, I heard footsteps near the door; the latch yielded, and in came our two lovers, looking so handsome that one had no feeling of shame in looking on at their little-concealed love-making; for indeed it seemed as if all the world must be in love with them. As for old Hammond, he looked on them like an artist who has just painted a picture nearly as well as he thought he could when he began it, and was perfectly happy. He said:

"Sit down, sit down, young folk, and don't make a noise. Our guest here has still some questions to ask me."

"Well, I should suppose so," said Dick; "you have only been three hours and a half together; and it isn't to be hoped that the history of two centuries could be told in three hours and a half: let alone that, for all I know, you may have been wandering into the realms of geography and craftsmanship."

"As to noise, my dear kinsman," said Clara, "you will very soon be disturbed by the noise of the dinner-bell, which I should think will be very pleasant music to our guest, who breakfasted early, it seems, and probably had a tiring day yesterday."

I said: "Well, since you have spoken the word, I begin to feel that it is so; but I have been feeding myself with wonder this long time past: really, it's quite true," quoth I, as I saw her smile, O so prettily!

But just then from some tower high up in the air came the sound of silvery chimes playing a sweet clear tune, that sounded to my unaccustomed ears like the song of the first blackbird in the spring, and called a rush of memories to my mind, some of bad times, some of good, but all sweetened now into mere pleasure.

"No more questions now before dinner," said Clara; and she took my hand as an affectionate child would, and led me out of the room and down stairs into the forecourt of the Museum, leaving the two Hammonds to follow as they pleased.

We went into the market-place which I had been in before, a thinnish stream of elegantly[1] dressed people going in along with us. We turned into the cloister and came to a richly moulded and carved doorway, where a very pretty dark-haired young girl gave us each a beautiful bunch of summer flowers, and we entered a hall much bigger than that of the Hammersmith Guest House, more elaborate in its architecture and perhaps more beautiful. I found it difficult to keep my eyes off the wall-pictures (for I thought it bad manners to stare at Clara all the time, though she was quite worth it). I saw at a glance that their subjects were taken from queer old world myths and imaginations which in yesterday's world only about half a dozen people in the country knew anything about; and when the two Hammonds sat down opposite to us, I said to the old man, pointing to the frieze:

"How strange to see such subjects here!"

"Why?" said he. "I don't see why you should be surprised; everybody knows the tales; and they are graceful and pleasant subjects, not too tragic for a place where people mostly eat and drink and amuse themselves, and yet full of incident."

I smiled, and said: "Well, I scarcely expected to find record of the Seven Swans and the King of the Golden Mountain and Faithful Henry, and such curious pleasant imaginations as Jacob Grimm got together from the childhood of the world, barely lingering even in his time: I should have thought you would have forgotten such childishness by this time."

The old man smiled, and said nothing; but Dick turned rather red, and broke out:

"What *do* you mean, Guest? I think them very beautiful, I mean not only the pictures, but the stories; and when we were children we used to imagine them going on in every wood-end, by the bight of every stream: every house in the fields was the Fairyland King's House to us. Don't you remember, Clara?"

"Yes," she said; and it seemed to me as if a slight cloud came over her fair face. I was going to speak to her on the subject, when the

[1] "Elegant," I mean, as a Persian pattern is elegant; not like a rich "elegant" lady out for a morning call. I should rather call that *genteel*.

pretty waitresses came to us smiling, and chattering sweetly like reed warblers by the river-side, and fell to giving us our dinner. As to this, as at our breakfast, everything was cooked and served with a daintiness which showed that those who had prepared it were interested in it; but there was no excess either of quantity or of gourmandise; everything was simple, though so excellent of its kind; and it was made clear to us that this was no feast, only an ordinary meal. The glass, crockery, and plate were very beautiful to my eyes, used to the study of mediæval art; but a nineteenth-century club-haunter would, I daresay, have found them rough and lacking in finish; the crockery being lead-glazed pot-ware, though beautifully ornamented; the only porcelain being here and there a piece of old oriental ware. The glass, again, though elegant and quaint, and very varied in form, was somewhat bubbled and hornier in texture than the commercial articles of the nineteenth century. The furniture and general fittings of the hall were much of apiece with the table-gear, beautiful in form and highly ornamented, but without the commercial "finish" of the joiners and cabinet-makers of our time. Withal, there was a total absence of what the nineteenth century calls "comfort"—that is, stuffy inconvenience; so that, even apart from the delightful excitement of the day, I had never eaten my dinner so pleasantly before.

When we had done eating, and were sitting a little while, with a bottle of very good Bordeaux wine before us, Clara came back to the question of the subject-matter of the pictures, as though it had troubled her.

She looked up at them, and said: "How is it that though we are so interested with our life for the most part, yet when people take to writing poems or painting pictures they seldom deal with our modern life, or if they do, take good care to make their poems or pictures unlike that life? Are we not good enough to paint ourselves? How is it that we find the dreadful times of the past so interesting to us—in pictures and poetry?"

Old Hammond smiled. "It always was so, and I suppose always will be," said he, "however it may be explained. It is true that in the nineteenth century, when there was so little art and so much talk about it, there was a theory that art and imaginative literature ought to deal with contemporary life; but they never did so; for, if there was any pretence of it, the author always took care (as Clara hinted just now) to disguise, or exaggerate, or idealise, and in some way or another make it strange; so that, for all the verisimilitude there was, he might just as well have dealt with the times of the Pharaohs."

"Well," said Dick, "surely it is but natural to like these things strange; just as when we were children, as I said just now, we used to pretend to be so-and-so in such-and-such a place. That's what these pictures and poems do; and why shouldn't they?"

"Thou has hit it, Dick," quoth old Hammond; "it is the child-like part of us that produces works of imagination. When we are children time passes so slow with us that we seem to have time for everything."

He sighed, and then smiled and said: "At least let us rejoice that we have got back our childhood again. I drink to the days that are!"

"Second childhood," said I in a low voice, and then blushed at my double rudeness, and hoped that he hadn't heard. But he had, and turned to me smiling, and said: "Yes, why not? And for my part, I hope it may last long; and that the world's next period of wise and unhappy manhood, if that should happen, will speedily lead us to a third childhood: if indeed this age be not our third. Meantime, my friend, you must know that we are too happy, both individually and collectively, to trouble ourselves about what is to come hereafter."

"Well, for my part," said Clara, "I wish we were interesting enough to be written or painted about."

Dick answered her with some lover's speech, impossible to be written down, and then we sat quiet a little.

CHAPTER XVII

HOW THE CHANGE CAME

Dick broke the silence at last, saying: "Guest, forgive us for a little after-dinner dulness. What would you like to do? Shall we have out Greylocks and trot back to Hammersmith? or will you come with us and hear some Welsh folk sing in a hall close by here? or would you like presently to come with me into the City and see some really fine building? or—what shall it be?"

"Well," said I, "as I am a stranger, I must let you choose for me."

In point of fact, I did not by any means want to be 'amused' just then; and also I rather felt as if the old man, with his knowledge of past times, and even a kind of inverted sympathy for them caused by his active hatred of them, was as it were a blanket for me against the cold of this very new world, where I was, so to say, stripped bare of every habitual thought and way of acting; and I did not want to leave him too soon. He came to my rescue at once, and said:

"Wait a bit, Dick; there is someone else to be consulted besides you and the guest here, and that is I. I am not going to lose the pleasure of his company just now, especially as I know he has something else to ask me. So go to your Welshmen, by all means; but first of all bring us another bottle of wine to this nook, and then be off as soon as you like; and come again and fetch our friend to go westward, but not too soon."

Dick nodded smilingly, and the old man and I were soon alone in the great hall, the afternoon sun gleaming on the red wine in our tall quaint-shaped glasses. Then said Hammond:

"Does anything especially puzzle you about our way of living, now you have heard a good deal and seen a little of it?"

Said I: "I think what puzzles me most is how it all came about."

"It well may," said he, "so great as the change is. It would be difficult indeed to tell you the whole story, perhaps impossible: knowledge, discontent, treachery, disappointment, ruin, misery, despair—those who worked for the change because they could see further than other people went through all these phases of suffering; and doubtless all the time the most of men looked on, not knowing what was doing, thinking it all a matter of course, like the rising and setting of the sun—and indeed it was so."

"Tell me one thing, if you can," said I. "Did the change, the 'revolution' it used to be called, come peacefully?"

"Peacefully?" said he; "what peace was there amongst those poor confused wretches of the nineteenth century? It was war from beginning to end: bitter war, till hope and pleasure put an end to it."

"Do you mean actual fighting with weapons?" said I, "or the strikes and lock-outs and starvation of which we have heard?"

"Both, both," he said. "As a matter of fact, the history of the terrible period of transition from commercial slavery to freedom may thus be summarised. When the hope of realising a communal condition of life for all men arose, quite late in the nineteenth century, the power of the middle classes, the then tyrants of society, was so enormous and crushing, that to almost all men, even those who had, you may say despite themselves, despite their reason and judgment, conceived such hopes, it seemed a dream. So much was this the case that some of those more enlightened men who were then called Socialists, although they well knew, and even stated in public, that the only reasonable condition of Society was that of pure Communism (such as you now see around you), yet shrunk from what seemed to them the barren task of preaching the realisation of a happy dream. Looking back now, we can see that the great motive-power of the change was a longing for freedom and equality, akin if you please to the unreasonable passion of the lover; a sickness of heart that rejected with loathing the aimless solitary life of the well-to-do educated man of that time: phrases, my dear friend, which have lost their meaning to us of the present day; so far removed we are from the dreadful facts which they represent.

"Well, these men, though conscious of this feeling, had no faith in it, as a means of bringing about the change. Nor was that wonderful: for looking around them they saw the huge mass of the oppressed classes too much burdened with the misery of their lives, and too much overwhelmed by the selfishness of misery, to be able to form a conception of any escape from it except by the ordinary way prescribed by the system of slavery under which they lived; which was nothing more than a remote chance of climbing out of the oppressed into the oppressing class.

"Therefore, though they knew that the only reasonable aim for those who would better the world was a condition of equality; in their impatience and despair they managed to convince themselves that if they could by hook or by crook get the machinery of production and the management of property so altered that the 'lower classes' (so the horrible word ran) might have their slavery somewhat ameliorated, they would be ready to fit into this machinery, and would use it for bettering their condition still more and still more, until at last the result would be a practical equality (they were very fond of using the word 'practical'), because 'the rich' would be forced to pay so much for keeping 'the poor' in a tolerable condition that the condition of riches would become no longer valuable and would gradually die out. Do you follow me?"

"Partly," said I. "Go on."

Said old Hammond: "Well, since you follow me, you will see that as a theory this was not altogether unreasonable; but 'practically,' it turned out a failure."

"How so?" said I.

"Well, don't you see," said he, "because it involved the making of a machinery by those who didn't know what they wanted the machines to do. So far as the masses of the oppressed class furthered this scheme of improvement, they did it to get themselves improved slave-rations—as many of them as could. And if those classes had really been incapable of being touched by that instinct which produced the passion for freedom and equality aforesaid, what would have happened, I think, would have been this: that a certain part of the working-classes would have been so far improved in condition that they would have approached the condition of the middling rich men; but below them would have been a great class of most miserable slaves, whose slavery would have been far more hopeless than the older class-slavery had been."

"What stood in the way of this?" said I.

"Why, of course," said he, "just that instinct for freedom aforesaid. It is true that the slave-class could not conceive the happiness
of a free life. Yet they grew to understand (and very speedily too)
that they were oppressed by their masters, and they assumed, you
see how justly, that they could do without them, though perhaps
they scarce knew how; so that it came to this, that though they could
not look forward to the happiness or peace of the freeman, they did
at least look forward to the war which a vague hope told them would
bring that peace about."

"Could you tell me rather more closely what actually took place?"
said I; for I thought *him* rather vague here.

"Yes," he said, "I can. That machinery of life for the use of people
who didn't know what they wanted of it, and which was known at
the time as State Socialism, was partly put in motion, though in a
very piecemeal way. But it did not work smoothly; it was, of course,
resisted at every turn by the capitalists; and no wonder, for it tended
more and more to upset the commercial system I have told you of,
without providing anything really effective in its place. The result
was growing confusion, great suffering amongst the working classes,
and, as a consequence, great discontent. For a long time matters
went on like this. The power of the upper classes had lessened, as
their command over wealth lessened, and they could not carry
things wholly by the high hand as they had been used to in earlier
days. So far the State Socialists were justified by the result. On the
other hand, the working classes were ill-organised, and growing
poorer in reality, in spite of the gains (also real in the long run)
which they had forced from the masters. Thus matters hung in the
balance; the masters could not reduce their slaves to complete sub-
jection, though they put down some feeble and partial riots easily
enough. The workers forced their masters to grant them ameliorations, real or imaginary, of their condition, but could not force freedom from them. At last came a great crash. To explain this you
must understand that very great progress had been made amongst
the workers, though as before said but little in the direction of improved livelihood."

I played the innocent and said: "In what direction could they
improve, if not in livelihood?"

Said he: "In the power to bring about a state of things in which
livelihood would be full, and easy to gain. They had at last learned
how to combine after a long period of mistakes and disasters. The
workmen had now a regular organisation in the struggle against
their masters, a struggle which for more than half a century had
been accepted as an inevitable part of the conditions of the modern

system of labour and production. This combination had now taken the form of a federation of all or almost all the recognised wage-paid employments, and it was by its means that those betterments of the condition of the workmen had been forced from the masters: and though they were not seldom mixed up with the rioting that happened, especially in the earlier days of their organisation, it by no means formed an essential part of their tactics; indeed at the time I am now speaking of they had got to be so strong that most commonly the mere threat of a 'strike' was enough to gain any minor point: because they had given up the foolish tactics of the ancient trades unions of calling out of work a part only of the workers of such and such an industry, and supporting them while out of work on the labour of those that remained in. By this time they had a biggish fund of money for the support of strikes, and could stop a certain industry altogether for a time if they so determined."

Said I: "Was there not a serious danger of such moneys being misused—of jobbery, in fact?"

Old Hammond wriggled uneasily on his seat, and said:

"Though all this happened so long ago, I still feel the pain of mere shame when I have to tell you that it was more than a danger: that such rascality often happened; indeed more than once the whole combination seemed dropping to pieces because of it: but at the time of which I am telling, things looked so threatening, and to the workmen at least the necessity of their dealing with the fast-gathering trouble which the labour-struggle had brought about, was so clear, that the conditions of the times had begot a deep seriousness amongst all reasonable people; a determination which put aside all non-essentials, and which to thinking men was ominous of the swiftly-approaching change: such an element was too dangerous for mere traitors and self-seekers, and one by one they were thrust out and mostly joined the declared reactionaries."

"How about those ameliorations," said I; "what were they? or rather of what nature?"

Said he: "Some of them, and these of the most practical importance to the men's livelihood, were yielded by the masters by direct compulsion on the part of the men; the new conditions of labour so gained were indeed only customary, enforced by no law: but, once established, the masters durst not attempt to withdraw them in face of the growing power of the combined workers. Some again were steps on the path of 'State Socialism;' the most important of which can be speedily summed up. At the end of the nineteenth century the cry arose for compelling the masters to employ their men a less number of hours in the day: this cry gathered volume quickly, and the masters had to yield to it. But it was, of course, clear that unless this meant a higher price for work per hour, it would be a mere nullity, and that the masters unless forced, would reduce it to that. Therefore after a long struggle another law was passed fixing a minimum price for labour in the most important industries; which again had to be supplemented by a law fixing the maximum price on the chief wares then considered necessary for a workman's life."

"You were getting perilously near to the late Roman poor-rates," said I, smiling, "and the doling out of bread to the proletariat."

"So many said at the time," said the old man drily; "and it has long been a commonplace that that slough awaits State Socialism in the end, if it gets to the end, which as you know it did not with us. However it went further than this minimum and maximum business, which by the by we can now see was necessary. The Government now found it imperative on them to meet the outcry of the master class at the approaching destruction of commerce (as desirable, had they known it, as the extinction of the cholera, which has since happily taken place). And they were forced to meet it by a measure hostile to the masters, the establishment of government factories for the production of necessary wares, and markets for their sale. These measures taken altogether did do something: they were in fact of the nature of regulations made by the commander of a beleaguered city. But of course to the privileged classes it seemed as if the end of the world were come when such laws were enacted.

"Nor was that altogether without a warrant: the spread of communistic theories, and the partial practice of State Socialism had at first disturbed, and at last almost paralysed the marvellous system of commerce under which the old world had lived so feverishly, and had produced for some few a life of gambler's pleasure, and for many, or most, a life of mere misery: over and over again came 'bad times' as they were called, and indeed they were bad enough for the wage-slaves. The year 1952 was one of the worst of these times; the workmen suffered dreadfully: the partial, inefficient government factories, which were terribly jobbed, all but broke down, and a vast part of the population had for the time being to be fed on undisguised 'charity' as it was called.

"The Combined Workers watched the situation with mingled hope and anxiety. They had already formulated their general demands; but now by a solemn and universal vote of the whole of their federated societies, they insisted on the first step being taken toward carrying out their demands: this step would have led directly to handing over the management of the whole natural resources of the country, together with the machinery for using them into the power of the Combined Workers, and the reduction of the privileged classes into the position of pensioners obviously dependent on the pleasure of the workers. The 'Resolution,' as it was called, which was widely published in the newspapers of the day, was in fact a declaration of war, and was so accepted by the master class. They began henceforward to prepare for a firm stand against the 'brutal and ferocious Communism of the day,' as they phrased it. And as they were in many ways still very powerful, or seemed so to be, they still hoped by means of brute force to regain some of what they had lost, and perhaps in the end the whole of it. It was said amongst them on all hands that it had been a great mistake of the various governments not to have resisted sooner; and the liberals and radicals (the name as perhaps you may know of the more democratically inclined part of the ruling classes) were much blamed for having led the world to this pass by their mis-timed pedantry and foolish sentimentality: and one Gladstone, or Gledstein (probably, judging by this name, of Scandinavian descent), a notable politician of the nineteenth century, was especially singled out for reprobation in this respect. I need scarcely point out to you the absurdity of all this. But terrible tragedy lay hidden behind this grinning through a horse-collar of the reactionary party. 'The insatiable greed of the lower classes must be repressed'—'The people must be taught a lesson'—these were the sacramental phrases current amongst the reactionists, and ominous enough they were."

The old man stopped to look keenly at my attentive and wondering face; and then said:

"I know, dear guest, that I have been using words and phrases which few people amongst us could understand without long and laborious explanation; and not even then perhaps. But since you have not yet gone to sleep, and since I am speaking to you as to a being from another planet, I may venture to ask you if you have followed me thus far?"

"O yes," said I, "I quite understand: pray go on; a great deal of what you have been saying was commonplace with us—when—when—"

"Yes," said he gravely, "when you were dwelling in the other planet. Well, now for the crash aforesaid.

"On some comparatively trifling occasion a great meeting was summoned by the workmen leaders to meet in Trafalgar Square (about the right to meet in which place there had for years and years been bickering). The civic bourgeois guard (called the police) attacked the said meeting with bludgeons, according to their custom; many people were hurt in the *mêlée,* of whom five in all died, either trampled to death on the spot, or from the effects of their cudgelling; the meeting was scattered, and some hundred of prisoners cast into gaol. A similar meeting had been treated in the same way a few days before at a place called Manchester, which has now disappeared. Thus the 'lesson' began. The whole country was thrown into a ferment by this; meetings were held which attempted some rough organisation for the holding of another meeting to retort on the authorities. A huge crowd assembled in Trafalgar Square and the neighbourhood (then a place of crowded streets), and was too big for the bludgeon-armed police to cope with; there was a good deal of dry-blow fighting; three or four of the people were killed, and half a score of policemen were crushed to death in the throng, and the rest got away as they could. This was a victory for the people as far as it went. The next day all London (remember what it was in those days) was in a state of turmoil. Many of the rich fled into the country; the executive got together soldiery, but did not dare to use them; and the police could not be massed in any one place, because riots or threats of riots were everywhere. But in Manchester, where the people were not so courageous or not so desperate as in London, several of the popular leaders were arrested. In London a convention of leaders was got together from the Federation of Combined Workmen, and sat under the old revolutionary name of the Committee of Public Safety; but as they had no drilled and armed body of men to direct, they attempted no aggressive measures, but only placarded the walls with somewhat vague appeals to the workmen not to allow themselves to be trampled upon. However, they called a meeting in Trafalgar Square for the day fortnight of the last-mentioned skirmish.

"Meantime the town grew no quieter, and business came pretty much to an end. The newspapers—then, as always hitherto, almost entirely in the hands of the masters—clamoured to the Government for repressive measures; the rich citizens were enrolled as an extra body of police, and armed with bludgeons like them; many of these were strong, well-fed, full-blooded young men, and had plenty of stomach for fighting; but the Government did not dare to use them, and contented itself with getting full powers voted to it by the Parliament for suppressing any revolt, and bringing up more and more soldiers to London. Thus passed the week after the great meeting; almost as large a one was held on the Sunday, which went off peaceably on the whole, as no opposition to it was offered, and again the people cried 'victory.' But on the Monday the people woke up to find that they were hungry. During the last few days there had been groups of men parading the streets asking (or, if you please, demanding) money to buy food; and what for good will, what for fear, the richer people gave them a good deal. The authorities of the parishes also (I haven't time to explain that phrase at present) gave willy-nilly what provisions they could to wandering people; and the Government, by means of its feeble national workshops, also fed a good number of half-starved folk. But in addition to this, several bakers' shops and other provision stores had been emptied without a great deal of disturbance. So far, so good. But on the Monday in question the Committee of Public Safety, on the one hand afraid of general unorganised pillage, and on the other emboldened by the wavering conduct of the authorities, sent a deputation provided with carts and all necessary gear to clear out two or three big provision stores in the centre of the town, leaving papers with the shop managers promising to pay the price of them: and also in the part of the town where they were strongest they took possession of several bakers' shops and set men at work in them for the benefit of the people; —all of which was done with little or no disturbance, the police assisting in keeping order at the sack of the stores, as they would have done at a big fire.

"But at this last stroke the reactionaries were so alarmed, that they were determined to force the executive into action. The newspapers next day all blazed into the fury of frightened people, and threatened the people, the Government, and everybody they could think of, unless 'order were at once restored.' A deputation of leading commercial people waited on the Government and told them that if they did not at once arrest the Committee of Public Safety, they themselves would gather a body of men, arm them, and fall on 'the incendiaries,' as they called them.

"They, together with a number of the newspaper editors, had a long interview with the heads of the Government and two or three military men, the deftest in their art that the country could furnish. The deputation came away from that interview, says a contemporary eye-witness, smiling and satisfied, and said no more about raising an anti-popular army, but that afternoon left London with their families for their country seats or elsewhere.

"The next morning the Government proclaimed a state of siege in London,—a thing common enough amongst the absolutist governments on the Continent, but unheard-of in England in those days. They appointed the youngest and cleverest of their generals to command the proclaimed district; a man who had won a certain sort of reputation in the disgraceful wars in which the country had been long engaged from time to time. The newspapers were in ecstacies, and all the most fervent of the reactionaries now came to the front;

men who in ordinary times were forced to keep their opinions to themselves or their immediate circle, but who began to look forward to crushing once for all the Socialist, and even democratic tendencies, which, said they, had been treated with such foolish indulgence for the last sixty years.

"But the clever general took no visible action; and yet only a few of the minor newspapers abused him; thoughtful men gathered from this that a plot was hatching. As for the Committee of Public Safety, whatever they thought of their position, they had now gone too far to draw back; and many of them, it seems, thought that the Government would not act. They went on quietly organising their food supply, which was a miserable driblet when all is said; and also as a retort to the state of siege, they armed as many men as they could in the quarter where they were strongest, but did not attempt to drill or organise them, thinking, perhaps, that they could not at the best turn them into trained soldiers till they had some breathing space. The clever general, his soldiers, and the police did not meddle with all this in the least in the world; and things were quieter in London that week-end; though there were riots in many places of the provinces, which were quelled by the authorities without much trouble. The most serious of these were at Glasgow and Bristol.

"Well, the Sunday of the meeting came, and great crowds came to Trafalgar Square in procession, the greater part of the Committee amongst them, surrounded by their band of men armed somehow or other. The streets were quite peaceful and quiet, though there were many spectators to see the procession pass. Trafalgar Square had no body of police in it; the people took quiet possession of it, and the meeting began. The armed men stood round the principal platform, and there were a few others armed amidst the general crowd; but by far the greater part were unarmed.

"Most people thought the meeting would go off peaceably; but the members of the Committee had heard from various quarters that something would be attempted against them; but these rumours were vague, and they had no idea of what threatened. They soon found out.

"For before the streets about the Square were filled, a body of soldiers poured into it from the north-west corner and took up their places by the houses that stood on the west side. The people growled at the sight of the red-coats; the armed men of the Committee stood undecided, not knowing what to do; and indeed this new influx so jammed the crowd together that, unorganised as they were, they had little chance of working through it. They had scarcely grasped the fact of their enemies being there, when another column of soldiers,

pouring out of the streets which led into the great southern road going down to the Parliament House (still existing, and called the
Dung Market), and also from the embankment by the side of the
Thames, marched up, pushing the crowd into a denser and denser
mass, and formed along the south side of the Square. Then any of
those who could see what was going on, knew at once that they were
in a trap, and could only wonder what would be done with them.

"The closely-packed crowd would not or could not budge, except
under the influence of the height of terror, which was soon to be
supplied to them. A few of the armed men struggled to the front, or
climbed up to the base of the monument which then stood there,
that they might face the wall of hidden fire before them; and to most
men (there were many women amongst them) it seemed as if the
end of the world had come, and to-day seemed strangely different
from yesterday. No sooner were the soldiers drawn up aforesaid than,
says an eye-witness, 'a glittering officer on horseback came prancing
out from the ranks on the south, and read something from a paper
which he held in his hand; which something, very few heard; but I
was told afterwards that it was an order for us to disperse, and a
warning that he had legal right to fire on the crowd else, and that he
would do so. The crowd took it as a challenge of some sort, and a
hoarse threatening roar went up from them; and after that there was
comparative silence for a little, till the officer had got back into the
ranks. I was near the edge of the crowd, towards the soldiers,' says
this eye-witness, 'and I saw three little machines being wheeled out
in front of the ranks, which I knew for mechanical guns. I cried
out, "Throw yourselves down! they are going to fire!" But no one
scarcely could throw himself down, so tight as the crowd were
packed. I heard a sharp order given, and wondered where I should
be the next minute; and then— It was as if the earth had opened,
and hell had come up bodily amidst us. It is no use trying to describe
the scene that followed. Deep lanes were mowed amidst the thick
crowd; the dead and dying covered the ground, and the shrieks and
wails and cries of horror filled all the air, till it seemed as if there
was nothing else in the world but murder and death. Those of our
armed men who were still unhurt cheered wildly and opened a scat-
tering fire on the soldiers. One or two soldiers fell; and I saw the
officers going up and down the ranks urging the men to fire again;
but they received the orders in sullen silence, and let the butts of
their guns fall. Only one sergeant ran to a machine-gun and began to
set it going; but a tall young man, an officer too, ran out of the ranks
and dragged him back by the collar; and the soldiers stood there
motionless while the horror-stricken crowd, nearly wholly unarmed

(for most of the armed men had fallen in that first discharge), drifted out of the Square. I was told afterwards that the soldiers on the west side had fired also, and done their part of the slaughter. How I got out of the Square I scarcely know: I went, not feeling the ground under me, what with rage and terror and despair.'

"So says our eye-witness. The number of the slain on the side of the people in that shooting during a minute was prodigious; but it was not easy to come at the truth about it; it was probably between one and two thousand. Of the soldiers, six were killed outright, and a dozen wounded."

I listened, trembling with excitement. The old man's eyes glittered and his face flushed as he spoke, and told the tale of what I had often thought might happen. Yet I wondered that he should have got so elated about a mere massacre, and I said:

"How fearful! And I suppose that this massacre put an end to the whole revolution for that time?"

"No, no," cried old Hammond; "it began it!"

He filled his glass and mine, and stood up and cried out, "Drink this glass to the memory of those who died there, for indeed it would be a long tale to tell how much we owe them."

I drank, and he sat down again and went on.

"That massacre of Trafalgar Square began the civil war, though, like all such events, it gathered head slowly, and people scarcely knew what a crisis they were acting in.

"Terrible as the massacre was, and hideous and overpowering as the first terror had been, when the people had time to think about it, their feeling was one of anger rather than fear; although the military organisation of the state of siege was now carried out without shrinking by the clever young general. For though the ruling-classes when the news spread next morning felt one gasp of horror and even dread, yet the Government and their immediate backers felt that now the wine was drawn and must be drunk. However, even the most reactionary of the capitalist papers, with two exceptions, stunned by the tremendous news, simply gave an account of what had taken place, without making any comment upon it. The exceptions were one, a so-called 'liberal' paper (the Government of the day was of that complexion), which, after a preamble in which it declared its undeviating sympathy with the cause of labour, proceeded to point out that in times of revolutionary disturbance it behoved the Government to be just but firm, and that by far the most merciful way of dealing with the poor madmen who were attacking the very foundations of society (which had made them mad and poor) was to shoot them at once, so as to stop others from drifting into a position in which they would run a chance of being shot. In short, it praised the determined action of the Government as the *acme* of human wisdom and mercy, and exulted in the inauguration of an epoch of reasonable democracy free from the tyrannical fads of Socialism.

"The other exception was a paper thought to be one of the most violent opponents of democracy, and so it was; but the editor of it found his manhood, and spoke for himself and not for his paper. In a few simple, indignant words he asked people to consider what a society was worth which had to be defended by the massacre of unarmed citizens, and called on the Government to withdraw their state of siege and put the general and his officers who fired on the people on their trial for murder. He went further, and declared that whatever his opinion might be as to the doctrines of the Socialists, he for one should throw in his lot with the people, until the Government atoned for their atrocity by showing that they were prepared to listen to the demands of men who knew what they wanted, and whom the decrepitude of society forced into pushing their demands in some way or other.

"Of course, this editor was immediately arrested by the military power; but his bold words were already in the hands of the public, and produced a great effect: so great an effect that the Government, after some vacillation, withdrew the state of siege; though at the same time it strengthened the military organisation and made it more stringent. Three of the Committee of Public Safety had been slain in Trafalgar Square: of the rest, the greater part went back to their old place of meeting, and there awaited the event calmly. They were arrested there on the Monday morning, and would have been shot at once by the general, who was a mere military machine, if the Government had not shrunk before the responsibility of killing men without any trial. There was at first a talk of trying them by a special commission of judges, as it was called—i.e., before a set of men bound to find them guilty, and whose business it was to do so. But with the Government the cold fit had succeeded to the hot one; and the prisoners were brought before a jury at the assizes. There a fresh blow awaited the Government; for in spite of the judge's charge, which distinctly instructed the jury to find the prisoners guilty, they were acquitted, and the jury added to their verdict a presentment, in which they condemned the action of the soldiery, in the queer phraseology of the day, as 'rash, unfortunate, and unnecessary.' The Committee of Public Safety renewed its sittings, and from thenceforth was a popular rallying-point in opposition to the Parliament. The Government now gave way on all sides, and made a show of yielding to the demands of the people, though there was a widespread plot for effecting a *coup d'état* set on foot between the leaders of the two so-called opposing parties in the parliamentary faction fight. The well-meaning part of the public was overjoyed, and thought that all danger of a civil war was over. The victory of the people was celebrated by huge meetings held in the parks and elsewhere, in memory of the victims of the great massacre.

"But the measures passed for the relief of the workers, though to the upper classes they seemed ruinously revolutionary, were not thorough enough to give the people food and a decent life, and they had to be supplemented by unwritten enactments without legality to back them. Although the Government and Parliament had the law-courts, the army, and 'society' at their backs, the Committee of Public Safety began to be a force in the country, and really represented the producing classes. It began to improve immensely in the days which followed on the acquittal of its members. Its old members had little administrative capacity, though with the exception of a few self-seekers and traitors, they were honest, courageous men, and many of them were endowed with considerable talent of other kinds. But now that the times called for immediate action, came forward the men capable of setting it on foot; and a new network of workmen's associations grew up very speedily, whose avowed single object was the tiding over of the ship of the community into a simple condition of Communism; and as they practically undertook also the management of the ordinary labour-war, they soon became the mouthpiece and intermediary of the whole of the working classes; and the manufacturing profit-grinders now found themselves powerless before this combination: unless *their* committee, Parliament, plucked up courage to begin the civil war again, and to shoot right and left, they were bound to yield to the demands of the men whom they employed, and pay higher and higher wages for shorter and shorter day's work. Yet one ally they had, and that was the rapidly approaching breakdown of the whole system founded on the World-Market and its supply; which now became so clear to all people, that the middle classes, shocked for the moment into condemnation of the Government for the great massacre, turned round nearly in a mass, and called on the Government to look to matters, and put an end to the tyranny of the Socialist leaders.

"Thus stimulated, the reactionist plot exploded probably before it was ripe; but this time the people and their leaders were forewarned, and, before the reactionaries could get under way, had taken the steps they thought necessary.

"The Liberal Government (clearly by collusion) was beaten by the Conservatives, though the latter were nominally much in the minority. The popular representatives in the House understood pretty well what this meant, and after an attempt to fight the matter out by divisions in the House of Commons, they made a protest, left the House, and came in a body to the Committee of Public Safety: and the civil war began again in good earnest.

"Yet its first act was not one of mere fighting. The new Tory Government determined to act, yet durst not re-enact the state of siege, but it sent a body of soldiers and police to arrest the Committee of Public Safety in the lump. They made no resistance, though they might have done so, as they had now a considerable body of men who were quite prepared for extremities. But they were determined to try first a weapon which they thought stronger than street fighting.

"The members of the Committee went off quietly to prison; but they had left their soul and their organisation behind them. For they depended not on a carefully arranged centre with all kinds of checks and counter-checks about it, but on a huge mass of people in thorough sympathy with the movement, bound together by a great number of links of small centres with very simple instructions. These instructions were now carried out.

"The next morning, when the leaders of the reaction were chuckling at the effect which the report in the newspapers of their stroke would have upon the public—no newspapers appeared; and it was only towards noon that a few straggling sheets, about the size of the gazettes of the seventeenth century, worked by policemen, soldiers, managers, and presswriters, were dribbled through the streets. They were greedily seized on and read; but by this time the serious part of their news was stale, and people did not need to be told that the GENERAL STRIKE had begun. The railways did not run, the telegraph-wires were unserved; flesh, fish, and green stuff brought to market was allowed to lie there still packed and perishing; the thousands of middle-class families, who were utterly dependant for the next meal on the workers, made frantic efforts through their more energetic members to cater for the needs of the day, and amongst those of them who could throw off the fear of what was to follow, there was, I am told, a certain enjoyment of this unexpected picnic —a forecast of the days to come, in which all labour grew pleasant.

"So passed the first day, and towards evening the Government grew quite distracted. They had but one resource for putting down any popular movement—to wit, mere brute-force; but there was nothing for them against which to use their army and police: no armed bodies appeared in the streets; the offices of the Federated Workmen were now, in appearance, at least, turned into places for the relief of people thrown out of work, and under the circumstances, they durst not arrest the men engaged in such business, all the more, as even that night many quite respectable people applied at these offices for relief, and swallowed down the charity of the revolutionists along with their supper. So the Government massed soldiers and police here and there—and sat still for that night, fully expecting on the morrow some manifesto from 'the rebels,' as they now began to be called, which would give them an opportunity of acting in some way or another. They were disappointed. The ordinary newspapers gave up the struggle that morning, and only one very violent reactionary paper (called the Daily Telegraph) attempted an appearance, and rated 'the rebels' in good set terms for their folly and ingratitude in tearing out the bowels of their 'common mother,' the English Nation, for the benefit of a few greedy paid agitators, and the fools whom they were deluding. On the other hand, the Socialist papers (of which three only, representing somewhat different schools, were published in London) came out full to the throat of well-printed matter. They were greedily bought by the whole public, who, of course, like the Government, expected a manifesto in them. But they found no word of reference to the great subject. It seemed as if their editors had ransacked their drawers for articles which would have been in place forty years before, under the technical name of educational articles. Most of these were admirable and straight forward expositions of the doctrines & practice of Socialism, free from haste and spite and hard words, and came upon the public with a kind of May-day freshness, amidst the worry and terror of the moment; and though the knowing well understood that the meaning of this move in the game was mere defiance, and a token of irreconcilable hostility to the then rulers of society, and though, also, they were meant for nothing else by 'the rebels,' yet they really had their effect as 'educational articles.' However, 'education' of another kind was acting upon the public with irresistible power, and probably cleared their heads a little.

"As to the Government, they were absolutely terrified by this act of 'boycotting' (the slang word then current for such acts of abstention). Their counsels became wild and vacillating to the last degree: one hour they were for giving way for the present till they could hatch another plot; the next they all but sent an order for the arrest in the lump of all the workmen's committees; the next they were on the point of ordering their brisk young general to take any excuse that offered for another massacre. But when they called to mind that the soldiery in that 'Battle' of Trafalgar Square were so daunted by the slaughter which they had made, that they could not be got to fire a second volley, they shrank back again from the dreadful courage necessary for carrying out another massacre. Meantime the prisoners, brought the second time before the magistrates under a strong escort of soldiers, were the second time remanded.

"The strike went on this day also. The workmen's committees were extended, and gave relief to great numbers of people, for they had organised a considerable amount of production of food by men whom they could depend upon. Quite a number of well-to-do people were now compelled to seek relief of them. But another curious thing happened: a band of young men of the upper classes armed themselves, and coolly went marauding in the streets, taking what suited them of such eatables and portables that they came across in the shops which had ventured to open. This operation they carried out in Oxford Street, then a great street of shops of all kinds. The Government, being at that hour in one of their yielding moods, thought this a fine opportunity for showing their impartiality in the maintenance of 'order,' and sent to arrest these hungry rich youths; who, however, surprised the police by a valiant resistance, so that all but three escaped. The Government did not gain the reputation for impartiality which they expected from this move; for they forgot that there were no evening papers; and the account of the skirmish spread wide indeed, but in a distorted form; for it was mostly told simply as an exploit of the starving people from the East-end; and everybody thought it was but natural for the Government to put them down when and where they could.

"That evening the rebel prisoners were visited in their cells by *very* polite and sympathetic persons, who pointed out to them what a suicidal course they were following, and how dangerous these extreme courses were for the popular cause. Says one of the prisoners: 'It was great sport comparing notes when we came out anent the attempt of the Government to "get at" us separately in prison, and how we answered the blandishments of the highly "intelligent and refined" persons set on to pump us. One laughed; another told extravagant long-bow stories to the envoy; a third held a sulky silence; a fourth damned the polite spy and bade him hold his jaw—and that was all they got out of us.'

"So passed the second day of the great strike. It was clear to all thinking people that the third day would bring on the crisis; for the present suspense and ill-concealed terror was unendurable. The ruling classes, and the middle-class nonpoliticians who had been their real strength and support, were as sheep lacking a shepherd; they literally did not know what to do.

"One thing they found they had to do: try to get the 'rebels' to do something. So the next morning, the morning of the third day of the strike, when the members of the Committee of Public Safety appeared again before the magistrate, they found themselves treated with the greatest possible courtesy—in fact, rather as envoys and ambassadors than prisoners. In short, the magistrate had received his orders; and with no more to do than might come of a long stupid speech, which might have been written by Dickens in mockery, he discharged the prisoners, who went back to their meeting-place and at once began a due sitting. It was high time. For this third day the mass was fermenting indeed. There was, of course, a vast number of working people who were not organised in the least in the world; men who had been used to act as their masters drove them, or rather as the system drove, of which their masters were a part. That system was now falling to pieces, and the old pressure of the master having been taken off these poor men, it seemed likely that nothing but the mere animal necessities and passions of men would have any hold on them, and that mere general overturn would be the result. Doubtless this would have happened if it had not been that the huge mass had been leavened by Socialist opinion in the first place, and in the second place by actual contact with declared Socialists, many or indeed most of whom were members of those bodies of workmen above said.

"If anything of this kind had happened some years before, when the masters of labour were still looked upon as the natural rulers of the people, and even the poorest and most ignorant man leaned upon them for support, while they submitted to their fleecing, the entire break-up of all society would have followed. But the long series of years during which the workmen had learned to despise their rulers, had done away with their dependence upon them, and they were now beginning to trust (somewhat dangerously, as events proved) in the non-legal leaders whom events had thrust forward; and though most of these were now become mere figure-heads, their names and reputations were useful in this crisis as a stop-gap.

"The effect of the news, therefore, of the release of the Committee gave the Government some breathing time: for it was received with the greatest joy by the workers, and even the well-to-do saw in it a respite from the mere destruction which they had begun to dread, and the fear of which most of them attributed to the weakness of the Government. As far as the passing hour went, perhaps they were right in this."

"How do you mean?" said I. "What could the Government have

done? I often used to think that they would be helpless in such a crisis."

Said old Hammond: "Of course I don't doubt that in the long run matters would have come about as they did. But if the Government could have treated their army as a real army, and used them strategically as a general would have done, looking on the people as a mere open enemy to be shot at and dispersed wherever they turned up, they would probably have gained the victory at the time."

"But would the soldiers have acted against the people in this way?" said I.

Said he: "I think from all I have heard that they would have done so if they had met bodies of men armed however badly, and however badly they had been organised. It seems also as if before the Trafalgar Square massacre they might as a whole have been depended upon to fire upon an unarmed crowd, though they were much honeycombed by Socialism. The reason for this was that they dreaded the use by apparently unarmed men of an explosive called dynamite, of which many loud boasts were made by the workers on the eve of these events; although it turned out to be of little use as a material for war in the way that was expected. Of course the officers of the soldiery fanned this fear to the utmost, so that the rank and file probably thought on that occasion that they were being led into a desperate battle with men who were really armed, and whose weapon was the more dreadful, because it was concealed. After that massacre, however, it was at all times doubtful if the regular soldiers would fire upon an unarmed or half-armed crowd."

Said I: "The regular soldiers? Then there were other combatants against the people?"

"Yes," said he, "we shall come to that presently."

"Certainly," I said, "you had better go on straight with your story. I see that time is wearing."

Said Hammond: "The Government lost no time in coming to terms with the Committee of Public Safety; for indeed they could think of nothing else than the danger of the moment. They sent a duly accredited envoy to treat with these men, who somehow had obtained dominion over people's minds, while the formal rulers had no hold except over their bodies. There is no need at present to go into the details of the truce (for such it was) between these high contracting parties, the Government of the empire of Great Britain and a handful of working-men (as they were called in scorn in those days), amongst whom, indeed, were some very capable and 'square-headed' persons, though, as aforesaid, the abler men were not then the recognised leaders. The upshot of it was that all the definite claims of the people had to be granted. We can now see that most of these claims were of themselves not worth either demanding or resisting; but they were looked on at that time as most important, and they were at least tokens of revolt against the miserable system of life which was then beginning to tumble to pieces. One claim, however, was of the utmost immediate importance, and this the Government tried hard to evade; but as they were not dealing with fools, they had to yield at last. This was the claim of recognition and formal status for the Committee of Public Safety, and all the associations which it fostered under its wing. This it is clear meant two things: first, amnesty for 'the rebels,' great and small, who, without a distinct act of civil war, could no longer be attacked; and next, a continuance of the organised revolution. Only one point the Government could gain, and that was a name. The dreadful revolutionary title was dropped, and the body, with its branches, acted under the respectable name of the 'Board of Conciliation and its local offices.' Carrying this name, it became the leader of the people in the civil war which soon followed."

"O," said I, somewhat startled, "so the civil war went on, in spite of all that had happened?"

"So it was," said he. "In fact, it was this very legal recognition which made the civil war possible in the ordinary sense of war; it took the struggle out of the element of mere massacres on one side, and endurance plus strikes on the other."

"And can you tell me in what kind of way the war was carried on?" said I.

"Yes," he said; "we have records and to spare of all that; and the essence of them I can give you in a few words. As I told you, the rank and file of the army was not to be trusted by the reactionists; but the officers generally were prepared for anything, for they were mostly the very stupidest men in the country. Whatever the Government might do, a great part of the upper and middle classes were determined to set on foot a counter-revolution; for the Communism which now loomed ahead seemed quite unendurable to them. Bands of young men, like the marauders in the great strike of whom I told you just now, armed themselves and drilled, and began on any opportunity or pretence to skirmish with the people in the streets. The Government neither helped them nor put them down, but stood by, hoping that something might come of it. These 'Friends of Order,' as they were called, had some successes at first, and grew bolder; they got many officers of the regular army to help them, and by their means laid hold of munitions of war of all kinds. One part of their

tactics consisted in their guarding and even garrisoning the big factories of the period: they held at one time, for instance, the whole
of that place called Manchester which I spoke of just now. A sort
of irregular war was carried on with varied success all over the country; and at last the Government, which at first pretended to ignore
the struggle, or treat it as mere rioting, definitely declared for 'the
Friends of Order,' and joined to their bands whatsoever of the regular army they could get together, and made a desperate effort to
overwhelm 'the rebels,' as they were now once more called, and as
indeed they called themselves.

"It was too late. All ideas of peace on a basis of compromise had disappeared on either side. The end, it was seen clearly, must be either
absolute slavery for all but the privileged, or a system of life founded
on equality and Communism. The sloth, the hopelessness, and if I
may say so, the cowardice of the last century, had given place to the
eager, restless heroism of a declared revolutionary period. I will not
say that the people of that time foresaw the life we are leading now,
but there was a general instinct amongst them towards the essential
part of that life, and many men saw clearly beyond the desperate
struggle of the day into the peace which it was to bring about. The
men of that day who were on the side of freedom were not unhappy,
I think, though they were harassed by hopes and fears, and sometimes torn by doubts, and the conflict of duties hard to reconcile."

"But how did the people, the revolutionists, carry on the war?
What were the elements of success on their side?"

I put this question, because I wanted to bring the old man back
to the definite history, and take him out of the musing mood so
natural to an old man.

He answered: "Well, they did not lack organisers; for the very
conflict itself, in days when, as I told you, men of any strength of
mind cast away all consideration for the ordinary business of life,
developed the necessary talent amongst them. Indeed, from all I have
read and heard, I much doubt whether, without this seemingly dreadful civil war, the due talent for administration would have been
developed amongst the working-men. Anyhow, it was there, and they
soon got leaders far more than equal to the best men amongst the
reactionaries. For the rest, they had no difficulty about the material
of their army; for that revolutionary instinct so acted on the ordinary
soldier in the ranks that the greater part, certainly the best part, of the
soldiers joined the side of the people. But the main element of their
success was this, that wherever the working people were not coerced,
they worked, not for the reactionists, but for 'the rebels.' The reactionists could get no work done for them outside the districts where

they were all-powerful: and even in those districts they were harassed by continual risings; and in all cases and everywhere got nothing done without obstruction and black looks and sulkiness; so that not only were their armies quite worn out with the difficulties which they had to meet, but the non-combatants who were on their side were so worried and beset with hatred and a thousand little troubles and annoyances that life became almost unendurable to them on those terms. Not a few of them actually died of the worry; many committed suicide. Of course, a vast number of them joined actively in the cause of reaction, and found some solace to their misery in the eagerness of conflict. Lastly, many thousands gave way and submitted to 'the rebels;' and as the numbers of these latter increased, it at last became clear to all men that the cause which was once hopeless, was now triumphant, and that the hopeless cause was that of slavery and privilege."

CHAPTER XVIII

THE BEGINNING OF THE NEW LIFE

"Well," said I, "so you got clear out of all your trouble. Were people satisfied with the new order of things when it came?"

"People?" he said. "Well, surely all must have been glad of peace when it came; especially when they found, as they must have found, that after all, they—even the once rich—were not living very badly. As to those who had been poor, all through the war, which lasted about two years, their condition had been bettering, in spite of the struggle; and when peace came at last, in a very short time they made great strides towards a decent life. The great difficulty was that the once-poor had such a feeble conception of the real pleasure of life; so to say, they did not ask enough, did not know how to ask enough, from the new state of things. It was perhaps rather a good than an evil thing that the necessity for restoring the wealth destroyed during the war forced them into working at first almost as hard as they had been used to before the Revolution. For all historians are agreed that there never was a war in which there was so much destruction of wares, and instruments for making them as in this civil war."

"I am rather surprised at that," said I.

"Are you? I don't see why," said Hammond.

"Why," I said, "because the party of order would surely look upon the wealth as their own property, no share of which, if they could help it, should go to their slaves, supposing they conquered. And on the other hand, it was just for the possession of that wealth that 'the rebels' were fighting, and I should have thought, especially when they saw that they were winning, that they would have been careful to destroy as little as possible of what was so soon to be their own."

"It was as I have told you, however," said he. "The party of order, when they recovered from their first cowardice of surprise—or, if you please, when they fairly saw that, whatever happened, they would be ruined, fought with great bitterness, and cared little what they did, so long as they injured the enemies who had destroyed the sweets of life for them. As to 'the rebels' I have told you that the outbreak of actual war made them careless of trying to save the wretched scraps of wealth that they had. It was a common saying amongst them, Let the country be cleared of everything except valiant living men, rather than that we fall into slavery again!"

He sat silently thinking a little while, and then said:

"When the conflict was once really begun, it was seen how little of any value there was in the old world of slavery and inequality. Don't you see what it means? In the times which you are thinking of, and of which you seem to know so much, there was no hope; nothing but the dull jog of the mill-horse under compulsion of collar and whip; but in that fighting-time that followed, all was hope: 'the rebels' at least felt themselves strong enough to build up the world again from its dry bones,—and they did it, too!" said the old man, his eyes glittering under his beetling brows. He went on: "And their opponents at least and at last learned something about the reality of life, and its sorrows, which they—their class, I mean—had once known nothing of. In short, the two combatants, the workman and the gentleman, between them—"

"Between them," said I, quickly, "they destroyed commercialism!"

"Yes, yes, YES," said he; "that is it. Nor could it have been destroyed otherwise; except, perhaps, by the whole of society gradually falling into lower depths, till it should at last reach a condition as rude as barbarism, but lacking both the hope and the pleasures of barbarism. Surely the sharper, shorter remedy was the happiest."

"Most surely," said I.

"Yes," said the old man, "the world was being brought to its second birth; how could that take place without a tragedy? Moreover, think of it. The spirit of the new days, of our days, was to be delight in the life of the world; intense and overweening love of the very skin and surface of the earth on which man dwells, such as a lover has in the fair flesh of the woman he loves; this, I say, was to be the new spirit of the time. All other moods save this had been exhausted: the unceasing criticism, the boundless curiosity in the ways and thoughts of man, which was the mood of the ancient Greek, to whom these things were not so much a means, as an end, was gone past recovery; nor had there been really any shadow of it in the so-called science of the nineteenth century, which, as you must know, was in the main an appendage to the commercial system; nay, not seldom an appendage to the police of that system. In spite of appearances, it was limited and cowardly, because it did not really believe in itself. It was the outcome, as it was the sole relief, of the unhappiness of the period which made life so bitter even to the rich, and which, as you may see with your bodily eyes, the great change has swept away. More akin to our way of looking at life was the spirit of the Middle Ages, to whom heaven and the life of the next world was such a reality, that it became to them a part of the life upon the earth; which accordingly they loved and adorned, in spite of the ascetic doctrines of their formal creed, which bade them contemn it.

"But that also, with its assured belief in heaven and hell as two countries in which to live, has gone, and now we do, both in word and in deed, believe in the continuous life of the world of men, and as it were, add every day of that common life to the little stock of days which our own mere individual experience wins for us: and consequently we are happy. Do you wonder at it? In times past, indeed, men were told to love their kind, to believe in the religion of humanity and so forth. But look you, just in the degree that a man had elevation of mind and refinement enough to be able to value this idea, was he repelled by the obvious aspect of the individuals composing the mass which he was to worship; and he could only evade that repulsion by making a conventional abstraction of mankind that had little actual or historical relation to the race; which to his eyes was divided into blind tyrants on the one hand and apathetic degraded slaves on the other. But now, where is the difficulty in accepting the religion of humanity, when the men and women who go to make up humanity are free, happy, and energetic at least, and most commonly beautiful of body also, and surrounded by beautiful things of their own fashioning, and a nature bettered and not worsened by contact with mankind? This is what this age of the world has reserved for us."

"It seems true," said I, "or ought to be, if what my eyes have seen is a token of the general life you lead. Can you now tell me anything of your progress after the years of the struggle?"

Said he: "I could easily tell you more than you have time to listen to; but I can at least hint at one of the chief difficulties which had to be met: and that was, that when men began to settle down after the war, and their labour had pretty much filled up the gap in wealth caused by the destruction of that war, a kind of disappointment seemed coming over us, and the prophecies of some of the reactionists of past times seemed as if they would come true, and a dull level of utilitarian comfort be the end for a while of our aspirations and success. The loss of the competitive spur to exertion had not, indeed, done anything to interfere with the necessary production of the community, but how if it should make men dull by giving them too much time for thought or idle musing? But, after all, this dull thunder-cloud only threatened us, and then passed over. Probably, from what I have told you before, you will have a guess at the remedy for such a disaster; remembering always that many of the things which used to be produced—slave-wares for the poor and mere wealth-wasting wares for the rich—ceased to be made. That remedy was, in short, the production of what used to be called art, but which has no name amongst us now, because it has become a necessary part of the labour of every man who produces."

Said I: "What! had men any time or opportunity for cultivating the fine arts amidst the desperate struggle for life and freedom that you have told me of?"

Said Hammond: "You must not suppose that the new form of art was founded chiefly on the memory of the art of the past; although, strange to say, the civil war was much less destructive of art than of other things, and though what of art existed under the old forms, revived in a wonderful way during the latter part of the struggle, especially as regards music and poetry. The art or work-pleasure, as one ought to call it, of which I am now speaking, sprung up almost spontaneously, it seems, from a kind of instinct amongst people, no longer driven desperately to painful and terrible overwork, to do the best they could with the work in hand—to make it excellent of its kind; and when that had gone on for a little, a craving for beauty seemed to awaken in men's minds, and they began rudely and awkwardly to ornament the wares which they made; and when they had once set to work at that, it soon began to grow. All this was much helped by the abolition of the squalor which our immediate ancestors put up with so coolly; and by the leisurely, but not stupid, country-life which now grew (as I told you before) to be common amongst us. Thus at last and by slow degrees we got pleasure into our work; then we became conscious of that pleasure, and cultivated it, and took care that we had our fill of it; and then all was gained, and we were happy. So may it be for ages and ages!"

The old man fell into a reverie, not altogether without melancholy I thought; but I would not break it. Suddenly he started, and said:

"Well, dear guest, here are come Dick and Clara to fetch you away, and there is an end of my talk; which I daresay you will not be sorry for; the long day is coming to an end, and you will have a pleasant ride back to Hammersmith."

CHAPTER XXII

HAMPTON COURT AND A PRAISER OF PAST TIMES

Clara and Dick, full of their renewed love for one another, ride back to Hammersmith with William. The next day the three of them row up the Thames and reach Runnymede at dusk, where they are invited by a malcontented old man to spend the night.

We went up a paved path between the roses, and straight into a very pretty room, panelled and carved, and as clean as a new pin; but the chief ornament of which was a young woman, light-haired and grey-eyed, but with her face and hands and bare feet tanned quite brown with the sun. Though she was very lightly clad, that was clearly from choice, not from poverty, though these were the first cottage-dwellers I had come across; for her gown was of silk, and on her wrists were bracelets that seemed to me of great value. She was lying on a sheep-skin near the window, but jumped up as soon as we entered, and when she saw the guests behind the old man, she clapped her hands and cried out with pleasure, and when she got us into the middle of the room, fairly danced round us in delight of our company.

"What!" said the old man, "you are pleased, are you, Ellen?"

The girl danced up to him and threw her arms round him, and said: "Yes I am, and so ought you to be, grandfather."

"Well, well, I am," said he, "as much as I can be pleased. Guests, please be seated."

This seemed rather strange to us; stranger, I suspect, to my friends than to me; but Dick took the opportuniy of both the host and his grand-daughter being out of the room to say to me, softly: "A grumbler: there are a few of them still. Once upon a time, I am told, they were quite a nuisance."

The old man came in as he spoke and sat down beside us with a sigh, which, indeed, seemed fetched up as if he wanted us to take notice of it; but just then the girl came in with the victuals, and the carle missed his mark, what between our hunger generally and that I was pretty busy watching the grand-daughter moving about as beautiful as a picture.

Everything to eat and drink, though it was somewhat different to what we had had in London, was better than good, but the old man eyed rather sulkily the chief dish on the table, on which lay a leash of fine perch, and said:

"H'm, perch! I am sorry we can't do better for you, guests. The time was when we might have had a good piece of salmon up from London for you; but the times have grown mean and petty."

"Yes, but you might have had it now," said the girl, giggling, "if you had known that they were coming."

"It's our fault for not bringing it with us, neighbours," said Dick, good-humouredly. "But if the times have grown petty, at any rate the perch haven't; that fellow in the middle there must have weighed a good two pounds when he was showing his dark stripes and red fins to the minnows yonder. And as to the salmon, why, neighbour, my friend here, who comes from the outlands, was quite surprised yesterday morning when I told him we had plenty of salmon at Hammersmith. I am sure I have heard nothing of the times worsening."

He looked a little uncomfortable. And the old man, turning to me, said very courteously:

"Well, sir, I am happy to see a man from over the water; but I really must appeal to you to say whether on the whole you are not better off in your country; where I suppose, from what our guest says, you are brisker and more alive, because you have not wholly got rid of competition. You see, I have read not a few books of the past days, and certainly *they* are much more alive than those which are written now; and good sound unlimited competition was the condition under which they were written,—if we didn't know that from the record of history, we should know it from the books themselves. There is a spirit of adventure in them, and signs of a capacity to extract good out of evil which our literature quite lacks now; and I cannot help thinking that our moralists and historians exaggerate hugely the unhappiness of the past days, in which such splendid works of imagination and intellect were produced."

Clara listened to him with restless eyes, as if she were excited and pleased; Dick knitted his brow and looked still more uncomfortable, but said nothing. Indeed, the old man gradually, as he warmed to his subject, dropped his sneering manner, and both spoke and looked very seriously. But the girl broke out before I could deliver myself of the answer I was framing:

"Books, books! always books, grandfather! When will you understand that after all it is the world we live in which interests us; the world of which we are a part, and which we can never love too

much? Look!" she said, throwing open the casement wider and showing us the white light sparkling between the black shadows of the
moonlit garden, through which ran a little shiver of the summer
night-wind, "look! these are our books in these days!—and these,"
she said, stepping lightly up to the two lovers and laying a hand on
each of their shoulders; "and the guest there, with his over-sea knowledge and experience;—yes, and even you, grandfather" (a smile ran
over her face as she spoke), "with all your grumbling and wishing
yourself back again in the good old days,—in which, as far as I can
make out, a harmless and lazy old man like you would either have
pretty nearly starved, or have had to pay soldiers and people to take
the folk's victuals and clothes and houses away from them by force.
Yes, these are our books; and if we want more, can we not find work
to do in the beautiful buildings that we raise up all over the country
(and I know there was nothing like them in past times), wherein
a man can put forth whatever is in him, and make his hands set
forth his mind and his soul."

She paused a little, and I for my part could not help staring at her,
and thinking that if she were a book, the pictures in it were most
lovely. The colour mantled in her delicate sun-burnt cheeks; her
grey eyes, light amidst the tan of her face, kindly looked on us all
as she spoke. She paused, and said again:

"As for your books, they were well enough for times when intelligent people had but little else in which they could take pleasure,
and when they must needs supplement the sordid miseries of their
own lives with imaginations of the lives of other people. But I say
flatly that in spite of all their cleverness and vigour, and capacity for
story-telling, there is something loathsome about them. Some of
them, indeed, do here and there show some feeling for those whom
the history-books call 'poor,' and of the misery of whose lives we have
some inkling; but presently they give it up, and towards the end of
the story we must be contented to see the hero and heroine living
happily in an island of bliss on other people's troubles; and that after
a long series of sham troubles (or mostly sham) of their own making, illustrated by dreary introspective nonsense about their feelings
and aspirations, and all the rest of it; while the world must even
then have gone on its way, and dug and sewed and baked and built
and carpentered round about these useless—animals."

"There!" said the old man, reverting to his dry sulky manner again.
"There's eloquence! I suppose you like it?"

"Yes," said I, very emphatically.

"Well," said he, "now the storm of eloquence has lulled for a little, suppose you answer my question?—that is, if you like, you know," quoth he, with a sudden access of courtesy.

"What question?" said I. For I must confess that Ellen's strange and almost wild beauty had put it out of my head.

Said he: "First of all (excuse my catechising), is there competition in life, after the old kind, in the country whence you come?"

"Yes," said I, "it is the rule there." And I wondered as I spoke what fresh complications I should get into as a result of this answer.

"Question two," said the carle: "Are you not on the whole much freer, more energetic—in a word, healthier and happier—for it?"

I smiled. "You wouldn't talk so if you had any idea of our life. To me you seem here as if you were living in heaven compared with us of the country from which I came."

"Heaven?" said he: "you like heaven, do you?"

"Yes," said I—snappishly, I am afraid; for I was beginning rather to resent his formula.

"Well, I am far from sure that I do," quoth he. "I think one may do more with one's life than sitting on a damp cloud and singing hymns."

I was rather nettled by this inconsequence, and said: "Well, neighbour, to be short, and without using metaphors, in the land whence I come, where the competition which produced those literary works which you admire so much is still the rule, most people are thoroughly unhappy; here, to me at least, most people seem thoroughly happy."

"No offence, Guest—no offence," said he; "but let me ask you; you like that, do you?"

His formula, put with such obstinate persistence, made us all laugh heartily; and even the old man joined in the laughter on the sly. However, he was by no means beaten, and said presently:

"From all I can hear, I should judge that a young woman so beautiful as my dear Ellen yonder would have been a lady, as they called it in the old time, and wouldn't have had to wear a few rags of silk as she does now, or to have browned herself in the sun as she has to do now. What do you say to that, eh?"

Here Clara, who had been pretty much silent hitherto, struck in, and said: "Well, really, I don't think that you would have mended matters, or that they want mending. Don't you see that she is dressed deliciously for this beautiful weather? And as for the sun-burning of your hayfields, why, I hope to pick up some of that for myself when we get a little higher up the river. Look if I don't need a little sun on my pasty white skin!"

And she stripped up the sleeve from her arm and laid it beside Ellen's who was now sitting next her. To say the truth, it was rather amusing to me to see Clara putting herself forward as a town-bred fine lady, for she was as well-knit and clean-skinned a girl as might be met with anywhere at the best. Dick stroked the beautiful arm rather shyly, and pulled down the sleeve again, while she blushed at his touch; and the old man said laughingly: "Well, I suppose you *do* like that; don't you?"

Ellen kissed her new friend, and we all sat silent for a little, till she broke out into a sweet shrill song, and held us all entranced with the wonder of her clear voice; and the old grumbler sat looking at her lovingly. The other young people sang also in due time; and then Ellen showed us to our beds in small cottage chambers, fragrant and clean as the ideal of the old pastoral poets; and the pleasure of the evening quite extinguished my fear of the last night, that I should wake up in the old miserable world of worn-out pleasures, and hopes that were half fears.

CHAPTER XXVII

THE UPPER WATERS

Clara, Dick and William continue their boat excursion on the Thames.

. . . And so went our ways into what once would have been the deeper country under the foot-hills of the White Horse; and though the contrast between half-cocknified and wholly unsophisticated country existed no longer, a feeling of exultation rose within me (as it used to do) at sight of the familiar and still unchanged hills of the Berkshire range.

We stopped at Wallingford for our mid-day meal; of course, all signs of squalor and poverty had disappeared from the streets of the ancient town, and many ugly houses had been taken down and many pretty new ones built, but I thought it curious, that the town still looked like the old place I remembered so well; for indeed it looked like that ought to have looked.

At dinner we fell in with an old, but very bright and intelligent man, who seemed in a country way to be another edition of old Hammond. He had an extraordinary detailed knowledge of the ancient history of the countryside from the time of Alfred to the days of the Parliamentary Wars, many events of which, as you may know, were enacted round about Wallingford. But, what was more interesting to us, he had detailed record of the period of the change to the present state of things, and told us a great deal about it, and especially of that exodus of the people from the town to the country, and the gradual recovery by the town-bred people on one side, and the country-bred people on the other, of those arts of life which they had each lost; which loss, as he told us, had at one time gone so far that not only was it impossible to find a carpenter or a smith in a village or small country town, but that people in such places had even forgotten how to bake bread, and that at Wallingford, for instance, the bread came down with the newspapers by an early train from London, worked in some way, the explanation of which I could not understand. He told us also that the townspeople who came into the country used to pick up the agricultural arts by carefully watching the way in which the machines worked, gathering an idea of handicraft from machinery; because at that time almost everything in and about the fields was done by elaborate machines used quite unintelligently by the labourers. On the other hand, the old men amongst the labourers managed to teach the younger ones gradually a little artizanship, such as the use of the saw and the plane, the work of the smithy, and so forth; for once more, by that time it was as much as—or rather, more than—a man could do to fix an ash pole to a rake by handiwork; so that it would take a machine worth a thousand pounds, a group of workmen, and half a day's travelling, to do five shillings' worth of work. He showed us, among other things, an account of a certain village council who were working hard at all this business; and the record of their intense earnestness in getting to the bottom of some matter which in time past would have been thought quite trivial, as, for example, the due proportions of alkali and oil for soap-making for the village wash, or the exact heat of the water into which a leg of mutton should be plunged for boiling—all this joined to the utter absence of anything like party feeling, which even in a village assembly would certainly have made its appearance in an earlier epoch, was very amusing, and at the same time instructive.

This old man, whose name was Henry Morsom, took us, after our meal and a rest, into a biggish hall which contained a large collection of articles of manufacture and art from the last days of the machine period to that day; and he went over them with us, and explained them with great care. They also were very interesting, showing the transition from the make-shift work of the machines (which was at about its worst a little after the civil war before told of) into the first years of the new handicraft period. Of course, there was much overlapping of the periods: and at first the new handwork came in very slowly.

"You must remember," said the old antiquary, "that the handicraft was not the result of what used to be called material necessity: on the contrary, by that time the machines had been so much improved that almost all necessary work might have been done by them: and indeed many people at that time, and before it, used to think that machinery would entirely supersede handicraft; which certainly, on the face of it, seemed more than likely. But there was another opinion, far less logical, prevalent amongst the rich people before the days of freedom, which did not die out at once after that epoch had begun. This opinion, which from all I can learn seemed as natural then, as it seems absurd now, was, that while the ordinary daily work of the world would be done entirely by automatic machinery, the energies of the more intelligent part of mankind would be set free to follow the higher forms of the arts, as well as science and the study of history. It was strange, was it not, that they should thus ignore that aspiration after complete equality which we now recognise as the bond of all happy human society?"

I did not answer, but thought the more. Dick looked thoughtful, and said:

"Strange, neighbour? Well, I don't know. I have often heard my old kinsman say the one aim of all people before our time was to avoid work, or at least they thought it was; so of course the work which their daily life *forced* them to do, seemed more like work than that which they *seemed* to choose for themselves."

"True enough," said Morsom. "Anyhow, they soon began to find out their mistake, and that only slaves and slave-holders could live solely by setting machines going."

Clara broke in here, flushing a little as she spoke: "Was not their mistake once more bred of the life of slavery that they had been living?—a life which was always looking upon everything, except mankind, animate and inanimate—'nature,' as people used to call it —as one thing, and mankind as another. It was natural to people thinking in this way, that they should try to make 'nature' their slave, since they thought 'nature' was something outside them."

"Surely," said Morsom; "and they were puzzled as to what to do, till they found the feeling against a mechanical life, which had begun before the Great Change amongst people who had leisure to think of such things, was spreading insensibly; till at last under the guise of pleasure that was not supposed to be work, work that was pleasure began to push out the mechanical toil, which they had once hoped at the best to reduce to narrow limits indeed, but never to get rid of; and which, moreover, they found they could not limit as they had hoped to do."

"When did this new revolution gather head?" said I.

"In the half-century that followed the Great Change," said Morsom, "it began to be noteworthy; machine after machine was quietly dropped under the excuse that the machines could not produce works of art, and that works of art were more and more called for. Look here," he said, "here are some of the works of that time— rough and unskilful in handiwork, but solid and showing some sense of pleasure in the making."

"They are very curious," said I, taking up a piece of pottery from amongst the specimens which the antiquary was showing us; "not a bit like the work of either savages or barbarians, and yet with what would once have been called a hatred of civilisation impressed upon them."

"Yes," said Morsom, "you must not look for delicacy there: in that period you could only have got that from a man who was practically a slave. But now, you see," said he, leading me on a little, "we have learned the trick of handicraft, and have added the utmost refinement of workmanship to the freedom of fancy and imagination."

I looked, and wondered indeed at the deftness and abundance of beauty of the work of men who had at last learned to accept life itself as a pleasure, and the satisfaction of the common needs of mankind and the preparation for them, as work fit for the best of the race. I mused silently; but at last I said:

"What is to come after this?"

The old man laughed. "I don't know," said he; "we will meet it when it comes."

Moving further up the Thames, Clara, Dick, and William meet Ellen, a coincidence that pleases William, and she joins the excursion party.

CHAPTER XXX

THE JOURNEY'S END

On we went. In spite of my new-born excitement about Ellen, and my gathering fear of where it would land me, I could not help taking abundant interest in the condition of the river and its banks; all the more as she never seemed weary of the changing picture, but looked at every yard of flowery bank and gurgling eddy with the same kind of affectionate interest which I myself once had so fully, as I used to think, and perhaps had not altogether lost even in this strangely changed society with all its wonders. Ellen seemed delighted with my pleasure at this, that, or the other piece of carefulness in dealing with the river: the nursing of pretty corners; the ingenuity in dealing with difficulties of water-engineering, so that the most obviously useful works looked beautiful and natural also. All this, I say, pleased me hugely, and she was pleased at my pleasure —but rather puzzled too.

"You seem astonished," she said, just after we had passed a mill [2] which spanned all the stream save the water-way for traffic, but which was as beautiful in its way as a Gothic cathedral—"You seem astonished at this being so pleasant to look at."

"Yes," I said, "in a way I am; though I don't see why it should not be."

"Ah!" she said, looking at me admiringly, yet with a lurking smile in her face, "you know all about the history of the past. Were they not always careful about this little stream which now adds so much pleasantness to the country-side? It would always be easy to manage this little river. Ah! I forgot, though," she said, as her eye caught mine, "in the days we are thinking of pleasure was wholly neglected in such matters. But how did they manage the river in the days that you—" Lived in she was going to say; but correcting herself, said: "in the days of which you have record?"

"They *mis*managed it," quoth I. "Up to the first half of the nineteenth century, when it was still more or less of a highway for the country people, some care was taken of the river and its banks; and though I don't suppose any one troubled himself about its aspect, yet it was trim and beautiful. But when the railways—of which no doubt you have heard—came into power, they would not allow the people of the country to use either the natural or artificial waterways, of which latter there were a great many. I suppose when we get higher up we shall see one of these; a very important one, which one of these railways entirely closed to the public, so that they might force people to send their goods by their private road, and so tax them as heavily as they could."

Ellen laughed heartily. "Well," she said, "that is not stated clearly enough in our history-books, and it is worth knowing. But certainly the people of those days must have been a curiously lazy set. We are

[2] I should have said that all along the Thames there were abundance of mills used for various purposes; none of which were in any degree unsightly, and many strikingly beautiful; and the gardens about them marvels of loveliness.

not either fidgety or quarrelsome now, but if any one tried such a piece of folly on us, we should use the said waterways, whoever gainsaid us: surely that would be simple enough. However, I remember other cases of this stupidity: when I was on the Rhine two years ago, I remember they showed us ruins of old castles, which, according to what we heard, must have been made for pretty much the same purpose as the railways were. But I am interrupting your history of the river: pray go on."

"It is both short and stupid enough," said I. "The river having lost its practical or commercial value—that is, being of no use to make money of—"

She nodded. "I understand what that queer phrase means," said she. "Go on!"

"Well, it was utterly neglected, till at last it became a nuisance—"

"Yes," quoth Ellen, "I understand: like the railways and the robber knights. Yes?"

"So then they turned the make-shift business on to it, and handed it over to a body up in London, who from time to time, in order to show that they had something to do, did some damage here and there,—cut down trees, destroying the banks thereby; dredged the river (where it was not needed always), and threw the dredgings on the fields so as to spoil them; and so forth. But for the most part they practised 'masterly inactivity,' as it was then called—that is, they drew their salaries, and let things alone."

"Drew their salaries," she said. "I know that means that they were allowed to take an extra lot of other people's goods for doing nothing. And if that had been all, it really might have been worth while to let them do so, if you couldn't find any other way of keeping them quiet; but it seems to me that being so paid, they could not help doing something, and that something was bound to be mischief,—because," said she, kindling with sudden anger, "the whole business was founded on lies and false pretensions. I don't mean only these river-guardians, but all these master-people I have read of."

"Yes," said I, "how happy you are to have got out of the parsimony of oppression!"

"Why do you sigh?" she said, kindly and somewhat anxiously. "You seem to think that it will not last?"

"It will last for you," quoth I.

"But why not for you?" said she. "Surely it is for all the world; and if your country is somewhat backward, it will come into line before long. Or," she said quickly, "are you thinking that you must soon go back again? I will make my proposal which I told you of at once, and so perhaps put an end to your anxiety. I was going to propose that you should live with us where we are going. I feel quite old friends with you, and should be sorry to lose you." Then she smiled on me, and said: "Do you know, I begin to suspect you of wanting to nurse a sham sorrow, like the ridiculous characters in some of those queer old novels that I have come across now and then."

I really had almost begun to suspect it myself, but I refused to admit so much; so I sighed no more, but fell to giving my delightful companion what little pieces of history I knew about the river and its borderlands; and the time passed pleasantly enough; and between the two of us (she was a better sculler than I was, and seemed quite tireless) we kept up fairly well with Dick, hot as the afternoon was, and swallowed up the way at a great rate. At last we passed under another ancient bridge; and through meadows bordered at first with huge elm-trees mingled with sweet chestnut of younger but very elegant growth; and the meadows widened out so much that it seemed as if the trees must now be on the bents only, or about the houses, except for the growth of willows on the immediate banks; so that the wide stretch of grass was little broken here. Dick got very much excited now, and often stood up in the boat to cry out to us that this was such and such a field, and so forth; and we caught fire at his enthusiasm for the hayfield and its harvest, and pulled our best.

At last as we were passing through a reach of the river where on the side of the towing-path was a highish bank with a thick whispering bed of reeds before it, and on the other side a higher bank, clothed with willows that dipped into the stream and crowned by ancient elm-trees, we saw bright figures coming along close to the bank, as if they were looking for something; as, indeed, they were, and we—that is, Dick and his company—were what they were looking for. Dick lay on his oars, and we followed his example. He gave a joyous shout to the people on the bank, which was echoed back from it in many voices, deep and sweetly shrill; for there were above a dozen persons, both men, women, and children. A tall handsome woman, with black wavy hair and deep-set grey eyes, came forward on the bank and waved her hand gracefully to us, and said:

"Dick, my friend, we have almost had to wait for you! What excuse have you to make for your slavish punctuality? Why didn't you take us by surprise, and come yesterday?"

"O," said Dick, with an almost imperceptible jerk of his head toward our boat, "we didn't want to come too quick up the water; there is so much to see for those who have not been up here before."

"True, true," said the stately lady, for stately is the word that must be used for her; "and we want them to get to know the wet way from the east thoroughly well, since they must often use it now. But come ashore at once, Dick, and you, dear neighbours; there is a break in the reeds and a good landing-place just round the corner. We can carry up your things, or send some of the lads after them."

"No, no," said Dick; "it is easier going by water, though it is but a step. Besides, I want to bring my friend here to the proper place. We will go on to the Ford; and you can talk to us from the bank as we paddle along."

He pulled his sculls through the water, and on we went, turning a sharp angle and going north a little. Presently we saw before us a bank of elm-trees, which told us of a house amidst them, though I looked in vain for the grey walls that I expected to see there. As we went, the folk on the bank talked indeed, mingling their kind voices with the cuckoo's song, the sweet strong whistle of the black-birds, and the ceaseless note of the corn-crake as he crept through the long grass of the mowing-field; whence came waves of fragrance from the flowering clover amidst of the ripe grass.

In a few minutes we had passed through a deep eddying pool into the sharp stream that ran from the ford, and beached our craft on a tiny strand of limestone-gravel, and stepped ashore into the arms of our up-river friends, our journey done.

I disentangled myself from the merry throng, and mounting on the cart-road that ran along the river some feet above the water, I looked round about me. The river came down through a wide meadow on my left, which was grey now with the ripened seeding grasses; the gleaming water was lost presently by a turn of the bank, but over the meadow I could see the mingled gables of a building where I knew the lock must be, and which now seemed to combine a mill with it. A low wooded ridge bounded the river-plain to the south and south-east, whence we had come, and a few low houses lay about its feet and up its slope. I turned a little to my right, and through the hawthorn sprays and long shoots of the wild roses could see the flat country spreading out far away under the sun of the calm evening, till something that might be called hills with a look of sheep-pastures about them bounded it with a soft blue line. Before me, the elm-boughs still hid most of what houses there might be in this river-side dwelling of men; but to the right of the cart-road a few grey buildings of the simplest kind showed here and there.

There I stood in a dreamy mood, and rubbed my eyes as if I were not wholly awake, and half expected to see the gay-clad company of beautiful men and women change to two or three spindle-legged back-bowed men and haggard, hollow-eyed, ill-favoured women, who once wore down the soil of this land with their heavy hopeless feet, from day to day, and season to season, and year to year. But no change came as yet, and my heart swelled with joy as I thought of all the beautiful grey villages, from the river to the plain and the plain to the uplands, which I could picture to myself so well, all peopled now with this happy and lovely folk, who had cast away riches and attained to wealth.

CHAPTER XXXI

AN OLD HOUSE AMONGST NEW FOLK

As I stood there Ellen detached herself from our happy friends who still stood on the little strand and came up to me. She took me by the hand, and said softly, "Take me on to the house at once; we need not wait for the others: I had rather not."

I had a mind to say that I did not know the way thither, and that the river-side dwellers should lead; but almost without my will my feet moved on along the road they knew. The raised way led us into a little field bounded by a backwater of the river on one side; on the right hand we could see a cluster of small houses and barns, new and old, and before us a grey stone barn and a wall partly over-grown with ivy, over which a few grey gables showed. The village road ended in the shallow of the aforesaid backwater. We crossed the road, and again almost without my will my hand raised the latch of a door in the wall, and we stood presently on a stone path which led up to the old house to which fate in the shape of Dick had so strangely brought me in this new world of men. My companion gave a sigh of pleased surprise and enjoyment; nor did I wonder, for the garden between the wall and the house was redolent of the June flowers, and the roses were rolling over one another with that delicious superabundance of small well-tended gardens which at first sight takes away all thought from the beholder save that of beauty. The blackbirds were singing their loudest, the doves were cooing on the roof-ridge, the rooks in the high elm-trees beyond were garrulous among the young leaves, and the swifts wheeled whining about the gables. And the house itself was a fit guardian for all the beauty of this heart of summer.

Once again Ellen echoed my thoughts as she said: "Yes, friend, this is what I came out for to see; this many-gabled old house built by the simple country-folk of the long-past times, regardless of all the turmoil that was going on in cities and courts, is lovely still amidst all the beauty which these latter days have created; and I do not wonder at our friends tending it carefully and making much of it. It seems to me as if it had waited for these happy days, and held in it the gathered crumbs of happiness of the confused and turbulent past."

She led me up close to the house, and laid her shapely sun-browned hand and arm on the lichened wall as if to embrace it, and cried out, "O me! O me! How I love the earth, and the seasons, and weather, and all things that deal with it, and all that grows out of it,—as this has done!"

I could not answer her, or say a word. Her exultation and pleasure were so keen and exquisite, and her beauty, so delicate, yet so interfused with energy, expressed it so fully, that any added word would have been commonplace and futile. I dreaded lest the others should come in suddenly and break the spell she had cast about me; but we stood there a while by the corner of the big gable of the house, and no one came. I heard the merry voices some way off presently, and knew that they were going along the river to the great meadow on the other side of the house and garden.

We drew back a little, and looked up at the house: the door and the windows were open to the fragrant sun-cured air; from the upper window-sills hung festoons of flowers in honour of the festival, as if the others shared in the love for the old house.

"Come in," said Ellen. "I hope nothing will spoil it inside; but I don't think it will. Come! we must go back presently to the others. They have gone on to the tents; for surely they must have tents pitched for the haymakers—the house would not hold a tithe of the folk, I am sure."

She led me on to the door, murmuring little above her breath as she did so, "The earth and the growth of it and the life of it! If I could but say or show how I love it!"

We went in, and found no soul in any room as we wandered from room to room,—from the rose-covered porch to the strange and quaint garrets amongst the great timbers of the roof, where of old time the tillers and herdsmen of the manor slept, but which a-nights seemed now, by the small size of the beds, and the litter of useless and disregarded matters—bunches of dying flowers, feathers of birds, shells of starling's eggs, caddis worms in mugs, and the like— seemed to be inhabited for the time by children.

Everywhere there was but little furniture, and that only the most necessary, and of the simplest forms. The extravagant love of ornament which I had noted in this people elsewhere seemed here to have given place to the feeling that the house itself and its associations was the ornament of the country life amidst which it had been left stranded from old times, and that to re-ornament it would but take away its use as a piece of natural beauty.

We sat down at last in a room over the wall which Ellen had caressed, and which was still hung with old tapestry, originally of no artistic value, but now faded into pleasant grey tones which harmonised thoroughly well with the quiet of the place, and which would have been ill-supplanted by brighter and more striking decoration.

I asked a few random questions of Ellen as we sat there, but scarcely listened to her answers, and presently became silent, and then scarce conscious of anything, but that I was there in that old room, the doves crooning from the roofs of the barn and dovecot beyond the window opposite to me.

My thought returned to me after what I think was but a minute or two, but which, as in a vivid dream, seemed as if it had lasted a long time, when I saw Ellen sitting, looking all the fuller of life and pleasure and desire from the contrast with the grey faded tapestry with its futile design, which was now only bearable because it had grown so faint and feeble.

She looked at me kindly, but as if she read me through and through. She said: "You have begun again your never-ending contrast between the past and the present. Is it not so?"

"True," said I. "I was thinking of what you, with your capacity and intelligence, joined to your love of pleasure, and your impatience of unreasonable restraint—of what you would have been in that past. And even now, when all is won and has been for a long time, my heart is sickened with thinking of all the waste of life that has gone on for so many years."

"So many centuries," she said, "so many ages!"

"True," I said; "too true," and sat silent again.

She rose up and said: "Come, I must not let you go off into a dream again so soon. If we must lose you, I want you to see all that you can see first before you go back again."

"Lose me?" I said—"go back again? Am I not to go up to the North with you? What do you mean?"

She smiled somewhat sadly, and said: "Not yet; we will not talk of that yet. Only, what were you thinking of just now?"

I said falteringly: "I was saying to myself, The past, the present? Should she not have said the contrast of the present with the future: of blind despair with hope?"

"I knew it," she said. Then she caught my hand and said excitedly, "Come, while there is yet time! Come!" And she led me out of the room; and as we were going downstairs and out of the house into the garden by a little side door which opened out of a curious lobby, she said in a calm voice, as if she wished me to forget her sudden nervousness: "Come! we ought to join the others before they come here looking for us And let me tell you, my friend, that I can see you are too apt to fall into mere dreamy musing: no doubt because you are not yet used to our life of repose amidst of energy; of work which is pleasure and pleasure which is work."

She paused a little, and as we came out into the lovely garden again, she said: "My friend, you were saying that you wondered what I should have been if I had lived in those past days of turmoil and oppression. Well, I think I have studied the history of them to know pretty well. I should have been one of the poor, for my father when he was working was a mere tiller of the soil. Well, I could not have borne that; therefore my beauty and cleverness and brightness" (she spoke with no blush or simper of false shame) "would have been sold to rich men, and my life would have been wasted indeed; for I know enough of that to know that I should have had no choice, no power of will over my life; and that I should never have bought pleasure from the rich men, or even opportunity of action, whereby I might have won some true excitement. I should have wrecked and wasted in one way or another, either by penury or by luxury. Is it not so?"

"Indeed it is," said I.

She was going to say something else, when a little gate in the fence, which led into a small elm-shaded field, was opened, and Dick came with hasty cheerfulness up the garden path, and was presently standing between us, a hand laid on the shoulder of each. He said: "Well, neighbours, I thought you two would like to see the old house quietly without a crowd in it. Isn't it a jewel of a house after its kind? Well, come along, for it is getting towards dinnertime. Perhaps you, Guest, would like a swim before we sit down to what I fancy will be a pretty long feast?"

"Yes," said, "I should like that."

"Well, good-bye for the present, neighbour Ellen," said Dick. "Here comes Clara to take care of you, as I fancy she is more at home amongst our friends here."

Clara came out of the fields as he spoke; and with one look at Ellen I turned and went with Dick, doubting, if I must say the truth, whether I should see her again.

CHAPTER XXXII

THE FEAST'S BEGINNING—THE END

Dick brought me at once into the little field which, as I had seen from the garden, was covered with gaily-coloured tents arranged in orderly lanes, about which were sitting and lying on the grass some fifty or sixty men, women, and children, all of them in the height of good temper and enjoyment—with their holiday mood on, so to say.

"You are thinking that we don't make a great show as to numbers," said Dick; "but you must remember that we shall have more to-morrow; because in this haymaking work there is room for a great many people who are not over-skilled in country matters: and there are many who lead sedentary lives, whom it would be unkind to deprive of their pleasure in the hayfield—scientific men and close students generally: so that the skilled workmen, outside those who are wanted as mowers, and foremen of the haymaking, stand aside, and take a little downright rest, which you know is good for them, whether they like it or not: or else they go to other country-sides, as I am doing here. You see, the scientific men and historians, and students generally, will not be wanted till we are fairly in the midst of the tedding, which of course will not be till the day after to-morrow." With that he brought me out of the little field on to a kind of causeway above the river-side meadow, and thence turning to the left on to a path through the mowing grass, which was thick and very tall, led on till we came to the river above the weir and its mill. There we had a delightful swim in the broad piece of water above the lock, where the river looked much bigger than its natural size from its being dammed up by the weir.

"Now we are in a fit mood for dinner," said Dick, when we had dressed and were going through the grass again; "and certainly of all the cheerful meals in the year, this one of haysel is the cheerfullest; not even excepting the corn-harvest feast; for then the year is beginning to fail, and one cannot help having a feeling behind all the gaiety, of the coming of the dark days, and the shorn fields and empty gardens; and the spring is almost too far off to look forward to. It is, then, in the autumn, when one almost believes in death."

"How strangely you talk," said I, "of such a constantly recurring and consequently commonplace matter as the sequence of the seasons." And indeed these people were like children about such things, and had what seemed to me a quite exaggerated interest in the weather, a fine day, a dark night, or a brilliant one, and the like.

"Strangely?" said he. "Is it strange to sympathise with the year and its gains and losses?"

"At any rate," said I, "if you look upon the course of the year as a beautiful and interesting drama, which is what I think you do, you should be as much pleased and interested with the winter and its trouble and pain as with this wonderful summer luxury."

"And am I not?" said Dick, rather warmly; "only I can't look upon it as if I were sitting in a theatre seeing the play going on before me, myself taking no part of it. It is difficult," said he, smiling good-humouredly, "for a non-literary man like me to explain myself properly, like that dear girl Ellen would; but I mean that I am part of it all, and feel the pain as well as the pleasure in my own person. It is not done for me by somebody else, merely that I may eat and drink and sleep; but I myself do my share of it."

In his way also, as Ellen in hers, I could see that Dick had that passionate love of the earth which was common to but few people at least, in the days I knew; in which the prevailing feeling amongst intellectual persons was a kind of sour distaste for the changing drama of the year, for the life of earth and its dealings with men. Indeed, in those days it was thought poetic and imaginative to look upon life as a thing to be borne, rather than enjoyed.

So I mused till Dick's laugh brought me back into the Oxford-shire hayfields. "One thing seems strange to me," said he—"that I must needs trouble myself about the winter and its scantiness, in the midst of the summer abundance. If it hadn't happened to me before, I should have thought it was your doing, Guest; that you had thrown a kind of evil charm over me. Now, you know," said he, suddenly, "that's only a joke, so you mustn't take it to heart."

"All right," said I; "I don't." Yet I did feel somewhat uneasy at his words, after all.

We crossed the causeway this time, and did not turn back to the house, but went along a path beside a field of wheat now almost ready to blossom. I said: "We do not dine in the house or garden, then?—as indeed I did not expect to do. Where do we meet, then? for I can see that the houses are mostly very small."

"Yes," said Dick, "you are right, they are small in this country-side: there are so many good old houses left, that people dwell a good deal in such small detached houses. As to our dinner, we are going to have our feast in the church. I wish, for your sake, it were as big and handsome as that of the old Roman town to the west, or the forest town to the north;[3] but, however, it will hold us all; and though it is a little thing, it is beautiful in its way."

This was somewhat new to me, this dinner in a church, and I thought of the church-ales of the Middle Ages; but I said nothing, and presently we came out into the road which ran through the village. Dick looked up and down it, and seeing only two straggling groups before us, said: "It seems as if we must be somewhat late; they are all gone on; and they will be sure to make a point of waiting for you, as the guest of guests, since you come from so far."

He hastened as he spoke, and I kept up with him, and presently we came to a little avenue of lime-trees which led us straight to the church porch, from whose open door came the sound of cheerful voices and laughter, and varied merriment.

"Yes," said Dick, "it's the coolest place for one thing, this hot evening. Come along; they will be glad to see you."

Indeed, in spite of my bath, I felt the weather more sultry and oppressive than on any day of our journey yet.

We went into the church, which was a simple little building with one little aisle divided from the nave by three round arches, a chancel, and a rather roomy transept for so small a building, the windows mostly of the graceful Oxfordshire fourteenth-century type. There was no modern architectural decoration in it; it looked, indeed, as if none had been attempted since the Puritans whitewashed the mediæval saints and histories on the wall. It was, however, gaily dressed up for this latter-day festival, with festoons of flowers from arch to arch, and great pitchers of flowers standing about on the floor; while under the west window hung two cross scythes, their blades polished white, and gleaming from out of the flowers that wreathed them. But its best ornament was the crowd of handsome, happy-looking men and women that were set down to table, and who, with their bright faces and rich hair over their gay holiday raiment, looked, as the Persian poet puts it, like a bed of tulips in the sun. Though the church was a small one, there was plenty of room; for a small church makes a biggish house; and on this evening there was no need to set cross tables along the transepts; though doubtless these would be wanted next day, when the learned men of whom Dick has been speaking should be come to take their more humble part in the haymaking.

I stood on the threshold with the expectant smile on my face of a man who is going to take part in a festivity which he is really prepared to enjoy. Dick, standing by me was looking round the com-

---

[3] Cirencester and Burford he must have meant.

pany with an air of proprietorship in them, I thought. Opposite me sat Clara and Ellen, with Dick's place open between them: they were smiling, but their beautiful faces were each turned towards the neighbours on either side, who were talking to them, and they did not seem to see me. I turned to Dick, expecting him to lead me forward, and he turned his face to me; but strange to say, though it was as smiling and cheerful as ever, it made no response to my glance—nay, he seemed to take no heed at all of my presence, and I noticed that none of the company looked at me. A pang shot through me, as of some disaster long expected and suddenly realised. Dick moved on a little without a word to me. I was not three yards from the two women who, though they had been my companions for such a short time, had really, as I thought, become my friends. Clara's face was turned full upon me now, but she also did not seem to see me, though I know I was trying to catch her eye with an appealing look. I turned to Ellen, and she *did* seem to recognise me for an instant; but her bright face turned sad directly, and she shook her head with a mournful look, and the next moment all consciousness of my presence had faded from her face.

I felt lonely and sick at heart past the power of words to describe. I hung about a minute longer, and then turned and went out of the porch again and through the lime-avenue into the road, while the blackbirds sang their strongest from the bushes about me in the hot June evening.

Once more without any conscious effort of will I set my face toward the old house by the ford, but as I turned round the corner which led to the remains of the village cross, I came upon a figure strangely contrasting with the joyous, beautiful people I had left behind in the church. It was a man who looked old, but whom I knew from habit, now half-forgotten, was really not much more than fifty. His face was rugged, and grimed rather than dirty; his eyes dull and bleared; his body bent, his calves thin and spindly, his feet dragging and limping. His clothing was a mixture of dirt and rags long overfamiliar to me. As I passed he touched his hat with some real good-will and courtesy, and much servility.

Inexpressibly shocked, I hurried past him and hastened along the road that led to the river and the lower end of the village; but suddenly I saw as it were a black cloud rolling along to meet me, like a nightmare of my childish days; and for a while I was conscious of nothing else than being in the dark, and whether I was walking, or sitting, or lying down, I could not tell.

*　　*　　*　　*　　*　　*

I lay in my bed in my house at dingy Hammersmith thinking about it all; and trying to consider if I was overwhelmed with despair at finding I had been dreaming a dream; and strange to say, I found that I was not so despairing.

Or indeed *was* it a dream? If so, why was I so conscious all along that I was really seeing all that new life from the outside, still wrapped up in the prejudices, the anxieties, the distrust of this time of doubt and struggle?

All along, though those friends were so real to me, I had been feeling as if I had no business amongst them: as though the time would come when they would reject me, and say, as Ellen's last mournful look seemed to say, "No, it will not do; you cannot be of us; you belong so entirely to the unhappiness of the past that our happiness even would weary you. Go back again, now you have seen us, and your outward eyes have learned that in spite of all the infallible maxims of your day there is yet a time of rest in store for the world, when mastery has changed into fellowship—but not before. Go back again, then, and while you live you will see all round you people engaged in making others live lives which are not their own, while they themselves care nothing for their own real lives—men who hate life though they fear death. Go back and be the happier for having seen us, for having added a little hope to your struggle. Go on living while you may, striving, with whatsoever pain and labour needs must be, to build up little by little the new day of fellowship, and rest, and happiness."

Yes, surely! and if others can see it as I have seen it, then it may be called a vision rather than a dream.

The End of News from Nowhere

Study Questions

1. What does Morris gain by presenting his utopian ideas in novel form? Consider the advantages of fiction as a persuasive literary device. How is the convention of the naive narrator exploited? Show how the love story of William and Ellen advances the theme.
2. Morris' society is postliterate as well as postindustrial. What is the purpose of education in this society? Why would the art of penmanship be considered more valuable than literary creativeness?

3. Morris' attack on the use of money does not seem to have a religious or a moral basis. Why is money so abjured? After all, the society is to a large extent product-oriented, and money is only a means of exchange.

4. The society has abandoned industrialism, the target of many nineteenth-century social reformers. Do you think twentieth-century electronics and technology could come under the same attack?

5. The description of the revolution that brings about the Great Change has an uncanny resemblance to many modern confrontations with the Establishment. What are the differences?

6. The city, London, has been transformed into a semirural area. How is the blending of city and country environments reflected in the attitudes and activities of the people?

7. Why is nineteenth-century idleness defined as if it were a biological disease?

8. Comment on this statement: "The lack of progress in Morris' society and its reluctance to advance human knowledge are signs of stagnation; such a society could not last very long."

PART B

UTOPIAN
ESSAYS

$\mathcal{I}$MMANUEL KANT (1724–1804) was a highly influential German philosopher of the Enlightenment who attempted to end the tyranny of religious dogmatism by establishing the authority of the human mind as the valid means to knowledge. According to Kant, nature is an organic whole whose composition and governing laws could be rationally described. Kant postulates a guiding purpose in the universe that orders and directs the progress of nature. The evidence of this progress is the advancement of human knowledge, which has led man out of a state of warring barbarism and will lead him to a peaceful world republic —but only if man accepts his duty to act according to reason.

Kant's optimism about the future happiness of the human race is expressed in his essay "Idea for a Universal History from a Cosmopolitan Point of View" (1784). Kant begins his thesis with a telling analogy: though the complicated laws that govern the progress of human history may be presently unknown, they nevertheless exist and operate much like the meteorological laws—similarly undiscovered—that pattern the seasons and ensure the growth of plants. From the broadest point of view the archetypal pattern or idea of history is discernible as a benevolent and purposeful development toward perfection. Man will have to suffer temporary social discontent, but such adversity sharpens his reason and forces him to adjust the constitution of society until it unifies all people in an ideal and universal culture. This formula was no abstract theory for Kant, and he worked in his own life for a world federation dedicated to the abolition of war.

IDEA FOR A UNIVERSAL HISTORY FROM A COSMOPOLITAN POINT OF VIEW [1]

Whatever concept one may hold, from a metaphysical point of view, concerning the freedom of the will, certainly its appearances, which are human actions, like every other natural event are deter-

[1] A statement in the "Short Notices" or the twelfth number of the *Gothaische Gelehrte Zeitung* of this year [1784], which no doubt was based on

mined by universal laws. However obscure their causes, history, which is concerned with narrating these appearances, permits us to hope that if we attend to the play of freedom of the human will in the large, we may be able to discern a regular movement in it, and that what seems complex and chaotic in the single individual may be seen from the standpoint of the human race as a whole to be a steady and progressive though slow evolution of its original endowment. Since the free will of man has obvious influence upon marriages, births, and deaths, they seem to be subject to no rule by which the number of them could be reckoned in advance. Yet the annual tables of them in the major countries prove that they occur according to laws as stable as [those of] the unstable weather, which we likewise cannot determine in advance, but which, in the large, maintain the growth of plants, the flow of rivers, and other natural events in an unbroken, uniform course. Individuals and even whole peoples think little on this. Each, according to his own inclination, follows his own purpose, often in opposition to others; yet each individual and people, as if following some guiding thread, go toward a natural but to each of them unknown goal; all work toward furthering it, even if they would set little store by it if they did know it.

Since men in their endeavors behave, on the whole, not just instinctively, like the brutes, nor yet like rational citizens of the world according to some agreed-on plan, no history of man conceived according to a plan seems to be possible, as it might be possible to have such a history of bees or beavers. One cannot suppress a certain indignation when one sees men's actions on the great world-stage and finds, beside the wisdom that appears here and there among individuals, everything in the large woven together from folly, childish vanity, even from childish malice and destructiveness. In the end, one does not know what to think of the human race, so conceited in its gifts. Since the philosopher cannot presuppose any [conscious] individual purpose among men in their great drama, there is no other expedient for him except to try to see if he can discover a natural purpose in this idiotic course of things human. In keeping with this

---

my conversation with a scholar who was traveling through, occasions this essay, without which that statement could not be understood.

[The notice said: "A favorite idea of Professor Kant's is that the ultimate purpose of the human race is to achieve the most perfect civic constitution, and he wishes that a philosophical historian might undertake to give us a history of humanity from this point of view, and to show to what extent humanity in various ages has approached or drawn away from this final purpose and what remains to be done in order to reach it."]

The footnotes within brackets are the translator's—RLC.

purpose, it might be possible to have a history with a definite natural plan for creatures who have no plan of their own.

We wish to see if we can succeed in finding a clue to such a history; we leave it to Nature to produce the man capable of composing it. Thus Nature produced Kepler, who subjected, in an unexpected way, the eccentric paths of the planets to definite laws; and she produced Newton, who explained these laws by a universal natural cause.

FIRST THESIS

All natural capacities of a creature are destined to evolve completely to their natural end.

Observation of both the outward form and inward structure of all animals confirms this of them. An organ that is of no use, an arrangement that does not achieve its purpose, are contradictions in the teleological theory of nature. If we give up this fundamental principle, we no longer have a lawful but an aimless course of nature, and blind chance takes the place of the guiding thread of reason.

SECOND THESIS

In man (as the only rational creature on earth) those natural capacities which are directed to the use of his reason are to be fully developed only in the race, not in the individual.

Reason in a creature is a faculty of widening the rules and purposes of the use of all its powers far beyond natural instinct; it acknowledges no limits to its projects. Reason itself does not work instinctively, but requires trial, practice, and instruction in order gradually to progress from one level of insight to another. Therefore a single man would have to live excessively long in order to learn to make full use of all his natural capacities. Since Nature has set only a short period for his life, she needs a perhaps unreckonable series of generations, each of which passes its own enlightenment to its successor in order finally to bring the seeds of enlightenment to that degree of development in our race which is completely suitable to Nature's purpose. This point of time must be, at least as an ideal, the goal of man's efforts, for otherwise his natural capacities would have to be counted as for the most part vain and aimless. This would destroy all practical principles, and Nature, whose wisdom must serve as the fundamental principle in judging all her other offspring, would thereby make man alone a contemptible plaything.

THIRD THESIS

Nature has willed that man should, by himself, produce every-thing that goes beyond the mechanical ordering of his animal existence, and that he should partake of no other happiness or perfection than that which he himself, independently of instinct, has created by his own reason.

Nature does nothing in vain, and in the use of means to her goals she is not prodigal. Her giving to man reason and the freedom of the will which depends upon it is clear indication of her purpose. Man accordingly was not to be guided by instinct, not nurtured and instructed with ready-made knowledge; rather, he should bring forth everything out of his own resources. Securing his own food, shelter, safety and defense (for which Nature gave him neither the horns of the bull, nor the claws of the lion, nor the fangs of the dog, but hands only), all amusement which can make life pleasant, insight and intelligence, finally even goodness of heart—all this should be wholly his own work. In this, Nature seems to have moved with the strictest parsimony, and to have measured her animal gifts precisely to the most stringent needs of a beginning existence, just as if she had willed that, if man ever did advance from the lowest barbarity to the highest skill and mental perfection and thereby worked himself up to happiness (so far as it is possible on earth), he alone should have the credit and should have only himself to thank—exactly as if she aimed more at his rational self-esteem than at his well-being. For along this march of human affairs, there was a host of troubles awaiting him. But it seems not to have concerned Nature that he should live well, but only that he should work himself upward so as to make himself, through his own actions, worthy of life and of well-being.

It remains strange that the earlier generations appear to carry through their toilsome labor only for the sake of the later, to prepare for them a foundation on which the later generations could erect the higher edifice which was Nature's goal, and yet that only the latest of the generations should have the good fortune to inhabit the building on which a long line of their ancestors had (unintentionally) labored without being permitted to partake of the fortune they had prepared. However puzzling this may be, it is necessary if one assumes that a species of animals should have reason, and, as a class of rational beings each of whom dies while the species is immortal, should develop their capacities to perfection.

FOURTH THESIS

The means employed by Nature to bring about the development of all the capacities of men is their antagonism in society, so far as this is, in the end, the cause of a lawful order among men.

By "antagonism" I mean the unsocial sociability of men, i.e., their propensity to enter into society, bound together with a mutual opposition which constantly threatens to break up the society. Man has an inclination to associate with others, because in society he feels himself to be more than man, i.e., as more than the developed form of his natural capacities. But he also has a strong propensity to isolate himself from others, because he finds in himself at the same time the unsocial characteristic of wishing to have everything go according to his own wish. Thus he expects opposition on all sides because, in knowing himself, he knows that he, on his own part, is inclined to oppose others. This opposition it is which awakens all his powers, brings him to conquer his inclination to laziness and, propelled by vainglory, lust for power, and avarice, to achieve a rank among his fellows whom he cannot tolerate but from whom he cannot withdraw. Thus are taken the first true steps from barbarism to culture, which consists in the social worth of man; thence gradually develop all talents, and taste is refined; through continued enlightenment the beginnings are laid for a way of thought which can in time convert the coarse, natural disposition for moral discrimination into definite practical principles, and thereby change a society of men driven together by their natural feelings into a moral whole. Without those in themselves unamiable characteristics of unsociability from whence opposition springs—characteristics each man must find in his own selfish pretensions—all talents would remain hidden, unborn in an Arcadian shepherd's life, with all its concord, contentment, and mutual affection. Men, good-natured as the sheep they herd, would hardly reach a higher worth than their beasts; they would not fill the empty place in creation by achieving their end, which is rational nature. Thanks be to Nature, then, for the incompatibility, for heartless competitive vanity, for the insatiable desire to possess and to rule! Without them, all the excellent natural capacities of humanity would forever sleep, undeveloped. Man wishes concord; but Nature knows better what is good for the race; she wills discord. He wishes to live comfortably and pleasantly; Nature wills that he should be plunged from sloth and passive contentment into labor and trouble, in order that he may find means of extricating himself from them.

The natural urges to this, the sources of unsociableness and mutual opposition from which so many evils arise, drive men to new exertions of their forces and thus to the manifold development of their capacities. They thereby perhaps show the ordering of a wise Creator and not the hand of an evil spirit, who bungled in his great work or spoiled it out of envy.

FIFTH THESIS

The greatest problem for the human race, to the solution of which Nature drives man, is the achievement of a universal civic society which administers law among men.

The highest purpose of Nature, which is the development of all the capacities which can be achieved by mankind, is attainable only in society, and more specifically in the society with the greatest freedom. Such a society is one in which there is mutual opposition among the members, together with the most exact definition of freedom and fixing of its limits so that it may be consistent with the freedom of others. Nature demands that humankind should itself achieve this goal like all its other destined goals. Thus a society in which freedom under external laws is associated in the highest degree with irresistible power, i.e., a perfectly just civic constitution, is the highest problem Nature assigns to the human race; for Nature can achieve her other purposes for mankind only upon the solution and completion of this assignment. Need forces men, so enamored otherwise of their boundless freedom, into this state of constraint. They are forced to it by the greatest of all needs, a need they themselves occasion inasmuch as their passions keep them from living long together in wild freedom. Once in such a preserve as a civic union, these same passions subsequently do the most good. It is just the same with trees in a forest: each needs the others, since each in seeking to take the air and sunlight from others must strive upward, and thereby each realizes a beautiful, straight stature, while those that live in isolated freedom put out branches at random and grow stunted, crooked, and twisted. All culture, art which adorns mankind, and the finest social order are fruits of unsociableness, which forces itself to discipline itself and so, by a contrived art, to develop the natural seeds to perfection.

SIXTH THESIS

This problem is the most difficult and the last to be solved by mankind.

The difficulty which the mere thought of this problem puts before our eyes is this. Man is an animal which, if it lives among others of its kind, requires a master. For he certainly abuses his freedom with respect to other men, and although as a reasonable being he wishes to have a law which limits the freedom of all, his selfish animal impulses tempt him, where possible, to exempt himself from them. He thus requires a master, who will break his will and force him to obey a will that is universally valid, under which each can be free. But whence does he get this master? Only from the human race. But then the master is himself an animal, and needs a master. Let him begin it as he will, it is not to be seen how he can procure a magistracy which can maintain public justice and which is itself just, whether it be a single person or a group of several elected persons. For each of them will always abuse his freedom if he has none above him to exercise force in accord with the laws. The highest master should be just in himself, and yet a man. This task is therefore the hardest of all; indeed, its complete solution is impossible, for from such crooked wood as man is made of, nothing perfectly straight can be built.[2] That it is the last problem to be solved follows also from this: it requires that there be a correct conception of a possible constitution, great experience gained in many paths of life, and—far beyond these—a good will ready to accept such a constitution. Three such things are very hard, and if they are ever to be found together, it will be very late and after many vain attempts.

[2] The role of man is very artificial. How it may be with the dwellers on other planets and their nature we do not know. If, however, we carry out well the mandate given us by Nature, we can perhaps flatter ourselves that we may claim among our neighbors in the cosmos no mean rank. Maybe among them each individual can perfectly attain his destiny in his own life. Among us, it is different; only the race can hope to attain it.

SEVENTH THESIS

The problem of establishing a perfect civic constitution is dependent upon the problem of a lawful external relation among states and cannot be solved without a solution of the latter problem.

What is the use of working toward a lawful civic constitution among individuals, i.e., toward the creation of a commonwealth? The same unsociability which drives man to this causes any single commonwealth to stand in unrestricted freedom in relation to others; consequently, each of them must expect from another precisely the evil which oppressed the individuals and forced them to enter into a lawful civic state. The friction among men, the inevitable antagonism, which is a mark of even the largest societies and political bodies, is used by Nature as a means to establish a condition of quiet and security. Through war, through the taxing and never-ending accumulation of armament, through the want which any state, even in peacetime, must suffer internally, Nature forces them to make at first inadequate and tentative attempts; finally, after devastations, revolutions, and even complete exhaustion, she brings them to that which reason could have told them at the beginning and with far less sad experience, to wit, to step from the lawless condition of savages into a league of nations. In a league of nations, even the smallest state could expect security and justice, not from its own power and by its own decrees, but only from this great league of nations (*Foedus Amphictyonum*[3]), from a united power acting according to decisions reached under the laws of their united will. However fantastical this idea may seem—and it was laughed at as fantastical by the Abbé de St. Pierre[4] and by Rousseau,[5] perhaps because they believed it was too near to realization—the necessary outcome of the destitution to which each man is brought by his fellows is to force the states to the same decision (hard though it be for them) that savage man also was reluctantly forced to take, namely, to give up

[3] [An allusion to the Amphictyonic League, a league of Greek tribes originally for the protection of a religious shrine, which later gained considerable political power.]

[4] [Charles-Irénée Castel, Abbé de Saint Pierre (1658–1743), in his *Projet de paix perpetuelle* (Utrecht, 1713). Trans. H. H. Bellot (London, 1927).]

[5] [In his *Extrait du projet de paix perpetuelle de M. l'Abbé de St. Pierre* (1760). Trans. C. E. Vaughn, *A Lasting Peace through the Federation of Europe* (London, 1917).]

their brutish freedom and to seek quiet and security under a lawful constitution.

All wars are accordingly so many attempts (not in the intention of man, but in the intention of Nature) to establish new relations among states, and through the destruction or at least the dismemberment of all of them to create new political bodies, which, again, either internally or externally, cannot maintain themselves and which must thus suffer like revolutions; until finally, through the best possible civic constitution and common agreement and legislation in external affairs, a state is created which, like a civic commonwealth, can maintain itself automatically.

[There are three questions here, which really come to one.] Would it be expected from an Epicurean concourse of efficient causes that states, like minute particles of matter in their chance contacts, should form all sorts of unions which in their turn are destroyed by new impacts, until once, finally, by chance a structure should arise which could maintain its existence—a fortunate accident that could hardly occur? Or are we not rather to suppose that Nature here follows a lawful course in gradually lifting our race from the lower levels of animality to the highest level of humanity, doing this by her own secret art, and developing in accord with her law all the original gifts of man in this apparently chaotic disorder? Or perhaps we should prefer to conclude that, from all these actions and counteractions of men in the large, absolutely nothing, at least nothing wise, is to issue? That everything should remain as it always was, that we cannot therefore tell but that discord, natural to our race, may not prepare for us a hell of evils, however civilized we may now be, by annihilating civilization and all cultural progress through barbarous devastation? (This is the fate we may well have to suffer under the rule of blind chance—which is in fact identical with lawless freedom—if there is no secret wise guidance in Nature.) These three questions, I say, mean about the same as this: Is it reasonable to assume a purposiveness in all the parts of Nature and to deny it to the whole?

Purposeless savagery held back the development of the capacities of our race; but finally, through the evil into which it plunged mankind, it forced our race to renounce this condition and to enter into a civic order in which those capacities could be developed. The same is done by the barbaric freedom of established states. Through wasting the powers of the commonwealths in armaments to be used against each other, through devastation brought on by war, and even more by the necessity of holding themselves in constant readiness for war, they stunt the full development of human nature. But because of the evils which thus arise, our race is forced to find, above the (in itself healthy) opposition of states which is a consequence of their freedom, a law of equilibrium and a united power to give it effect. Thus it is forced to institute a cosmopolitan condition to secure the external safety of each state.

Such a condition is not unattended by the danger that the vitality of mankind may fall asleep; but it is at least not without a principle of balance among men's actions and counteractions, without which they might be altogether destroyed. Until this last step to a union of states is taken, which is the halfway mark in the development of mankind, human nature must suffer the cruelest hardships under the guise of external well-being; and Rousseau was not far wrong in preferring the state of savages, so long, that is, as the last stage to which the human race must climb is not attained.

To a high degree we are, through art and science, *cultured*. We are *civilized*—perhaps too much for our own good—in all sorts of social grace and decorum. But to consider ourselves as having reached *morality*—for that, much is lacking. The ideal of morality belongs to culture; its use for some simulacrum of morality in the love of honor and outward decorum constitutes mere civilization. So long as states waste their forces in vain and violent self-expansion, and thereby constantly thwart the slow efforts to improve the minds of their citizens by even withdrawing all support from them, nothing in the way of a moral order is to be expected. For such an end, a long internal working of each political body toward the education of its citizens is required. Everything good that is not based on a morally good disposition, however, is nothing but pretense and glittering misery. In such a condition the human species will no doubt remain until, in the way I have described, it works its way out of the chaotic conditions of its international relations.

EIGHTH THESIS

The history of mankind can be seen, in the large, as the realization of Nature's secret plan to bring forth a perfectly constituted state as the only condition in which the capacities of mankind can be fully developed, and also bring forth that external relation among states which is perfectly adequate to this end.

This is a corollary to the preceding. Everyone can see that philosophy can have her belief in a millennium, but her millenarianism is not Utopian, since the Idea can help, though only from afar, to bring the millennium to pass. The only question is: Does Nature reveal anything of a path to this end? And I say: She reveals something, but very little. This great revolution seems to require so long for its completion that the short period during which humanity has been following this course permits us to determine its path and the relation of the parts to the whole with as little certainty as we can determine, from all previous astronomical observation, the path of the sun and his host of satellites among the fixed stars. Yet, on the fundamental premise of the systematic structure of the cosmos and from the little that has been observed, we can confidently infer the reality of such a revolution.

Moreover, human nature is so constituted that we cannot be indifferent to the most remote epoch our race may come to, if only we may expect it with certainty. Such indifference is even less possible for us, since it seems that our own intelligent action may hasten this happy time for our posterity. For that reason, even faint indications of approach to it are very important to us. At present, states are in such an artificial relation to each other that none of them can neglect its internal cultural development without losing power and influence among the others. Therefore the preservation of this natural end [culture], if not progress in it, is fairly well assured by the ambitions of states. Furthermore, civic freedom can hardly be infringed without the evil consequences being felt in all walks of life, especially in commerce, where the effect is loss of power of the state in its foreign relations. But this freedom spreads by degrees. When the citizen is hindered in seeking his own welfare in his own way, so long as it is consistent with the freedom of others, the vitality of the entire enterprise is sapped, and therewith the powers of the whole are diminished. Therefore limitations on personal actions are step by step removed, and general religious freedom is permitted. Enlightenment comes gradually, with intermittent folly and caprice, as a great good which must finally save men from the selfish aggrandizement of their masters, always assuming that the latter know their own interest. This enlightenment, and with it a certain commitment of heart which the enlightened man cannot fail to make to the good he clearly understands, must step by step ascend the throne and influence the principles of government.

Although, for instance, our world rulers at present have no money left over for public education and for anything that concerns what is best in the world, since all they have is already committed to future wars, they will still find it to their own interest at least not to hinder the weak and slow, independent efforts of their peoples in this work. In the end, war itself will be seen as not only so artificial, in outcome so uncertain for both sides, in aftereffects so painful in the form of an ever-growing war debt (a new invention) that cannot be met, that it will be regarded as a most dubious undertaking. The impact of any revolution on all states on our continent, so closely knit together through commerce, will be so obvious that the other states, driven by their own danger but without any legal basis, will offer themselves as arbiters, and thus they will prepare the way for a distant international government for which there is no precedent in world history. Although this government at present exists only as a rough outline, nevertheless in all the members there is rising a feeling which each has for the preservation of the whole. This gives hope finally that after many reformative revolutions, a universal cosmopolitan condition, which Nature has as her ultimate purpose, will come into being as the womb wherein all the original capacities of the human race can develop.

NINTH THESIS

A philosophical attempt to work out a universal history according to a natural plan directed to achieving the civic union of the human race must be regarded as possible and, indeed, as contributing to this end of Nature.

It is strange and apparently silly to wish to write a history in accordance with an Idea of how the course of the world must be if it it is to lead to certain rational ends. It seems that with such an Idea only a romance could be written. Nevertheless, if one may assume that Nature, even in the play of human freedom, works not without plan or purpose, this Idea could still be of use. Even if we are too blind to see the secret mechanism of its workings, this Idea may still serve as a guiding thread for presenting as a system, at least in broad outlines, what would otherwise be a planless conglomeration of human actions. For if one starts with Greek history, through which every older or contemporaneous history has been handed down or at least certified;[6] if one follows the influence of Greek history on the

---

[6] Only a learned public, which has lasted from its beginning to our own day, can certify ancient history. Outside it, everything else is *terra incognita;* and the history of peoples outside it can only be begun when they come into contact with it. This happened with the Jews in the time of the Ptolemies through the translation of the Bible into Greek, without which we would give little credence to their isolated narratives. From this point, when once properly fixed, we can retrace their history. And so with all other peoples. The first page of Thucydides, says Hume,* is the only beginning of all real history.

* ["Of the Populousness of Ancient Nations," in *Essays Moral, Political, and Literary,* eds. Green and Grose, Vol. I, p. 414.]

construction and misconstruction of the Roman state which swallowed up the Greek, then the Roman influence on the barbarians who in turn destroyed it, and so on down to our times; if one adds episodes from the national histories of other peoples insofar as they are known from the history of the enlightened nations, one will discover a regular progress in the constitution of states on our continent (which will probably give law, eventually, to all the others). If, further, one concentrates on the civic constitutions and their laws and on the relations among states, insofar as through the good they contained they served over long periods of time to elevate and adorn nations and their arts and sciences, while through the evil they contained they destroyed them, if only a germ of enlightenment was left to be further developed by this overthrow and a higher level was thus prepared—if, I say, one carries through this study, a guiding thread will be revealed. It can serve not only for clarifying the confused play of things human, and not only for the art of prophesying later political changes (a use which has already been made of history even when seen as the disconnected effect of lawless freedom), but for giving a consoling view of the future (which could not be reasonably hoped for without the presupposition of a natural plan) in which there will be exhibited in the distance how the human race finally achieves the condition in which all the seeds planted in it by Nature can fully develop and in which the destiny of the race can be fulfilled here on earth.

Such a justification of Nature—or, better, of Providence—is no unimportant reason for choosing a standpoint toward world history. For what is the good of esteeming the majesty and wisdom of Creation in the realm of brute nature and of recommending that we contemplate it, if that part of the great stage of supreme wisdom which contains the purpose of all the others—the history of mankind—must remain an unceasing reproach to it? If we are forced to turn our eyes from it in disgust, doubting that we can ever find a perfectly rational purpose in it and hoping for that only in another world?

That I would want to displace the work of practicing empirical historians with this Idea of world history, which is to some extent based upon an a priori principle, would be a misinterpretation of my intention. It is only a suggestion of what a philosophical mind (which would have to be well versed in history) could essay from another point of view. Otherwise the notorious complexity of a history of our time must naturally lead to serious doubt as to how our descendants will begin to grasp the burden of the history we shall leave to them after a few centuries. They will naturally value the history of earlier times, from which the documents may long since have disappeared, only from the point of view of what interests them, i.e., in answer to the question of what the various nations and governments have contributed to the goal of world citizenship, and what they have done to damage it. To consider this, so as to direct the ambitions of sovereigns and their agents to the only means by which their fame can be spread to later ages: this can be a minor motive for attempting such a philosophical history.

Study Questions

1. What is the difference between Kant's concept of nature and Diderot's? Which seems more benevolent?
2. According to Kant, what good stems from normal social discontent?
3. Why does Kant attack the view of utopia as an idyllic, pastoral retreat?
4. Kant believes that wars compel men to devise more compatible methods of coexistence. What kind of wars does he have in mind?
5. If a tyrannical ruler held Kant's view of history, what kind of society would he create to maintain his power?
6. Kant holds that the philosopher's mission in achieving world peace is to make the hidden pattern of nature evident to mankind. In what way does knowledge of the plan aid its progress? How does the philosopher's mission differ from that of the historian?

$\mathcal{R}$ALPH WALDO EMERSON (1803–1882)
preached, taught, wrote, and traveled in order to promulgate his belief in man's capacity to comprehend the spiritual essence of the
universe through inquiry and faith. In his early essays, Emerson explains that the faculty of reason, a unifying and synthesizing power,
gives man the ability to see the world as a manifestation of spirit and
to perceive the connection between himself, the external world, and
God. If we are to know ourselves, therefore, we must study nature.
Trusting in oneself and avoiding past models of experience become
the keys to sustaining this spiritual vision of the world. In the essay "Self-Reliance," Emerson advocated abandoning society altogether
because it limits man and severs his relationship with God. Emerson's idealism and his confidence in man's self-supportive ability
later weakened; he saw nature to be not as benevolent as he had con-
tended and realized that man's conditioning by his past, his human-
ness, and his environment are possible limitations to his freedom.
But he hoped that these influences working in conjunction with
the Divine Power might eventually liberate rather than restrict mankind.

In "War" (1838) Emerson argues that human thought and actions determine the physical conditions of society; men—not necessity—create a belligerent state. They can therefore as easily create a
peaceful one. But a new conception of heroism must first replace the
notion that soldiering and aggressiveness represent the noblest in
man. The new hero, through dedication to nonviolent resistance and
respect for the human community, could then transform the world
by the power of his convictions.

WAR[1]

The archangel Hope
Looks to the azure cope,
Waits through dark ages for the morn,
Defeated day by day, but unto Victory born.

IT has been a favorite study of modern philosophy to indicate the steps of human progress, to watch the rising of a thought in one man's mind, the communication of it to a few, to a small minority, its expansion and general reception, until it publishes itself to the world by destroying the existing laws and institutions, and the generation of new. Looked at in this general and historical way, many things wear a very different face from that they show near by, and one at a time,—and, particularly, war. War, which to sane men at the present day begins to look like an epidemic insanity, breaking out here and there like the cholera or influenza, infecting men's brains instead of their bowels,—when seen in the remote past, in the infancy of society, appears a part of the connection of events, and, in its place, necessary.

As far as history has preserved to us the slow unfoldings of any savage tribe, it is not easy to see how war could be avoided by such wild, passionate, needy, ungoverned, strong-bodied creatures. For in the infancy of society, when a thin population and improvidence make the supply of food and of shelter insufficient and very precarious, and when hunger, thirst, ague and frozen limbs universally take precedence of the wants of the mind and the heart, the necessities of the strong will certainly be satisfied at the cost of the weak, at whatever peril of future revenge. It is plain, too, that in the first dawnings of the religious sentiment, *that* blends itself with their passions and is oil to the fire. Not only every tribe has war-gods, religious festivals in victory, but *religious wars*.

The student of history acquiesces the more readily in this copious bloodshed of the early annals, bloodshed in God's name too, when he learns that it is a temporary and preparatory state, and does actively forward the culture of man. War educates the senses, calls into action the will, perfects the physical constitution, brings men into such swift and close collision in critical moments that man measures man.

[1] Delivered as a lecture in Boston, in March, 1838. Reprinted from "Æsthetic Papers," edited by Miss E. P. Peabody, 1849.

On its own scale, on the virtues it loves, it endures no counterfeit, but shakes the whole society until every atom falls in the place its specific gravity assigns it. It presently finds the value of good sense and of foresight, and Ulysses takes rank next to Achilles. The leaders, picked men of a courage and vigor tried and augmented in fifty battles, are emulous to distinguish themselves above each other by new merits, as clemency, hospitality, splendor of living. The people imitate the chiefs. The strong tribe, in which war has become an art, attack and conquer their neighbors, and teach them their arts and virtues. New territory, augmented numbers and extended interests call out new virtues and abilities, and the tribe makes long strides. And, finally, when much progress has been made, all its secrets of wisdom and art are disseminated by its invasions. Plutarch, in his essay "On the Fortune of Alexander," considers the invasion and conquest of the East by Alexander as one of the most bright and pleasing pages in history; and it must be owned he gives sound reason for his opinion. It had the effect of uniting into one great interest the divided commonwealths of Greece, and infusing a new and more enlarged public spirit into the councils of their statesmen. It carried the arts and language and philosophy of the Greeks into the sluggish and barbarous nations of Persia, Assyria and India. It introduced the arts of husbandry among tribes of hunters and shepherds. It weaned the Scythians and Persians from some cruel and licentious practices to a more civil way of life. It introduced the sacredness of marriage among them. It built seventy cities, and sowed the Greek customs and humane laws over Asia, and united hostile nations under one code. It brought different families of the human race together,—to blows at first, but afterwards to truce, to trade and to intermarriage. It would be very easy to show analogous benefits that have resulted from military movements of later ages.

Considerations of this kind lead us to a true view of the nature and office of war. We see it is the subject of all history; that it has been the principal employment of the most conspicuous men; that it is at this moment the delight of half the world, of almost all young and ignorant persons; that it is exhibited to us continually in the dumb show of brute nature, where war between tribes, and between individuals of the same tribe, perpetually rages. The microscope reveals miniature butchery in atomies and infinitely small biters that swim and fight in an illuminated drop of water; and the little globe is but a too faithful miniature of the large.

What does all this war, beginning from the lowest races and reaching up to man, signify? Is it not manifest that it covers a great and beneficent principle, which nature had deeply at heart? What is that principle?—It is self-help. Nature implants with life the instinct of self-help, perpetual struggle to be, to resist opposition, to attain to freedom, to attain to a mastery and the security of a permanent, self-defended being; and to each creature these objects are made so dear that it risks its life continually in the struggle for these ends.

But whilst this principle, necessarily, is inwrought into the fabric of every creature, yet it is but *one* instinct; and though a primary one, or we may say the very first, yet the appearance of the other instincts immediately modifies and controls this; turns its energies into harmless, useful and high courses, showing thereby what was its ultimate design; and, finally, takes out its fangs. The instinct of self-help is very early unfolded in the coarse and merely brute form of war, only in the childhood and imbecility of the other instincts, and remains in that form only until their development. It is the ignorant and childish part of mankind that is the fighting part. Idle and vacant minds want excitement, as all boys kill cats. Bull-baiting, cockpits and the boxer's ring are the enjoyment of the part of society whose animal nature alone has been developed. In some parts of this country, where the intellectual and moral faculties have as yet scarcely any culture, the absorbing topic of all conversation is whipping; who fought, and which whipped? Of man, boy, or beast, the only trait that much interests the speakers is the pugnacity. And why? Because the speaker has as yet no other image of manly activity and virtue, none of endurance, none of perseverance, none of charity, none of the attainment of truth. Put him into a circle of cultivated men, where the conversation broaches the great questions that besiege the human reason, and he would be dumb and unhappy, as an Indian in church.

To men of a sedate and mature spirit, in whom is any knowledge or mental activity, the detail of battle becomes insupportably tedious and revolting. It is like the talk of one of those monomaniacs whom we sometimes meet in society, who converse on horses; and Fontenelle expressed a volume of meaning when he said, "I hate war, for it spoils conversation."

Nothing is plainer than that the sympathy with war is a juvenile and temporary state. Not only the moral sentiment, but trade, learning and whatever makes intercourse, conspire to put it down. Trade, as all men know, is the antagonist of war. Wherever there is no property, the people will put on the knapsack for bread; but trade is instantly endangered and destroyed. And, moreover, trade brings men to look each other in the face, and gives the parties the knowledge that these enemies over sea or over the mountain are such men as we; who laugh and grieve, who love and fear, as we do. And learning and art, and especially religion, weave ties that make war look like fratricide, as it is. And as all history is the picture of war, as we have said, so it is no less true that it is the record of the mitigation and decline of war. Early in the eleventh and twelfth centuries, the Italian cities had grown so populous and strong, that they forced the rural nobility to dismantle their castles, which were dens of cruelty, and come and reside in the towns. The Popes, to their eternal honor, declared religious jubilees, during which all hostilities were suspended throughout Christendom, and man had a breathing space. The increase of civility has abolished the use of poison and of torture, once supposed as necessary as navies now. And, finally, the art of war, what with gunpowder and tactics, has made, as all men know, battles less frequent and less murderous.

By all these means, war has been steadily on the decline; and we read with astonishment of the beastly fighting of the old times. Only in Elizabeth's time, out of the European waters, piracy was all but universal. The proverb was,—"No peace beyond the line;" and the seaman shipped on the buccaneer's bargain, "No prey, no pay." The celebrated Cavendish, who was thought in his times a good Christian man, wrote thus to Lord Hunsdon, on his return from a voyage round the world:—"Sept. 1588. It hath pleased Almighty God to suffer me to circumpass the whole globe of the world, entering in at the Strait of Magellan, and returning by the Cape of Buena Esperança; in which voyage, I have either discovered or brought certain intelligence of all the rich places of the world, which were ever discovered by any Christian. I navigated along the coast of Chili, Peru, and New Spain, *where I made great spoils. I burnt and sunk nineteen sail of ships, small and great. All the villages and towns that ever I landed at, I burned and spoiled.* And had I not been discovered upon the coast, I had taken great quantity of treasure. The matter of most profit to me was a great ship of the king's, which I took at California," &c. And the good Cavendish piously begins this statement,—"It hath pleased Almighty God."

Indeed, our American annals have preserved the vestiges of barbarous warfare down to more recent times. I read in Williams's "History of Maine," that "Assacombuit, the Sagamore of the Anagunticook tribe, was remarkable for his turpitude and ferocity above all other known Indians; that, in 1705, Vaudreuil sent him to France, where he was introduced to the king. When he appeared at court, he lifted up his hand, and said, 'This hand has slain a hundred and fifty of your majesty's enemies within the territories of New England.' This so pleased the king that he knighted him, and ordered a pension of eight livres a day to be paid him during life."

This valuable person, on his return to America, took to killing his own neighbors and kindred, with such appetite that his tribe combined against him, and would have killed him had he not fled his country for ever.

The scandal which we feel in such facts certainly shows that we have got on a little. All history is the decline of war, though the slow decline. All that society has yet gained is mitigation: the doctrine of the right of war still remains.

For ages (for ideas work in ages, and animate vast societies of men) the human race has gone on under the tyranny—shall I so call it?—of this first brutish form of their effort to be men; that is, for ages they have shared so much of the nature of the lower animals, the tiger and the shark, and the savages of the water-drop. They have nearly exhausted all the good and all the evil of this form: they have held as fast to this degradation as their worst enemy could desire; but all things have an end, and so has this. The eternal germination of the better has unfolded new powers, new instincts, which were really concealed under this rough and base rind. The sublime question has startled one and another happy soul in different quarters of the globe,—Cannot love be, as well as hate? Would not love answer the same end, or even a better? Cannot peace be, as well as war?

This thought is no man's invention, neither St. Pierre's nor Rousseau's, but the rising of the general tide in the human soul,—and rising highest, and first made visible, in the most simple and pure souls, who have therefore announced it to us beforehand; but presently we all see it. It has now become so distinct as to be a social thought: societies can be formed on it. It is expounded, illustrated, defined, with different degrees of clearness; and its actualization, or the measures it should inspire, predicted according to the light of each seer.

The idea itself is the epoch; the fact that it has become so distinct to any small number of persons as to become a subject of prayer and hope, of concert and discussion,—*that* is the commanding fact. This having come, much more will follow. Revolutions go not backward. The star once risen, though only one man in the hemisphere has yet seen its upper limb in the horizon, will mount and mount, until it becomes visible to other men, to multitudes, and climbs the zenith of all eyes. And so it is not a great matter how long men refuse to believe the advent of peace: war is on its last legs; and a universal peace is as sure as is the prevalence of civilization over barbarism, of liberal governments over feudal forms. The question for us is only *How soon?*

That the project of peace should appear visionary to great numbers of sensible men; should appear laughable even, to numbers; should appear to the grave and good-natured to be embarrassed with extreme practical difficulties,—is very natural. 'This is a poor, tedious society of yours,' they say: 'we do not see what good can come of it. Peace! why, we are all at peace now. But if a foreign nation should wantonly insult or plunder our commerce, or, worse yet, should land on our shores to rob and kill, you would not have us sit, and be robbed and killed? You mistake the times; you overestimate the virtue of men. You forget that the quiet which now sleeps in cities and in farms, which lets the wagon go unguarded and the farmhouse unbolted, rests on the perfect understanding of all men that the musket, the halter and the jail stand behind there, ready to punish any disturber of it. All admit that this would be the best policy, if the world were all a church, if all men were the best men, if all would agree to accept this rule. But it is absurd for one nation to attempt it alone."

In the first place, we answer that we never make much account of objections which merely respect the actual state of the world at this moment, but which admit the general expediency and permanent excellence of the project. What is the best must be the true; and what is true,—that is, what is at bottom fit and agreeable to the constitution of man,—must at last prevail over all obstruction and all opposition. There is no good now enjoyed by society that was not once as problematical and visionary as this. It is the tendency of the true interest of man to become his desire and steadfast aim.

But, further, it is a lesson which all history teaches wise men, to put trust in ideas, and not in circumstances. We have all grown up in the sight of frigates and navy yards, of armed forts and islands, of arsenals and militia. The reference to any foreign register will inform us of the number of thousand or million men that are now under arms in the vast colonial system of the British empire, of Russia, Austria and France; and one is scared to find at what a cost the peace of the globe is kept. This vast apparatus of artillery, of fleets, of stone bastions and trenches and embankments; this incessant patrolling of sentinels; this waving of national flags; this reveille and evening gun; this martial music and endless playing of marches and singing of military and naval songs seem to us to constitute an imposing actual, which will not yield in centuries to the feeble, deprecatory voices of a handful of friends of peace.

Thus always we are daunted by the appearances; not seeing that their whole value lies at bottom in the state of mind. It is really a thought that built this portentous war-establishment, and a thought

shall also melt it away. Every nation and every man instantly surround themselves with a material apparatus which exactly corre-
sponds to their moral state, or their state of thought. Observe how
every truth and every error, each a *thought* of some man's mind,
clothes itself with societies, houses, cities, language, ceremonies,
newspapers. Observe the ideas of the present day,—orthodoxy, skep-
ticism, missions, popular education, temperance, anti-masonry, anti-
slavery; see how each of these abstractions has embodied itself in an
imposing apparatus in the community; and how timber, brick, lime
and stone have flown into convenient shape, obedient to the master-
idea reigning in the minds of many persons.

You shall hear, some day, of a wild fancy which some man has in
his brain, of the mischief of secret oaths. Come again one or two
years afterwards, and you shall see it has built great houses of solid
wood and brick and mortar. You shall see a hundred presses printing a million sheets; you shall see men and horses and wheels made
to walk, run and roll for it: this great body of matter thus executing
that one man's wild thought. This happens daily, yearly about us,
with half thoughts, often with flimsy lies, pieces of policy and speculation. With good nursing they will last three or four years before
they will come to nothing. But when a truth appears,—as, for instance, a perception in the wit of one Columbus that there is land
in the Western Sea; though he alone of all men has that thought,
and they all jeer,—it will build ships; it will build fleets; it will carry
over half Spain and half England; it will plant a colony, a state, nations and half a globe full of men.

We surround ourselves always, according to our freedom and
ability, with true images of ourselves in things, whether it be ships
or books or cannons or churches. The standing army, the arsenal,
the camp and the gibbet do not appertain to man. They only serve
as an index to show where man is now; what a bad, ungoverned
temper he has; what an ugly neighbor he is; how his affections halt;
how low his hope lies. He who loves the bristle of bayonets only
sees in their glitter what beforehand he feels in his heart. It is
avarice and hatred; it is that quivering lip, that cold, hating eye,
which built magazines and powder-houses.

It follows of course that the least change in the man will change
his circumstances; the least enlargement of his ideas, the least mitigation of his feelings in respect to other men; if, for example, he
could be inspired with a tender kindness to the souls of men, and
should come to feel that every man was another self with whom
he might come to join, as left hand works with right. Every degree of the ascendancy of this feeling would cause the most strik-

ing changes of external things: the tents would be struck; the men-of-war would rot ashore; the arms rust; the cannon would become street-posts; the pikes, a fisher's harpoon; the marching regiment would be a caravan of emigrants, *peaceful* pioneers at the fountains of the Wabash and the Missouri. And so it must and will be: bayonet and sword must first retreat a little from their ostentatious prominence; then quite hide themselves, as the sheriff's halter does now, inviting the attendance only of relations and friends; and then, lastly, will be transferred to the museums of the curious, as poisoning and torturing tools are at this day.

War and peace thus resolve themselves into a mercury of the state of cultivation. At a certain stage of his progress, the man fights, if he be of a sound body and mind. At a certain higher stage, he makes no offensive demonstration, but is alert to repel injury, and of an unconquerable heart. At a still higher stage, he comes into the region of holiness; passion has passed away from him; his warlike nature is all converted into an active medicinal principle; he sacrifices himself, and accepts with alacrity wearisome tasks of denial and charity; but, being attacked, he bears it and turns the other cheek, as one engaged, throughout his being, no longer to the service of an individual but to the common soul of all men.

Since the peace question has been before the public mind, those who affirm its right and expediency have naturally been met with objections more or less weighty. There are cases frequently put by the curious,—moral problems, like those problems in arithmetic which in long winter evenings the rustics try the hardness of their heads in ciphering out. And chiefly it is said,—Either accept this principle for better, for worse, carry it out to the end, and meet its absurd consequences; or else, if you pretend to set an arbitrary limit, a "Thus far, no farther," then give up the principle, and take that limit which the common-sense of all mankind has set, and which distinguishes offensive war as criminal, defensive war as just. Otherwise, if you go for no war, then be consistent, and give up self-defence in the highway, in your own house. Will you push it thus far? Will you stick to your principle of non-resistance when your strong-box is broken open, when your wife and babes are insulted and slaughtered in your sight? If you say yes, you only invite the robber and assassin; and a few bloody-minded desperadoes would soon butcher the good.

In reply to this charge of absurdity on the extreme peace doctrine, as shown in the supposed consequences, I wish to say that such deductions consider only one half of the fact. They look only at the passive side of the friend of peace, only at his passivity; they quite omit to consider his activity. But no man, it may be presumed, ever embraced the cause of peace and philanthropy for the sole end and satisfaction of being plundered and slain. A man does not come the length of the spirit of martyrdom without some active purpose, some equal motive, some flaming love. If you have a nation of men who have risen to that height of moral cultivation that they will not declare war or carry arms, for they have not so much madness left in their brains, you have a nation of lovers, of benefactors, of true, great and able men. Let me know more of that nation; I shall not find them defenceless, with idle hands springing at their sides. I shall find them men of love, honor and truth; men of an immense industry; men whose influence is felt to the end of the earth; men whose very look and voice carry the sentence of honor and shame; and all forces yield to their energy and persuasion. Whenever we see the doctrine of peace embraced by a nation, we may be assured it will not be one that invites injury; but one, on the contrary, which has a friend in the bottom of the heart of every man, even of the violent and the base; one against which no weapon can prosper; one which is looked upon as the asylum of the human race and has the tears and the blessings of mankind.

In the second place, as far as it respects individual action in difficult and extreme cases, I will say, such cases seldom or never occur to the good and just man; nor are we careful to say, or even to know, what in such crises is to be done. A wise man will never impawn his future being and action, and decide beforehand what he shall do in a given extreme event. Nature and God will instruct him in that hour.

The question naturally arises, How is this new aspiration of the human mind to be made visible and real? How is it to pass out of thoughts into things?

Not, certainly, in the first place, *in the way of routine and mere forms,*—the universal specific of modern politics; not by organizing a society, and going through a course of resolutions and public manifestoes, and being thus formally accredited to the public and to the civility of the newspapers. We have played this game to tediousness. In some of our cities they choose noted duellists as presidents and officers of anti-duelling societies. Men who love that bloated vanity called public opinion think all is well if they have once got their bantling through a sufficient course of speeches and cheerings, of one, two, or three public meetings; as if *they* could do anything: they vote and vote, cry hurrah on both sides, no man responsible, no man caring a pin. The next season, an Indian war, or an aggression on our commerce by Malays; or the party this man votes with have an appropriation to carry through Congress: instantly he wags his head the other way, and cries, Havoc and war!

This is not to be carried by public opinion, but by private opinion, by private conviction, by private, dear and earnest love. For the only hope of this cause is in the increased insight, and it is to be accomplished by the spontaneous teaching, of the cultivated soul, in its secret experience and meditation,—that it is now time that it should pass out of the state of beast into the state of man; it is to hear the voice of God, which bids the devils that have rended and torn him come out of him and let him now be clothed and walk forth in his right mind.

Nor, in the next place, is the peace principle to be carried into effect by fear. It can never be defended, it can never be executed, by cowards. Everything great must be done in the spirit of greatness. The manhood that has been in war must be transferred to the cause of peace, before war can lose its charm, and peace be venerable to men.

The attractiveness of war shows one thing through all the throats of artillery, the thunders of so many sieges, the sack of towns, the jousts of chivalry, the shock of hosts,—this namely, the conviction of man universally, that a man should be himself responsible, with goods, health and life, for his behavior; that he should not ask of the State protection; should ask nothing of the State; should be himself a kingdom and a state; fearing no man; quite willing to use the opportunities and advantages that good government throw in his way, but nothing daunted, and not really the poorer if government, law and order went by the board; because in himself reside infinite resources; because he is sure of himself, and never needs to ask another what in any crisis it behooves him to do.

What makes to us the attractiveness of the Greek heroes? of the Roman? What makes the attractiveness of that romantic style of living which is the material of ten thousand plays and romances, from Shakespeare to Scott; the feudal baron, the French, the English nobility, the Warwicks, Plantagenets? It is their absolute self-dependence. I do not wonder at the dislike some of the friends of peace have expressed at Shakespeare. The veriest churl and Jacobin cannot resist the influence of the style and manners of these haughty lords. We are affected, as boys and barbarians are, by the appearance of a few rich and wilful gentlemen who take their honor into their own keeping, defy the world, so confident are they of their courage and strength, and whose appearance is the arrival of so much life and virtue. In dangerous times they are presently tried, and therefore their name is a flourish of trumpets. They, at least, affect us as a reality. They are not shams, but the substance of which that age and world is made. They are true heroes for their time. They make what is in their minds the greatest sacrifice. They will, for an injurious word, peril all their state and wealth, and go to the field. Take away that principle of responsibleness, and they become pirates and ruffians.

This self-subsistency is the charm of war; for this self-subsistency is essential to our idea of man. But another age comes, a truer religion and ethics open, and a man puts himself under the dominion of principles. I see him to be the servant of truth, of love and of freedom, and immoveable in the waves of the crowd. The man of principle, that is, the man who, without any flourish of trumpets, titles of lordship or train of guards, without any notice of his action abroad, expecting none, takes in solitude the right step uniformly, on his private choice and disdaining consequences,—does not yield, in my imagination, to any man. He is willing to be hanged at his own gate, rather than consent to any compromise of his freedom or the suppression of his conviction. I regard no longer those names that so tingled in my ear. This is a baron of a better nobility and a stouter stomach.

The cause of peace is not the cause of cowardice. If peace is sought to be defended or preserved for the safety of the luxurious and the timid, it is a sham, and the peace will be base. War is better, and the peace will be broken. If peace is to be maintained, it must be by brave men, who have come up to the same height as the hero, namely, the will to carry their life in their hand, and stake it at any instant for their principle, but who have gone one step beyond the hero, and will not seek another man's life;—men who have, by their intellectual insight or else by their moral elevation, attained such a perception of their own intrinsic worth, that they do not think property or their own body a sufficient good to be saved by such dereliction of principle as treating a man like a sheep.

If the universal cry for reform of so many inveterate abuses, with which society rings,—if the desire of a large class of young men for a faith and hope, intellectual and religious, such as they have not yet found, be an omen to be trusted; if the disposition to rely more in study and in action on the unexplored riches of the human constitution,—if the search of the sublime laws of morals and the sources of hope and trust, in man, and not in books, in the present, and not in the past, proceed; if the rising generation can be provoked to think it unworthy to nestle into every abomination of the past, and shall feel the generous darings of austerity and virtue, then war has a short day, and human blood will cease to flow.

It is of little consequence in what manner, through what organs, this purpose of mercy and holiness is effected. The proposition of the Congress of Nations is undoubtedly that at which the present fabric of our society and the present course of events do point. But the mind, once prepared for the reign of principles, will easily find modes of expressing its will. There is the highest fitness in the place and time in which this enterprise is begun. Not in an obscure corner, not in a feudal Europe, not in an antiquated appanage where no onward step can be taken without rebellion, is this seed of benevolence laid in the furrow, with tears of hope; but in this broad America of God and man, where the forest is only now falling, or yet to fall, and the green earth opened to the inundation of emigrant men from all quarters of oppression and guilt; here, where not a family, not a few men, but mankind, shall say what shall be; here, we ask, Shall it be War, or shall it be Peace?

Study Questions

1. What rhetorical effects does Emerson create in his description of the brave men of peace? Characterize the style of these passages.
2. What does Emerson mean by calling war and peace the "mercury of the state of cultivation"?
3. Compare Emerson's estimate of the benefits of war with those of Kant. In your opinion, which one describes the effects of warfare more accurately? Would Kant agree with Emerson that it "is the ignorant and childish part of mankind that is the fighting part"?
4. In what way could Emerson's essay be used for the defense of a conscientious objector?
5. What is the connection between the self-help of the conqueror and the independence of the man of peace?
6. Emerson sees a natural antagonism between high culture and war. Does this apply today?
7. According to Emerson, what immunity from domination does a peaceful country have?

$\mathcal{H}$ENRY DAVID THOREAU (1817–1862) wrote on and lived according to a set of beliefs that constitute the philosophy of transcendentalism. A student and friend of Emerson, Thoreau led a less public life than did his teacher in an attempt to realize Emerson's program of solitude and self-reliance. Thoreau's animosity toward institutional schools of thought should deter us from attempting to systematize the tenets of his philosophy. We should instead respond to his random observations and diverse ideas with the informality with which he offered them in a number of works, including the popular *Walden* and "Civil Disobedience," as well as in the lesser-known essay reprinted below. Nevertheless, the foundation of Thoreau's approach to life, which emerges from and unifies the discursive surface of his writings, is easily stated. He believed that meditation, self-reliance, and purity would lead man to discover God's presence in the world about him; the momentary insight that God pervades the entire universe must become the primary way of viewing the world in order to live constantly in unison with God. The synthesis of the self and the external world with God is a transcendental union and results in the view and practice of life as an organic whole.

In "Life Without Principle" (1863), Thoreau surveys a wide range of worldly activities that prevent people from comprehending the spirituality of the universe. Engaged in their "business," they view everything as a commodity and thus fail to appreciate and love things for themselves. Theirs is a fallen world that has lost its potential for delight, and Thoreau alone seems to maintain a frame of mind that sees the world as an object of worship rather than of utility.

LIFE WITHOUT PRINCIPLE

At a lyceum, not long since, I felt that the lecturer had chosen a theme too foreign to himself, and so failed to interest me as much as he might have done. He described things not in or near to his heart, but toward his extremities and superficies. There was, in this sense, no truly central or centralizing thought in the lecture. I would have had him deal with his privatest experience, as the poet does. The greatest compliment that was ever paid me was when one asked me what *I thought,* and attended to my answer. I am surprised, as well as delighted, when this happens, it is such a rare use he would make of me, as if he were acquainted with the tool. Commonly, if men want anything of me, it is only to know how many acres I make of their land,—since I am a surveyor,—or, at most, what trivial news I have burdened myself with. They never will go to law for my meat; they prefer the shell. A man once came a considerable distance to ask me to lecture on Slavery; but on conversing with him, I found that he and his clique expected seven eighths of the lecture to be theirs, and only one eighth mine; so I declined. I take it for granted, when I am invited to lecture anywhere,—for I have had a little experience in that business,—that there is a desire to hear what *I think* on some subject, though I may be the greatest fool in the country,—and not that I should say pleasant things merely, or such as the audience will assent to; and I resolve, accordingly, that I will give them a strong dose of myself. They have sent for me, and engaged to pay for me, and I am determined that they shall have me, though I bore them beyond all precedent.

So now I would say something similar to you, my readers. Since *you* are my readers, and I have not been much of a traveler, I will not talk about people a thousand miles off, but come as near home as I can. As the time is short, I will leave out all the flattery, and retain all the criticism.

Let us consider the way in which we spend our lives.

This world is a place of business. What an infinite bustle! I am awaked almost every night by the panting of the locomotive. It interrupts my dreams. There is no sabbath. It would be glorious to see mankind at leisure for once. It is nothing but work, work, work. I cannot easily buy a blank-book to write thoughts in; they are commonly ruled for dollars and cents. An Irishman, seeing me making a minute in the fields, took it for granted that I was calculating my wages. If a man was tossed out of a window when an infant, and so made a cripple for life, or scared out of his wits by the Indians, it is regretted chiefly because he was thus incapacitated for—business! I think that there is nothing, not even crime, more opposed to poetry, to philosophy, ay, to life itself, than this incessant business.

There is a coarse and boisterous money-making fellow in the outskirts of our town, who is going to build a bank-wall under the hill along the edge of his meadow. The powers have put this into his head to keep him out of mischief, and he wishes me to spend three weeks digging there with him. The result will be that he will perhaps get some more money to hoard, and leave for his heirs to spend foolishly. If I do this, most will commend me as an industrious and hardworking man; but if I choose to devote myself to certain labors which yield more real profit, though but little money, they may be inclined to look on me as an idler. Nevertheless, as I do not need the police of meaningless labor to regulate me, and do not see anything absolutely praiseworthy in this fellow's undertaking any more than in many an enterprise of our own or foreign governments, however amusing it may be to him or them, I prefer to finish my education at a different school.

If a man walk in the woods for love of them half of each day, he is in danger of being regarded as a loafer; but if he spends his whole day as a speculator, shearing off those woods and making earth bald before her time, he is esteemed an industrious and enterprising citizen. As if a town had no interest in its forests but to cut them down!

Most men would feel insulted if it were proposed to employ them in throwing stones over a wall, and then in throwing them back, merely that they might earn their wages. But many are no more worthily employed now. For instance: just after sunrise, one summer morning, I noticed one of my neighbors walking beside his team, which was slowly drawing a heavy hewn stone swung under the axle, surrounded by an atmosphere of industry,—his day's work begun,—his brow commenced to sweat,—a reproach to all sluggards and idlers,—pausing abreast the shoulders of his oxen, and half turning round with a flourish of his merciful whip, while they gained their length on him. And I thought, Such is the labor which the American Congress exists to protect,—honest, manly toil,—honest as the day is long,—that makes his bread taste sweet, and keeps society sweet,—which all men respect and have consecrated; one of the sacred band, doing the needful but irksome drudgery. Indeed, I felt a slight reproach, because I observed this from a window, and was not abroad and stirring about a similar business. The day went by, and at evening I passed the yard of another neighbor, who keeps many servants, and spends much money foolishly, while he adds nothing to the common stock, and there I saw the stone of the morning lying beside a whimsical structure intended to adorn this Lord Timothy Dexter's premises, and the dignity forthwith departed from the teamster's labor, in my eyes. In my opinion, the sun was made to light worthier toil than this. I may add that his employer has since run off, in debt to a good part of the town, and, after passing through Chancery, has settled somewhere else, there to become once more a patron of the arts.

The ways by which you may get money almost without exception lead downward. To have done anything by which you earned money *merely* is to have been truly idle or worse. If the laborer gets no more than the wages which his employer pays him, he is cheated, he cheats himself. If you would get money as a writer or lecturer, you must be popular, which is to go down perpendicularly. Those services which the community will most readily pay for, it is most disagreeable to render. You are paid for being something less than a man. The state does not commonly reward a genius any more wisely. Even the poet laureate would rather not have to celebrate the accidents of royalty. He must be bribed with a pipe of wine; and perhaps another poet is called away from his muse to gauge that very pipe. As for my own business, even that kind of surveying which I could do with most satisfaction my employers do not want. They would prefer that I should do my work coarsely and not too well, ay, not well enough. When I observe that there are different ways of surveying, my employer commonly asks which will give him the most land, not which is most correct. I once invented a rule for measuring cord-wood, and tried to introduce it in Boston; but the measurer there told me that the sellers did not wish to have their wood measured correctly,—that he was already too accurate for them, and therefore they commonly got their wood measured in Charlestown before crossing the bridge.

The aim of the laborer should be, not to get his living, to get "a good job," but to perform well a certain work; and, even in a pecuniary sense, it would be economy for a town to pay its laborers so well that they would not feel that they were working for low ends, as for a livelihood merely, but for scientific, or even moral ends. Do not hire a man who does your work for money, but him who does it for love of it.

It is remarkable that there are few men so well employed, so much to their minds, but that a little money or fame would commonly buy them off from their present pursuit. I see advertisements for *active* young men, as if activity were the whole of a young man's capital. Yet I have been surprised when one has with confidence proposed to me, a grown man, to embark in some enterprise of his, as if I had absolutely nothing to do, my life having been a complete failure hitherto. What a doubtful compliment this to pay me! As if he had met me half-way across the ocean beating up against the wind, but bound nowhere, and proposed to me to go along with him! If I did, what do you think the underwriters would say? No, no! I am not without employment at this stage of the voyage. To tell the truth, I saw an advertisement for able-bodied seamen, when I was a boy, sauntering in my native port, and as soon as I came of age I embarked.

The community has no bribe that will tempt a wise man. You may raise money enough to tunnel a mountain, but you cannot raise money enough to hire a man who is minding *his own* business. An efficient and valuable man does what he can, whether the community pay him for it or not. The inefficient offer their inefficiency to the highest bidder, and are forever expecting to be put into office. One would suppose that they were rarely disappointed.

Perhaps I am more than usually jealous with respect to my freedom. I feel that my connection with and obligation to society are still very slight and transient. Those slight labors which afford me a livelihood, and by which it is allowed that I am to some extent serviceable to my contemporaries, are as yet commonly a pleasure to me, and I am not often reminded that they are a necessity. So far I am successful. But I foresee that if my wants should be much increased, the labor required to supply them would become a drudgery. If I should sell both my forenoons and afternoons to society, as most appear to do, I am sure that for me there would be nothing left worth living for. I trust that I shall never thus sell my birthright for a mess of pottage. I wish to suggest that a man may be very industrious, and yet not spend his time well. There is no more fatal blunderer than he who consumes the greater part of his life getting his living. All great enterprises are self-supporting. The poet, for instance, must sustain his body by his poetry, as a steam planing-mill feeds its boilers with the shavings it makes. You must get your living by loving. But as it is said of the merchants that ninety-seven in a hundred fail, so the life of men generally, tried by this standard, is a failure, and bankruptcy may be surely prophesied.

Merely to come into the world the heir of a fortune is not to be born, but to be still-born, rather. To be supported by the charity of friends, or a government pension,—provided you continue to breathe,—by whatever fine synonyms you describe these relations, is to go into the almshouse. On Sundays the poor debtor goes to church to take an account of stock, and finds, of course, that his outgoes have been greater than his income. In the Catholic Church, especially, they go into chancery, make a clean confession, give up all, and think to start again. Thus men will lie on their backs, talking about the fall of man, and never make an effort to get up.

As for the comparative demand which men make on life, it is an important difference between two, that the one is satisfied with a level success, that his marks can all be hit by point-blank shots, but the other, however low and unsuccessful his life may be, constantly elevates his aim, though at a very slight angle to the horizon. I should much rather be the last man,—though, as the Orientals say, "Greatness doth not approach him who is forever looking down; and all those who are looking high are growing poor."

It is remarkable that there is little or nothing to be remembered written on the subject of getting a living; how to make getting a living not merely honest and honorable, but altogether inviting and glorious; for if *getting* a living is not so, then living is not. One would think, from looking at literature, that this question had never disturbed a solitary individual's musings. Is it that men are too much disgusted with their experience to speak of it? The lesson of value which money teaches, which the Author of the Universe has taken so much pains to teach us, we are inclined to skip altogether. As for the means of living, it is wonderful how indifferent men of all classes are about it, even reformers, so called,—whether they inherit, or earn, or steal it. I think that Society has done nothing for us in this respect, or at least has undone what she has done. Cold and hunger seem more friendly to my nature than those methods which men have adopted and advise to ward them off.

The title *wise* is, for the most part, falsely applied. How can one be a wise man, if he does not know any better how to live than other men?—if he is only more cunning and intellectually subtle? Does Wisdom work in a tread-mill? or does she teach how to succeed *by her example*? Is there any such thing as wisdom not applied to life? Is she merely the miller who grinds the finest logic? It is pertinent to ask if Plato got his *living* in a better way or more successfully than his contemporaries,—or did he succumb to the difficulties of life like other men? Did he seem to prevail over some of them merely by indifference, or by assuming grand airs? or find it easier to live, because his aunt remembered him in her will? The ways in which most men get their living, that is, live, are mere makeshifts, and a shirking of the real business of life,—chiefly because they do not know, but partly because they do not mean, any better.

The rush to California, for instance, and the attitude, not merely of merchants, but of philosophers and prophets, so called, in relation to it, reflect the greatest disgrace on mankind. That so many are ready to live by luck, and so get the means of commanding the labor of others less lucky, without contributing any value to society! And that is called enterprise! I know of no more startling development of the immorality of trade, and all the common modes of getting a living. The philosophy and poetry and religion of such a mankind are not worth the dust of a puffball. The hog that gets his living by rooting, stirring up the soil so, would be ashamed of such company. If I could command the wealth of all the worlds by lifting my finger, I would not pay *such* a price for it. Even Mahomet knew that God did not make this world in jest. It makes God to be a moneyed gentleman who scatters a handful of pennies in order to see mankind scramble for them. The world's raffle! A subsistence in the domains of Nature a thing to be raffled for! What a comment, what a satire, on our institutions! The conclusion will be, that mankind will hang itself upon a tree. And have all the precepts in all the Bibles taught men only this? and is the last and most admirable invention of the human race only an improved muck-rake? Is this the ground on which Orientals and Occidentals meet? Did God direct us so to get our living, digging where we never planted,—and He would, perchance, reward us with lumps of gold?

God gave the righteous man a certificate entitling him to food and raiment, but the unrighteous man found a facsimile of the same in God's coffers, and appropriated it, and obtained food and raiment like the former. It is one of the most extensive systems of counterfeiting that the world has seen. I did not know that mankind was suffering for want of gold. I have seen a little of it. I know that it is very malleable, but not so malleable as wit. A grain of gold will gild a great surface, but not so much as a grain of wisdom.

The gold-digger in the ravines of the mountains is as much a gambler as his fellow in the saloons of San Francisco. What difference does it make whether you shake dirt or shake dice? If you win, society is the loser. The gold-digger is the enemy of the honest laborer, whatever checks and compensations there may be. It is not enough to tell me that you worked hard to get your gold. So does the Devil work hard. The way of transgressors may be hard in many respects. The humblest observer who goes to the mines sees and says that gold-digging is of the character of a lottery; the gold thus obtained is not the same thing with the wages of honest toil. But, practically, he forgets what he has seen, for he has seen only the fact, not the principle, and goes into trade there, that is, buys a ticket in what commonly proves another lottery, where the fact is not so obvious.

After reading Howitt's account of the Australian gold-diggings one evening, I had in my mind's eye, all night, the numerous valleys, with their streams, all cut up with foul pits, from ten to one hundred feet deep, and half a dozen feet across, as close as they can be dug, and partly filled with water,—the locality to which men furiously rush to probe for their fortunes,—uncertain where they shall break ground,—not knowing but the gold is under their camp itself,—sometimes digging one hundred and sixty feet before they strike the vein, or then missing it by a foot,—turned into demons, and regardless of each other's rights, in their thirst for riches,— whole valleys, for thirty miles, suddenly honeycombed by the pits of the miners, so that even hundreds are drowned in them,—standing in water, and covered with mud and clay, they work night and day, dying of exposure and disease. Having read this, and partly forgotten it, I was thinking, accidentally, of my own unsatisfactory life, doing as others do; and with that vision of the diggings still before me, I asked myself why I might not be washing some gold daily, though it were only the finest particles,—why I might not sink a shaft down to the gold within me, and work that mine. *There* is a Ballarat, a Bendigo for you,—what though it were a sulky-gully? At any rate, I might pursue some path, however solitary and narrow and crooked, in which I could walk with love and reverence. Wherever a man separates from the multitude, and goes his own way in this mood, there indeed is a fork in the road, though ordinary travelers may see only a gap in the paling. His solitary path across lots will turn out the *higher way* of the two.

Men rush to California and Australia as if the true gold were to be found in that direction; but that is to go to the very opposite extreme to where it lies. They go prospecting farther and farther away from the true lead, and are most unfortunate when they think themselves most successful. Is not our *native* soil auriferous? Does not a stream from the golden mountains flow through our native valley? and has not this for more than geologic ages been bringing down the shining particles and forming the nuggets for us? Yet, strange to tell, if a digger steal away, prospecting for this true gold, into the unexplored solitudes around us, there is no danger that any will dog his steps, and endeavor to supplant him. He may claim and undermine the whole valley even, both the cultivated and the uncultivated portions, his whole life long in peace, for no one will ever dispute his claim. They will not mind his cradles or his toms. He is not confined to a claim twelve feet square, as at Ballarat, but may mine anywhere, and wash the whole wide world in his tom.

Howitt says of the man who found the great nugget which weighed twenty-eight pounds, at the Bendigo diggings in Australia: "He soon began to drink; got a horse, and rode all about, generally at full gallop, and, when he met people, called out to inquire if they knew who he was, and then kindly informed them that he was 'the bloody wretch that had found the nugget.' At last he rode full speed against a tree, and nearly knocked his brains out." I think, however, there was no danger of that, for he had already knocked his brains out against the nugget. Howitt adds, "He is a hopelessly ruined man." But he is a type of the class. They are all fast men. Hear some of the names of the places where they dig: "Jackass Flat,"—"Sheep's-Head Gully,"—"Murderer's Bar," etc. Is there no satire in these names? Let them carry their ill-gotten wealth where they will, I am thinking it will still be "Jackass Flat," if not "Murderer's Bar," where they live.

The last resource of our energy has been the robbing of grave-yards on the Isthmus of Darien, an enterprise which appears to be but in its infancy; for, according to late accounts, an act has passed its second reading in the legislature of New Granada, regulating this kind of mining; and a correspondent of the "Tribune" writes: "In the dry season, when the weather will permit of the country being properly prospected, no doubt other rich *guacas* [that is, graveyards] will be found." To emigrants he says: "Do not come before December; take the Isthmus route in preference to the Boca del Toro one; bring no useless baggage, and do not cumber yourself with a tent; but a good pair of blankets will be necessary; a pick, shovel, and axe of good material will be almost all that is required:" advice which might have been taken from the "Burker's Guide." And he concludes with this line in Italics and small capitals: *"If you are doing well at home,* STAY THERE," which may fairly be interpreted to mean, "If you are getting a good living by robbing graveyards at home, stay there."

But why go to California for a text? She is the child of New England, bred at her own school and church.

It is remarkable that among all the preachers there are so few moral teachers. The prophets are employed in excusing the ways of men. Most reverend seniors, the *illuminati* of the age, tell me, with a gracious, reminiscent smile, betwixt an aspiration and a shudder, not to be too tender about these things,—to lump all that, that is, make a lump of gold of it. The highest advice I have heard on these subjects was groveling. The burden of it was,—It is not worth your while to undertake to reform the world in this particular. Do not ask how your bread is buttered; it will make you sick, if you do,—and the like. A man had better starve at once than lose his innocence in the process of getting his bread. If within the sophisticated man there is not an unsophisticated one, then he is but one of the Devil's angels. As we grow old, we live more coarsely, we relax a little in our disciplines, and, to some extent, cease to obey our finest instincts. But we should be fastidious to the extreme of sanity, disregarding the gibes of those who are more unfortunate than ourselves.

In our science and philosophy, even, there is commonly no true and absolute account of things. The spirit of sect and bigotry has planted its hoof amid the stars. You have only to discuss the problem, whether the stars are inhabited or not, in order to discover it. Why must we daub the heavens as well as the earth? It was an unfortunate discovery that Dr. Kane was a Mason, and that Sir John Franklin was another. But it was a more cruel suggestion that possibly that was the reason why the former went in search of the latter. There is not a popular magazine in this country that would dare to print a child's thought on important subjects without comment. It must be submitted to the D.D.'s. I would it were the chickadee-dees.

You come from attending the funeral of mankind to attend to a natural phenomenon. A little thought is sexton to all the world.

I hardly know an *intellectual* man, even, who is so broad and truly liberal that you can think aloud in his society. Most with whom you endeavor to talk soon come to a stand against some institution in which they appear to hold stock,—that is, some particular, not universal, way of viewing things. They will continually thrust their own low roof, with its narrow skylight, between you and the sky, when it is the unobstructed heavens you would view. Get out of the way with your cobwebs; wash your windows, I say! In some lyceums they tell me that they have voted to exclude the subject of religion. But how do I know what their religion is, and when I am near to or far from it? I have walked into such an arena and done my best to make a clean breast of what religion I have experienced, and the audience never suspected what I was about. The lecture was as harmless as moonshine to them. Whereas, if I had read to them the biography of the greatest scamps in history, they might have thought that I had written the lives of the deacons of their church. Ordinarily, the inquiry is, Where did you come from? or, Where are you going? That was a more pertinent question which I overheard one of my auditors put to another once,—"What does he lecture for?" It made me quake in my shoes.

To speak impartially, the best men that I know are not serene, a world in themselves. For the most part, they dwell in forms, and flatter and study effect only more finely than the rest. We select granite for the underpinning of our houses and barns; we build fences of stone; but we do not ourselves rest on an underpinning of granitic truth, the lowest primitive rock. Our sills are rotten. What stuff is the man made of who is not coexistent in our thought with the purest and subtilest truth? I often accuse my finest acquaintances of an immense frivolity; for, while there are manners and compliments we do not meet, we do not teach one another the lessons of honesty and sincerity that the brutes do, or of steadiness and solidity that the rocks do. The fault is commonly mutual, however; for we do not habitually demand any more of each other.

That excitement about Kossuth, consider how characteristic, but superficial, it was!—only another kind of politics or dancing. Men were making speeches to him all over the country, but each expressed only the thought, or the want of thought, of the multitude. No man stood on truth. They were merely banded together, as usual one leaning on another, and all together on nothing; as the Hindoos made the world rest on an elephant, the elephant on a tortoise, and the tortoise on a serpent, and had nothing to put under the serpent. For all fruit of that stir we have the Kossuth hat.

Just so hollow and ineffectual, for the most part, is our ordinary conversation. Surface meets surface. When our life ceases to be inward and private, conversation degenerates into mere gossip. We rarely meet a man who can tell us any news which he has not read in a newspaper, or been told by his neighbor; and, for the most part, the only difference between us and our fellow is that he has seen the newspaper, or been out to tea, and we have not. In proportion as our inward life fails, we go more constantly and desperately to the post-office. You may depend on it, that the poor fellow who walks away with the greatest number of letters, proud of his extensive correspondence, has not heard from himself this long while.

I do not know but it is too much to read one newspaper a week. I have tried it recently, and for so long it seems to me that I have not dwelt in my native region. The sun, the clouds, the snow, the trees say not so much to me. You cannot serve two masters. It requires more than a day's devotion to know and to possess the wealth of a day.

We may well be ashamed to tell what things we have read or heard in our day. I do not know why my news should be so trivial, —considering what one's dreams and expectations are, why the developments should be so paltry. The news we hear, for the most part, is not news to our genius. It is the stalest repetition. You are often tempted to ask why such stress is laid on a particular experience which you have had,—that, after twenty-five years, you should meet Hobbins, Registrar of Deeds, again on the sidewalk. Have you not budged an inch, then? Such is the daily news. Its facts appear to float in the atmosphere, insignificant as the sporules of fungi, and impinge on some neglected *thallus,* or surface of our minds, which affords a basis for them, and hence a parasitic growth. We should wash ourselves clean of such news. Of what consequence, though our planet explode, if there is no character involved in the explosion? In health we have not the least curiosity about such events. We do not live for idle amusement. I would not run round a corner to see the world blow up.

All summer, and far into the autumn, perchance, you unconsciously went by the newspapers and the news, and now you find it was because the morning and the evening were full of news to you. Your walks were full of incidents. You attended, not to the affairs of Europe, but to your own affairs in Massachusetts fields. If you chance to live and move and have your being in that thin stratum in which the events that make the news transpire,—thinner than the paper on which it is printed,—then these things will fill the world for you; but if you soar above or dive below that plane, you cannot remember nor be reminded of them. Really to see the sun rise or go down every day, so to relate ourselves to a universal fact, would preserve us sane forever. Nations! What are nations? Tartars, and Huns, and Chinamen! Like insects, they swarm. The historian strives in vain to make them memorable. It is for want of a man that there are so many men. It is individuals that populate the world. Any man thinking may say with the Spirit of Lodin,—

> "I look down from my height on nations,
> And they become ashes before me;—
> Calm is my dwelling in the clouds;
> Pleasant are the great fields of my rest."

Pray, let us live without being drawn by dogs, Esquimaux-fashion, tearing over hill and dale, and biting each other's ears.

Not without a slight shudder at the danger, I often perceive how near I had come to admitting into my mind the details of some trivial affair,—the news of the street; and I am astonished to observe how willing men are to lumber their minds with such rubbish,—to permit idle rumors and incidents of the most insignificant kind to intrude on ground which should be sacred to thought. Shall the mind be a public arena, where the affairs of the street and the gossip of the tea-table chiefly are discussed? Or shall it be a quarter of heaven itself,—an hypæthral temple, consecrated to the service of the gods? I find it so difficult to dispose of the few facts which to me are significant, that I hesitate to burden my attention with those which are insignificant, which only a divine mind could illustrate. Such is, for the most part, the news in newspapers and conversation. It is important to preserve the mind's chastity in this respect. Think of admitting the details of a single case of the criminal court into our thoughts, to stalk profanely through their very *sanctum sanctorum* for an hour, ay, for many hours! to make a very barroom of the mind's inmost apartment, as if for so long the dust of the street had occupied us,—the very street itself, with all its travel, its bustle, and filth, had passed through our thoughts' shrine! Would it not be an intellectual and moral suicide? When I have been compelled to sit spectator and auditor in a court-room for some hours, and have seen my neighbors, who were not compelled, stealing in from time to time, and tiptoeing about with washed hands and faces, it has appeared to my mind's eye, that, when they took off their hats, their ears suddenly expanded into vast hoppers for sound, between which even their narrow heads were crowded. Like the vanes of windmills, they caught the broad but shallow stream of sound, which, after a few titillating gyrations in their coggy brains, passed out the other side. I wondered if, when they got home, they were as careful to wash their ears as before their hands and faces. It has seemed to me, at such a time, that the auditors and the witnesses, the jury and the counsel, the judge and the criminal at the bar,—if I may presume him guilty before he is convicted,—were all equally criminal, and a thunderbolt might be expected to descend and consume them all together.

By all kinds of traps and signboards, threatening the extreme penalty of the divine law, exclude such trespassers from the only ground which can be sacred to you. It is so hard to forget what it is worse than useless to remember! If I am to be a thoroughfare, I prefer that it be of the mountain brooks, the Parnassian streams, and not the town sewers. There is inspiration, that gossip which comes to the ear of the attentive mind from the courts of heaven. There is the profane and stale revelation of the barroom and the police court. The same ear is fitted to receive both communications. Only the character of the hearer determines to which it shall be open, and to which closed. I believe that the mind can be permanently profaned by the habit of attending to trivial things, so that all our thoughts shall be tinged with triviality. Our very intellect shall be macadamized, as it were,—its foundation broken into fragments for the wheels of travel to roll over; and if you would know what will make the most durable pavement, surpassing rolled stones, spruce blocks, and asphaltum, you have only to look into some of our minds which have been subjected to this treatment so long.

If we have thus desecrated ourselves,—as who has not?—the remedy will be by wariness and devotion to reconsecrate ourselves, and make once more a fane of the mind. We should treat our minds, that is, ourselves, as innocent and ingenuous children, whose guardians we are, and be careful what objects and what subjects we thrust on their attention. Read not the Times. Read the Eternities. Conventionalities are at length as bad as impurities. Even the facts of science may dust the mind by their dryness, unless they are in a sense effaced each morning, or rather rendered fertile by the dews of fresh and living truth. Knowledge does not come to us by details, but in flashes of light from heaven. Yes, every thought that passes through the mind helps to wear and tear it, and to deepen the ruts, which, as in the streets of Pompeii, evince how much it has been used. How many things there are concerning which we might well deliberate whether we had better know them,—had better let their peddling-carts be driven, even at the slowest trot or walk, over that bridge of glorious span by which we trust to pass at last from the farthest brink of time to the nearest shore of eternity! Have we no culture, no refinement,—but skill only to live coarsely and serve the Devil?—to acquire a little worldly wealth, or fame, or liberty, and make a false show with it, as if we were all husk and shell, with no tender and living kernel to us? Shall our institutions be like those chestnut burs which contain abortive nuts, perfect only to prick the fingers?

America is said to be the arena on which the battle of freedom is to be fought; but surely it cannot be freedom in a merely political sense that is meant. Even if we grant that the American has freed himself from a political tyrant, he is still the slave of an economical and moral tyrant. Now that the republic—the *res-publica*—has been settled, it is time to look after the *res-privata*,—the private state,—to see, as the Roman senate charged its consuls, *"ne quid res-* PRIVATA *detrimenti caperet,"* that the *private* state receive no detriment.

Do we call this the land of the free? What is it to be free from King George and continue the slaves of King Prejudice? What is it to be born free and not to live free? What is the value of any political freedom, but as a means to moral freedom? Is it a freedom to be slaves, or a freedom to be free, of which we boast? We are a nation of politicians, concerned about the outmost defenses only of freedom. It is our children's children who may perchance be really free. We tax ourselves unjustly. There is a part of us which is not represented. It is taxation without representation. We quarter troops, we quarter fools and cattle of all sorts upon ourselves. We quarter our gross bodies on our poor souls, till the former eat up all the latter's substance.

With respect to a true culture and manhood, we are essentially provincial still, not metropolitan,—mere Jonathans. We are provincial, because we do not find at home our standards; because we do not worship truth, but the reflection of truth; because we are warped and narrowed by an exclusive devotion to trade and commerce and manufactures and agriculture and the like, which are but means, and not the end.

So is the English Parliament provincial. Mere country bumpkins, they betray themselves, when any more important question arises for them to settle, the Irish question, for instance,—the English question why did I not say? Their natures are subdued to what they work in. Their "good breeding" respects only secondary objects. The finest manners in the world are awkwardness and fatuity when contrasted with a finer intelligence. They appear but as the fashions of past days,—mere courtliness, knee-buckles and small-clothes, out of date. It is the vice, but not the excellence of manners, that they are continually being deserted by the character; they are cast-off clothes or shells, claiming the respect which belonged to the living creature. You are presented with the shells instead of the meat, and it is no excuse generally, that, in the case of some fishes, the shells are of more worth than the meat. The man who thrusts his manners upon me does as if he were to insist on introducing me to his cabinet of curiosities, when I wished to see himself. It was not in this sense that the poet Decker called Christ "the first true gentleman that ever breathed." I repeat that in this sense the most splendid court in Christendom is provincial, having authority to consult about Transalpine interests only, and not the affairs of Rome. A prætor or proconsul would suffice to settle the questions which absorb the attention of the English Parliament and the American Congress.

Government and legislation! these I thought were respectable professions. We have heard of heaven-born Numas, Lycurguses, and Solons, in the history of the world, whose *names* at least may stand for ideal legislators; but think of legislating to *regulate* the breeding of slaves, or the exportation of tobacco! What have divine legislators to do with the exportation or the importation of tobacco? what humane ones with the breeding of slaves? Suppose you were to submit the question to any son of God,—and has He no children in the Nineteenth Century? is it a family which is extinct?—in what condition would you get it again? What shall a State like Virginia say for itself at the last day, in which these have been the principal, the staple productions? What ground is there for patriotism in such a State? I derive my facts from statistical tables which the States themselves have published.

A commerce that whitens every sea in quest of nuts and raisins, and makes slaves of its sailors for this purpose! I saw, the other day, a vessel which had been wrecked, and many lives lost, and her cargo of rags, juniper berries, and bitter almonds were strewn along the shore. It seemed hardly worth the while to tempt the dangers of the sea between Leghorn and New York for the sake of a cargo of juniper berries and bitter almonds. America sending to the Old World for her bitters! Is not the sea-brine, is not shipwreck, bitter enough to make the cup of life go down here? Yet such, to a great extent, is our boasted commerce; and there are those who style themselves statesmen and philosophers who are so blind as to think that progress and civilization depend on precisely this kind of inter-change and activity,—the activity of flies about a molasses-hogshead. Very well, observes one, if men were oysters. And very well, answer I, if men were mosquitoes.

Lieutenant Herndon, whom our government sent to explore the Amazon, and, it is said, to extend the area of slavery, observed that there was wanting there "an industrious and active population, who know what the comforts of life are, and who have artificial wants to draw out the great resources of the country." But what are the "artificial wants" to be encouraged? Not the love of luxuries, like the tobacco and slaves of, I believe, his native Virginia, nor the ice and granite and other material wealth of our native New England; nor are "the great resources of a country" that fertility or barrenness of soil which produces these. The chief want, in every State that I have been into, was a high and earnest purpose in its inhabitants. This alone draws out "the great resources" of Nature, and at last taxes her beyond her resources; for man naturally dies out of her. When we want culture more than potatoes, and illumination more than sugar-plums, then the great resources of a world are taxed and drawn out, and the result, or staple production, is, not slaves, nor operatives, but men,—those rare fruits called heroes, saints, poets, philosophers, and redeemers.

In short, as a snow-drift is formed where there is a lull in the wind, so, one would say, where there is a lull of truth, an institution springs up. But the truth blows right on over it, nevertheless, and at length blows it down.

What is called politics is comparatively something so superficial and inhuman, that practically I have never fairly recognized that it concerns me at all. The newspapers, I perceive, devote some of their columns specially to politics or government without charge; and this, one would say, is all that saves it; but as I love literature and to some extent the truth also, I never read those columns at any rate. I do not wish to blunt my sense of right so much. I have not got to an-swer for having read a single President's Message. A strange age of the world this, when empires, kingdoms, and republics come a-beg-ging to a private man's door, and utter their complaints at his elbow!

I cannot take up a newspaper but I find that some wretched government or other, hard pushed and on its last legs, is interceding with
me, the reader, to vote for it,—more importunate than an Italian
beggar; and if I have a mind to look at its certificate, made, perchance, by some benevolent merchant's clerk, or the skipper that
brought it over, for it cannot speak a word of English itself, I shall
probably read of the eruption of some Vesuvius, or the overflowing
of some Po, true or forged, which brought it into this condition. I
do not hesitate, in such a case, to suggest work, or the almshouse; or
why not keep its castle in silence, as I do commonly? The poor
President, what with preserving his popularity and doing his duty,
is completely bewildered. The newspapers are the ruling power. Any
other government is reduced to a few marines at Fort Independence.
If a man neglects to read the Daily Times, government will go down
on its knees to him, for this is the only treason in these days.

Those things which now most engage the attention of men, as
politics and the daily routine, are, it is true, vital functions of human society, but should be unconsciously performed, like the corresponding functions of the physical body. They are *infra*-human,
a kind of vegetation. I sometimes awake to a half-consciousness
of them going on about me, as a man may become conscious of
some of the processes of digestion in a morbid state, and so have
the dyspepsia, as it is called. It is as if a thinker submitted himself to be rasped by the great gizzard of creation. Politics is, as
it were, the gizzard of society, full of grit and gravel, and the two
political parties are its two opposite halves,—sometimes split into
quarters, it may be, which grind on each other. Not only individuals, but states, have thus a confirmed dyspepsia, which expresses
itself, you can imagine by what sort of eloquence. Thus our life is
not altogether a forgetting, but also, alas! to a great extent, a remembering, of that which we should never have been conscious of, certainly not in our waking hours. Why should we not meet, not always as dyspeptics, to tell our bad dreams, but sometimes as *eupep*-
tics, to congratulate each other on the ever-glorious morning? I do
not make an exorbitant demand, surely.

Study Questions

1. What are the various meanings that the word "principle" acquires in the course of the essay?
2. Thoreau uses the phrase "honest manly toil" in an ironic sense. What are the implications of the word "manly"? Does Thoreau believe that leisure is "unmanly"? What view of masculinity emerges from the essay?
3. Many of Thoreau's metaphors and analogies transform abstractions such as thinking and politicking into material things and biological functions. What is the purpose of the transformations? How do they aid in defining what for Thoreau is real and worthy of our attention?
4. We probably know what stories would be considered newsworthy in the *Times,* the paper Thoreau warns us against reading. What kind of articles would you expect to find in the *Eternities?*
5. It is clear that Thoreau would be more comfortable in Diderot's Tahiti than in Campanella's City of the Sun. But how would he fit into Morris' society?
6. Are the abuses Thoreau cites the result of the effects of society on man, or are they inherent in every individual?
7. What would Thoreau think of Kant's idea that one man alone cannot achieve perfection?

$\mathcal{R}$OBERT L. HEILBRONER
is a member of the Graduate Faculty of the New School for Social Research in New York City. He is the author of numerous books, including *The Worldly Philosophers, The Limits of American Capitalism,* and *Economic Means and Social Ends.* His writing on economics makes him particularly suited to discuss the ecological crisis, since one of the major components of that crisis is the world production and distribution of life-sustaining goods. He has analyzed and warned of the inevitable dangers besetting twentieth-century society, and in *The Future As History* draws a conclusion that is echoed in the essay included here: "Optimism as a philosophy of historic expectations can no longer be considered a national virtue. It has become a dangerous national delusion."

The essay reprinted below, "Ecological Armageddon," first appeared in the *New York Review of Books* (April 23, 1970) as a review of a recent book by Paul and Anne Ehrlich, *Population, Resources, Environment.*

ECOLOGICAL ARMAGEDDON

Ecology has become the Thing. There are ecological politics, ecological jokes, ecological bookstores, advertisements, seminars, teach-ins, buttons. The automobile, symbol of ecological abuse, has been tried, sentenced to death, and formally executed in at least two universities (complete with burial of one victim). Publishing companies are fattening on books on the sonic boom, poisons in the things we eat, perils loose in the garden, the dangers of breathing. The *Saturday Review* has appended a regular monthly Ecological Supplement. In short, the ecological issue has assumed the dimensions of a vast popular fad, for which one can predict with reasonable assurance the trajectory of all such fads—a period of intense popular involvement, followed by growing boredom and gradual extinction, save for a diehard remnant of the faithful.

This would be a great tragedy, for I have slowly become convinced during the last twelve months that the ecological issue is not only of primary and lasting importance, but that it may indeed constitute the most dangerous and difficult challenge that humanity has ever faced. Since these are very large statements, let me attempt to substantiate them by drawing freely on the best single descriptive and analytic treatment of the subject that I have yet seen, *Population, Resources, Environment,* by Paul and Anne Ehrlich of Stanford University.[1] Rather than resort to the bothersome procedure of endlessly citing their arguments in quotation marks, I shall take the liberty of reproducing their case in a rather free paraphrase, as if it were my own, until we reach the end of the basic argument, after which I shall make clear some conclusions that I believe lie implicit, although not quite overt, in their work.

Ultimately, the ecological crisis represents our belated awakening to the fact that we live on what Kenneth Boulding has called, in the perfect phrase, our Spaceship Earth. As in all spaceships, sustained life requires that a meticulous balance be maintained between the life-support capability of the vehicle and the demands made by the inhabitants of the craft. Until quite recently, those demands have been well within the capability of the ship, both in terms of its ability to supply the physical and chemical requirements for continued existence and to absorb the waste products of the voyagers. This is not to say that the earth has been generous—short rations have been the lot of mankind for most of its history—nor is it to deny the recurrent advent of local ecological crises: witness the destruction of whole areas like the erstwhile granaries of North Africa. But famines have passed and there have always been new areas to move to. The idea that the earth as a whole was overtaxed is one that is new to our time.

For it is only in our time that we are reaching the ceiling of terrain-carrying capacity, not on a local but on a global basis. Indeed, as will soon become clear, we are well past that capacity, provided that the level of resource intake and waste output represented by the average American or European is taken as a standard to be achieved by all humanity. To put it bluntly, if we take as the price of a first-class ticket the resource requirements of those passengers who travel in the Northern Hemisphere of the Spaceship, we have now reached a point at which the steerage is condemned to live forever—or at least within the horizon of the technology presently visible—at a second-class level; or at which a considerable change in living habits must be imposed on first class if the ship is ever to be converted to a one-class cruise.

This strain on the carrying capacity of the vessel results from the

---

[1] W. H. Freeman and Co., San Francisco, 1970.

contemporary confluence of three distinct developments, each of which places tremendous or even unmanageable strains on the life-carrying capability of the planet and all of which together simply overload it. The first of these is the enormous strain imposed by the sheer burgeoning of population. The statistics of population growth are by now very well known: the earth's passenger list is growing at a rate that will give us some 4 billion humans by 1975, and that threatens to give us 8 billions by 2010. I say "threatens," since it is likely that the inability of the earth to carry so large a group will result in an actual population somewhat smaller than this, especially in the steerage, where the growth is most rapid and the available resources least plentiful.

We shall return to the population problem later. But meanwhile a second strain is placed on the earth by the simple cumulative effect of *existing* technology (combustion engines, the main industrial processes, present-day agricultural techniques, etc.). This strain is localized mainly in the first-class portions of the vessel where each new arrival on board is rapidly given a standard complement of capital equipment and where the rate of physical- and chemical-resource transformation per capita steadily mounts. The strain consists of the limited ability of the soil, the water, and the atmosphere of these favored regions to absorb the outpourings of these fast-growing industrial processes.

The most dramatic instance of this limited absorptive power is the rise in the carbon dioxide content of the air due to the steady growth of (largely industrial) combustion. By the year 2000, it seems beyond dispute that the CO_2 content of the air will have doubled, raising the heat-trapping properties of the atmosphere. This so-called greenhouse effect has been predicted to raise main global temperatures sufficiently to bring catastrophic potential consequences. One possibility is a sequence of climatic changes resulting from a melting of the Arctic ice floes that would result in the advent of a new Ice Age; another is the slumping of the Antarctic icecap into the sea with a consequent tidal wave that could wipe out a substantial portion of mankind and raise the sea level by sixty to a hundred feet.

These are all "iffy" scenarios, whose present significance may be limited to alerting us to the immensity of the ecological problem; happily they are of sufficient uncertainty not to cause us immediate worry (it is lucky they are, because it is extremely unlikely that all the massed technological and human energy on earth could arrest such changes once they began). Much closer to home is the burden placed on the earth's carrying capacity by the sheer requirements of a spreading industrial activity in terms of the fuel and mineral resources needed to maintain the going rate of output per person in the first-class cabins. To raise the existing (not the anticipated) population of the earth to American standards would require the annual extraction of 75 times as much iron, 100 times as much copper, 200 times as much lead, and 250 times as much tin as we now take from the earth. Only the known reserves of iron allow us to entertain such fantastic rates of mineral exploitation (and the capital investment needed to bring about such mining operations is in itself staggering to contemplate). All the other requirements exceed by far all known or reasonably anticipated ore reserves. And, to repeat, we have taken into account only today's level of population: to equip the prospective passengers of the year 2010 with this amount of basic raw materials would require a doubling of all the above figures.

I will revert later to the consequences of this prospect. First, however, let us pay attention to the third source of overload, this one traceable to the special environment-destroying potential of newly developed technologies. Of these the most important—and if it should ever come to full-scale war, of course the most lethal—is the threat posed by nuclear radiation. I shall not elaborate on this well-known (although not well-believed) danger, pausing to point out only that a massive nuclear holocaust would in all likelihood exert its principal effect in the Northern Hemisphere. The survivors in the South would be severely hampered in their efforts at reconstruction not only because most of the easily available resources of the world have already been used up, but because most of the technological know-how would have perished along with the populations up North.

But the threats of new technology are by no means limited to the specter of nuclear devastation. There is, immediately at hand, the known devastation of the new chemical pesticides that have now entered more or less irreversibly into the living tissue of the world's population. Most mothers' milk in the United States today—I now quote the Ehrlichs verbatim—"contains so much DDT that it would be declared illegal in interstate commerce if it were sold as cow's milk"; and the DDT intake of infants around the world is twice the daily allowable maximum set by the World Health Organization. We are already, in other words, being exposed to heavy dosages of chemicals whose effects we know to be dangerous, with what ultimate results we shall have to wait nervously to discover. (There is food for thought in the archeological evidence that one factor in the decline of Rome was the systematic poisoning of upper-class Romans from the lead with which they lined their wine containers.)

But the threat is not limited to pesticides. Barry Commoner predicts an agricultural crisis in the United States within fifty years from the action of our fertilizers, which will either ultimately destroy soil fertility or lead to pollution of the national water supply. At another corner of the new technology, the SST threatens not alone to shake us with its boom, but to affect the amount of cloud cover (and climate) by its contrails. And I have not even mentioned the standard pollution problems of smoke, industrial effluents into lakes and rivers, or solid wastes. Suffice it to report that a 1968 UNESCO conference concluded that man has only about twenty years to go before the planet starts to become uninhabitable because of air pollution alone. Of course, "starts to" is imprecise; I am reminded of a cartoon of an industrialist looking at his billowing smokestacks, in front of which a forlorn figure is holding up a placard that says: "We have only 35 years to go." The caption reads, "Boy, that shook me up for a minute. I though it said 3–5 years."

I have left until last the grimmest and gravest threat of all, speaking now on behalf of the steerage. This is the looming inability of the great green earth to bring forth sufficient food to maintain life, even at the miserable threshold of subsistence at which it is now endured by perhaps a third of the world's population. The problem here is the very strong likelihood that population growth will inexorably outpace whatever improvements in fertility and productivity we will be able to apply to the earth's mantle (including the watery fringes of the ocean where sea "farming" is at least technically imaginable). Here the race is basically between two forces: on the one hand, those that give promise that the rate of increase of population can be curbed (if not totally halted); and on the other, those that give promise of increasing the amount of sustenance we can wring from the soil.

Both these forces are subtly blended of technological and social factors. Take population growth. The great hope of every ecologist is that an effective birth-control technique—cheap, requiring little or no medical supervision, devoid of taboos or religious hindrances— will rapidly and effectively lower the present fertility rates which are doubling world population every 35 years (every 28 years in Africa; every 24 in Latin America). No such device is currently available, although the Pill, the IUD, vasectomies, abortions, condoms, coitus interruptus, and other known techniques could, of course, do the job, if the requisite equipment, persuasion (or coercion), instruction, etc., could be brought to the 80 to 90 percent of the world's people who know next to nothing about birth control.

It seems a fair conclusion that no such worldwide campaign is apt to be successful for at least a decade and maybe a generation, although there is always the hope that a "spontaneous" change in attitudes similar to that in Hungary or Japan will bring about a rapid halt to population growth. But even in this unlikely event, the sheer "momentum" of population growth still poses terrible problems. Malcom Potts, Secretary General of International Planned Parenthood has presented a shocking statistical calculation in this regard: he has pointed out that population growth in India is today adding a million mouths per month to the Indian subcontinent. If, by some miracle, fertility rates were to decline tomorrow by 50 percent in India, at the end of twenty years, owing to the already existing huge numbers of children who would be moving up into childbearing ages, population growth in India would still be taking place at the rate of a million per month.

The other element in the race is our ability to match population growth with food supplies, at least for a generation or so, while birth-control techniques and campaigns are perfected. Here the problem is also partly technological, partly social. The technological part involves the so-called Green Revolution—the development of seeds that are capable, at their best, of improving yields per acre by a factor of 300 percent, sometimes even more. The problem, however, is that these new seeds generally require irrigation and fertilizer to bring their benefits. If India alone were to apply fertilizer at the per capita level of the Netherlands, she would consume half the world's total output of fertilizer. This would require a hundredfold expansion of India's present level of fertilizer use. Irrigation, the other necessary input for most improved seeds, poses equally formidable requirements. E. A. Mason of the Oak Ridge National Laboratories has prepared preliminary estimates of the costs of nuclear-powered "agro-industrial complexes" in which desalted water and fertilizer would be produced for use on adjacent farms. It would require 23 such plants per year, each taking care of some three million people, just to keep pace with present population growth. Since it would take at least five years to get these plants into operation, we should begin work today on at least 125 such units. Assuming that no hitches were encountered and that the technology on paper could be easily translated into a technology *in situ*, the cost would amount to $315 billion.

There are, as well, other technical problems associated with the Green Revolution of an ecological nature—mainly the risk of introducing locally untried strains of plants that may be subject to epidemic disease. But putting those difficulties to the side, we must recognize as well the social obstacles that a successful Green Revolution must overcome. The new seeds can only be afforded by the upper level of peasantry—not merely because of their cost (and the cost of the required fertilizer) but because only a rich peasant can take the risk of having the crop turn out badly without himself suffering starvation. Hence the Green Revolution is likely to increase the strains of social stratification within the underdeveloped areas. Then, too, even a successful local crop does not always shed its benefits evenly across a nation but results all too often in local gluts that cannot be transported to starving areas because of transportation bottlenecks.

None of these discouraging remarks are intended in the slightest to disparage the Green Revolution, which represents the inspired work of dedicated men. But the difficulties must be kept in mind as a corrective to the lulling belief that "science" can easily offset the population boom with larger supplies of food. There is no doubt that supplies of food *can* be substantially increased—rats alone devour some 10 to 12 percent of India's crop, and insects can ravage up to half the stored crops of some underdeveloped area, so that even very "simple" methods of improved storage hold out important prospects of improving basic life-support, quite aside from the longer-term hopes of agronomy. Yet, at best these improvements will only stave off the day of reckoning. Ultimately the problem posed by Malthus must be faced—that population tends to increase geometrically, by doubling, and that agriculture does not, so that eventually population *must* face the limit of a food barrier. It is worth repeating the words of Malthus himself in this regard:

> Famine seems to be the last, the most dreadful resource of nature. The power of population is so much superior to the power in the earth to produce subsistence for man, that premature death must in some shape or other visit the human race. The vices of mankind are active and able ministers of depopulation . . . [S]hould they fail in this war of extermination, sickly seasons, epidemics, pestilence, and plague, advance in terrific array, and sweep off their thousands and ten thousands. Should success still be incomplete, gigantic inevitable famine stalks in the rear, and with one mighty blow, levels the population with the food of the world.

This Malthusian prophecy has been so often "refuted," as economists have pointed to the astonishing rates of growth of food output in the advanced nations, that there is a danger of dismissing the warnings of the Ehrlichs as merely another premature alarm. To do so would be a fearful mistake. For, unlike Malthus, who assumed that technology would remain constant, the Ehrlichs have made ample allowance for the growth of technological capability, and their approach to the impending catastrophe is not shrill. They merely point out that a mild version of the Malthusian solution is already upon us, for at least half a billion people are chronically hungry or outright starving, and another one and a half billion under- or malnourished. Thus we do not have to wait for "gigantic inevitable famine"; it has already come.

What is more important is that the Ehrlichs see the matter in a perspective fundamentally different from Malthus', not as a problem involving supply and demand but as one involving a total ecological equilibrium. The crisis, as the Ehrlichs see it, is thus both deeper and more complex than merely a shortage of food, although the latter is one of its more horrendous evidences. What threatens the Spaceship Earth is a profound imbalance between the totality of systems by which human life is maintained and the totality of demands, industrial as well as agricultural, technological as well as demographic, to which that life-support capacity is subjected.

I have no doubt that one can fault bits and pieces of the Ehrlichs' analysis, and there is a note of determined pessimism in their work that leads me to suspect (or at least hope) that there is somewhat more time for adaptation than they suggest. Yet I do not see how their basic conclusion can be denied. Beginning within our lifetimes and rising rapidly to crisis proportions in our children's, humankind faces a challenge comparable to none in its history, with the possible exception of the forced migrations of the Ice Age. It is with the responses to this crisis that I wish to end this essay, for, telling and courageous as the Ehrlichs' analysis is, I do not believe that even they have fully faced up to the implications that their own findings present.

The first of these I have already stated: it is the clear conclusion that the underdeveloped countries can *never* hope to achieve parity with the developed countries. Given our present and prospective technology, there are simply not enough resources to permit a "Western" rate of industrial exploitation to be expanded to a population of four billion—much less eight billion—persons. It may well be that most of the population in the underdeveloped world has no ambition to reach Western standards—indeed, does not even know that such a thing as "development" is on the agenda. But the elites of these nations, for all their rhetorical rejection of Western (and especially American) styles of life, do tend to picture a Western standard as the ultimate end of their activities. As it becomes clear that such an objective is impossible, a profound reorientation of views must take place within the underdeveloped nations.

What such a reorientation will be it is impossible to say. For the near-term future, the outlook for the most population-oppressed areas will be a continuous battle against food shortages, coupled with the permanent impairment of the intelligence of much of the surviving population due to protein deficiencies in childhood. This pressure of population may lead to aggressive searches for *Lebensraum,* or, as I have frequently written, it may culminate in revolutions of desperation. In the long run, of course, there is the possibility of considerable growth (although nothing resembling the attainment of a Western standard of consumption). But no quick substantial improvement in their condition seems feasible within the next generation at least. The visions of Sir Charles Snow or Soviet Academician Sakharov for a gigantic transfer of wealth from the rich nations to the poor (20 percent of GNP is proposed) are simply fantasies. Since much of GNP is spatially nontransferrable or inappropriate, such a massive levy against GNP would imply shipments of up to 50 percent of much movable output. How this enormous flood of goods would be transported, allocated, absorbed, or maintained—*not to mention relinquished by the donor countries*—is nowhere analyzed by the proponents of such massive aid.

The implications of the ecological crisis for the advanced nations are not any less severe, although they are of a different kind. For it is clear that free industrial growth is just as disastrous for the Western nations as free population growth for those of the East and South. The worship in the West of a growing Gross National Product must be recognized as not only a deceptive but a very dangerous avatar; Kenneth Boulding has begun a campaign, in which I shall join him, to label this statistical monster Gross National Cost.

The necessity to bring our economic activities into a sustainable relationship with the resource capabilities and waste-absorption properties of the world, will pose two problems for the West. On the simpler level, a whole series of technological problems must be met. Fume-free transportation must be developed on land and air. The cult of disposablity must be replaced by that of reusability. Population stability must be attained through tax and other inducements, both to conserve resources and to preserve reasonable population densities. Many of these problems will tax our ingenuity, technical and socio-political, but the main problem they pose is not whether, but *how soon,* they can be solved.

But there is another, deeper question that the developed nations face—at least those that have capitalist economies. This problem can be stated as a crucial test as to who was right—John Stuart Mill or Karl Marx. Mill maintained, in his *Principles of Economics*, that the terminus of capitalist evolution would be a stationary state, in which the return to capital had fallen to insignificance, and a redistributive tax system would be able to capture any flows of income to the holders of scarce resources, such as land. In effect, he prophesied the transformation of capitalism, in an environment of abundance, into a balanced economy, in which the capitalist, both as the generator of change and as the main claimant on the surplus generated by change, would in fact undergo a painless euthanasia.

The Marxian view is, of course, quite the opposite. The very essence of capitalism, according to Marx, is expansion—which is to say, the capitalist, as a historical "type," finds his raison d'être in the insatiable search for additional money-wealth gained through the constant growth of the economic system. The idea of a "stationary" capitalism is, in Marxian eyes, a contradiction in terms, on a logical part with a democratic aristocracy or an industrial feudalism.

Is the Millian or the Marxian view correct? I do not think that we can yet say. Some economic growth is certainly compatible with a stabilized rate of resource use and disposal, for growth could take the form of the expenditure of additional labor on the improvement (aesthetic or technical) of the national environment. Indeed, insofar as education or cultural activity are forms of national output that require little resource use and result in little waste product, national output could be indefinitely expanded through these and similar activities. But there is no doubt that the main avenue of traditional capitalist accumulation would have to be considerably constrained; that net investment in mining and manufacturing would effectively cease; that the rate and kind of technological change would need to be supervised and probably greatly reduced; and that, as a consequence, the flow of profits would almost certainly fall.

Is this imaginable within a capitalist setting—that is, in a nation in which the business ideology permeates the views of nearly all groups and classes, and establishes the bounds of what is possible and natural, and what is not? Ordinarily I do not see how such a question could be answered in any way but negatively, for it is tantamount to asking a dominant class to acquiesce in the elimination of the very activities that sustain it. But this is an extraordinary challenge that may evoke an extraordinary response. Like the challenge posed by war, the ecological crisis affects all classes, and therefore may be sufficient to induce sociological changes that would be unthinkable in ordinary circumstances. The capitalist and managerial classes may see—perhaps even more clearly than the consuming masses—the nature and nearness of the ecological crisis, and may recognize that their only salvation (as human beings, let alone privileged human beings) is an occupational migration into governmental or other posts of power, or they may come to accept a smaller share of the national surplus, simply because they recognize that there is no alternative. When the enemy is nature, in other words, rather than another social class, it is at least imaginable that adjustments could be made that would be impossible in ordinary circumstances.[2]

There is, however, one last possibility to which I must also call attention. It is the possibility that the ecological crisis will simply result in the decline, or even destruction of Western civilization, and of the hegemony of the scientific-technological view that has achieved so much and cost us so dearly. Great challenges do not always bring great responses, especially when those responses must be sustained over long periods of time and require dramatic changes in life styles and attitudes. Even educated men today are able to deny the reality of the crisis they face: there is wild talk of farming the seas, of transporting men to the planets, of unspecified "miracles" of technology that will avert disaster. Glib as they are, however, at least these suggestions have a certain responsibility when compared with another and much more worrisome response: *je m'en fiche.* Can we really persuade the citizens of the Western world who are just now entering the heady atmosphere of a high-consumption way of life, that conservation, stability, frugality and a deep concern for the distant future must take priority over the personal indulgence for which they have been culturally prepared and which they are about to experience for the first time? Not the least danger of the ecological crisis, as I see it, is that tens and hundreds of millions will shrug their shoulders at the prospects ahead ("What has posterity ever done for us?"), and that the increasingly visible approach of ecological Armageddon will bring not repentance but Saturnalia.

Yet I cannot end this essay on such a note. For it seems to me that the ecological enthusiasts may be right when they speak of the deteriorating environment as providing the *possibility* for a new political rallying ground. If a New Deal, capable of engaging both

[2] Let me add a warning that it is not only capitalists who must make an unprecedented ideological adjustment. Socialists must also come to terms with the abandonment of the goal of industrial superabundance on which their vision of a transformed society rests. The stationary equilibrium imposed by the constraints of ecology requires at the very least a reformulation of the kind of economic society toward which socialism sets its course.

the efforts and the beliefs of this nation, is the last great hope to which we cling in the face of what seems otherwise to be an inevitable gradual worsening and coarsening of our style of life, it is possible that a determined effort to arrest the ecological decay might prove to be its underlying theme. Such an issue, immediate in the experience of all, carries an appeal that might allow vast improvements to be worked in the American environment, both urban and industrial. I cannot estimate the likelihood of such a political awakening, dependent as these matters are on the dice of personality and the outcome of events at home and abroad. But however slim the possibility of bringing about such a change, it does at least make the ecological crisis, unquestionably the gravest long-run threat of our times, potentially the source of its greatest short-term promise.

Study Questions

1. "Armageddon" means apocalyptic war—the battle that ultimately decides which of two opposing sides, such as the forces of good and evil, is victorious. Who are the parties fighting the "ecological armageddon"? In this context, would it be accurate to rename Emerson's essay "Psychological Armageddon"? Consider both parts of the new title.
2. Why does Heilbroner refer to the Ehrlichs' book as if it were his own? Why do the nature of his subject matter and his attitude toward it require a very personal framework?
3. The essay begins with a comical list of ecological fads. What is the purpose of this humorous opening? Does it do more than just soften the grim news that follows?
4. Trace the development of the metaphor of the earth as a spaceship. How does the metaphor determine diction and tone?
5. What laws seem to underlie the progression of the earth to the crisis point that Heilbroner predicts? Compare the operation of these laws with the laws and patterns that Kant sees guiding human destiny.
6. What does Heilbroner mean by the phrase "the dice of personality"?
7. In your opinion, which seems a more insurmountable crisis—the deteriorating environment or the reluctance of people to change their habits and attitudes?

MISCELLANEOUS
STATEMENTS

Chapter 2

The word that Ī-sā'iah the son of Ā'mŏz saw concerning Judah and Jerusalem.

2 And it shall come to pass in the last days, *that* the mountain of the Lord's house shall be established in the top of the mountains, and shall be exalted above the hills; and all nations shall flow unto it.

3 And many people shall go and say, Come ye, and let us go up to the mountain of the Lord, to the house of the God of Jacob; and he will teach us of his ways, and we will walk in his paths: for out of Zion shall go forth the law, and the word of the Lord from Jerusalem.

4 And he shall judge among the nations, and shall rebuke many people: and they shall beat their swords into plowshares, and their spears into pruning hooks: nation shall not lift up sword against nation, neither shall they learn war any more.

5 O house of Jacob, come ye, and let us walk in the light of the Lord.

Chapter 11

And there shall come forth a rod out of the stem of Jesse, and a Branch shall grow out of his roots:

2 And the Spirit of the Lord shall rest upon him, the spirit of wisdom and understanding, the spirit of counsel and might, the spirit of knowledge and of the fear of the Lord;

3 And shall make him of quick understanding in the fear of the Lord: and he shall not judge after the sight of his eyes, neither reprove after the hearing of his ears:

4 But with righteousness shall he judge the poor, and reprove with equity for the meek of the earth: and he shall smite the earth with the rod of his mouth, and with the breath of his lips shall he slay the wicked.

5 And righteousness shall be the girdle of his loins, and faithfulness the girdle of his reins.

6 The wolf also shall dwell with the lamb, and the leopard shall

lie down with the kid; and the calf and the young lion and the fat-
ling together; and a little child shall lead them.

7 And the cow and the bear shall feed; their young ones shall lie
down together: and the lion shall eat straw like the ox.

8 And the sucking child shall play on the hole of the asp, and the
weaned child shall put his hand on the cockatrice' den.

9 They shall not hurt nor destroy in all my holy mountain: for
the earth shall be full of the knowledge of the LORD, as the waters
cover the sea.

Chapter 32

Behold, a King shall reign in righteousness, and princes shall rule
in judgment.

2 And a man shall be as a hiding place from the wind, and a
covert from the tempest; as rivers of water in a dry place, as the
shadow of a great rock in a weary land.

3 And the eyes of them that see shall not be dim, and the ears of
them that hear shall hearken.

4 The heart also of the rash shall understand knowledge, and the
tongue of the stammerers shall be ready to speak plainly.

5 The vile person shall be no more called liberal, nor the churl
said *to be* bountiful.

6 For the vile person will speak villainy, and his heart will work
iniquity, to practise hypocrisy, and to utter error against the LORD,
to make empty the soul of the hungry; and he will cause the drink
of the thirsty to fail.

7 The instruments also of the churl *are* evil: he deviseth wicked
devices to destroy the poor with lying words, even when the needy
speaketh right.

8 But the liberal deviseth liberal things; and by liberal things
shall he stand.

9 ¶ Rise up, ye women that are at ease; hear my voice, ye careless
daughters; give ear unto my speech.

10 Many days and years shall ye be troubled, ye careless women:
for the vintage shall fail, the gathering shall not come.

11 Tremble, ye women that are at ease; be troubled, ye careless
ones: strip you, and make you bare, and gird *sackcloth* upon *your*
loins.

12 They shall lament for the teats, for the pleasant fields, for the
fruitful vine.

13 Upon the land of my people shall come up thorns *and* briers;
yea, upon all the houses of joy *in* the joyous city:

14 Because the palaces shall be forsaken; the multitude of the city shall be left; the forts and towers shall be for dens for ever, a joy of wild asses, a pasture of flocks;

15 Until the Spirit be poured upon us from on high, and the wilderness be a fruitful field, and the fruitful field be counted for a forest.

16 Then judgment shall dwell in the wilderness, and righteousness remain in the fruitful field.

17 And the work of righteousness shall be peace; and the effect of righteousness, quietness and assurance for ever.

18 And my people shall dwell in a peaceable habitation, and in sure dwellings, and in quiet resting places;

19 When it shall hail, coming down on the forest; and the city shall be low in a low place.

20 Blessed *are* ye that sow beside all waters, that send forth *thither* the feet of the ox and the ass.

Chapter 33

Woe to thee that spoilest, and thou *wast* not spoiled; and dealest treacherously, and they dealt not treacherously with thee! when thou shalt cease to spoil, thou shalt be spoiled; *and* when thou shalt make an end to deal treacherously, they shall deal treacherously with thee.

2 O Lord, be gracious unto us; we have waited for thee: be thou their arm every morning, our salvation also in the time of trouble.

3 At the noise of the tumult the people fled; at the lifting up of thyself the nations were scattered.

4 And your spoil shall be gathered *like* the gathering of the caterpillar: as the running to and fro of locusts shall he run upon them.

5 The Lord is exalted; for he dwelleth on high: he hath filled Zion with judgment and righteousness.

6 And wisdom and knowledge shall be the stability of thy times, *and* strength of salvation: the fear of the Lord *is* his treasure.

7 Behold, their valiant ones shall cry without: the ambassadors of peace shall weep bitterly.

8 The highways lie waste, the wayfaring man ceaseth: he hath broken the covenant, he hath despised the cities, he regardeth no man.

9 The earth mourneth *and* languisheth: Lebanon is ashamed *and* hewn down: Shăr'ŏn is like a wilderness; and Bā'shăn and Cär'mĕl shake off *their fruits.*

10 Now will I rise, saith the Lord; now will I be exalted; now will I lift up myself.

11 Ye shall conceive chaff, ye shall bring forth stubble: your breath, *as* fire, shall devour you.

12 And the people shall be *as* the burnings of lime: *as* thorns cut up shall they be burned in the fire.

13 ¶ Hear, ye *that are* far off, what I have done; and, ye *that are* near, acknowledge my might.

14 The sinners in Zion are afraid; fearfulness hath surprised the hypocrites. Who among us shall dwell with the devouring fire? who among us shall dwell with everlasting burnings?

15 He that walketh righteously, and speaketh uprightly; he that despiseth the gain of oppressions, that shaketh his hands from holding of bribes, that stoppeth his ears from hearing of blood, and shutteth his eyes from seeing evil;

16 He shall dwell on high; his place of defense *shall be* the munitions of rocks: bread shall be given him; his waters *shall be* sure.

17 Thine eyes shall see the King in his beauty: they shall behold the land that is very far off.

18 Thine heart shall meditate terror. Where *is* the scribe? where *is* the receiver? where *is* he that counted the towers?

19 Thou shalt not see a fierce people, a people of a deeper speech than thou canst perceive; of a stammering tongue, *that thou canst* not understand.

20 Look upon Zion, the city of our solemnities: thine eyes shall see Jerusalem a quiet habitation, a tabernacle *that* shall not be taken down; not one of the stakes thereof shall ever be removed, neither shall any of the cords thereof be broken.

21 But there the glorious LORD *will be* unto us a place of broad rivers *and* streams; wherein shall go no galley with oars, neither shall gallant ship pass thereby.

22 For the LORD *is* our judge, the LORD *is* our lawgiver, the LORD *is* our King; he will save us.

23 Thy tacklings are loosed; they could not well strengthen their mast; they could not spread the sail: then is the prey of a great spoil divided; the lame take the prey.

24 And the inhabitant shall not say, I am sick: the people that dwell therein *shall be* forgiven *their* iniquity.

Chapter 34

Come near, ye nations, to hear; and hearken, ye people: let the earth hear, and all that is therein; the world, and all things that come forth of it.

2 For the indignation of the LORD *is* upon all nations, and *his* fury upon all their armies: he hath utterly destroyed them, he hath delivered them to the slaughter.

3 Their slain also shall be cast out, and their stink shall come up out of their carcasses, and the mountains shall be melted with their blood.

4 And all the host of heaven shall be dissolved, and the heavens shall be rolled together as a scroll: and all their host shall fall down, as the leaf falleth off from the vine, and as a falling *fig* from the fig tree.

5 For my sword shall be bathed in heaven: behold, it shall come down upon Ĭd'ū-mē'á, and upon the people of my curse, to judgment.

6 The sword of the LORD is filled with blood, it is made fat with fatness, *and* with the blood of lambs and goats, with the fat of the kidneys of rams: for the LORD hath a sacrifice in Bŏz'ràh, and a great slaughter in the land of Id'ū-mē-á.

7 And the unicorns shall come down with them, and the bullocks with the bulls; and their land shall be soaked with blood, and their dust made fat with fatness.

8 For *it is* the day of the LORD's vengeance, *and* the year of recompenses for the controversy of Zion.

9 And the streams thereof shall be turned into pitch, and the dust thereof into brimstone, and the land thereof shall become burning pitch.

10 It shall not be quenched night nor day; the smoke thereof shall go up for ever: from generation to generation it shall lie waste; none shall pass through it for ever and ever.

11 ¶ But the cormorant and the bittern shall possess it; the owl also and the raven shall dwell in it: and he shall stretch out upon it the line of confusion, and the stones of emptiness.

12 They shall call the nobles thereof to the kingdom, but none *shall be* there, and all her princes shall be nothing.

13 And thorns shall come up in her palaces, nettles and brambles in the fortresses thereof: and it shall be a habitation of dragons, *and* a court for owls.

14 The wild beasts of the desert shall also meet with the wild

beasts of the island, and the satyr shall cry to his fellow; the screech owl also shall rest there, and find for herself a place of rest.

15 There shall the great owl make her nest, and lay, and hatch, and gather under her shadow: there shall the vultures also be gathered, every one with her mate.

16 ¶ Seek ye out of the book of the LORD, and read: no one of these shall fail, none shall want her mate: for my mouth it hath commanded, and his spirit it hath gathered them.

17 And he hath cast the lot for them, and his hand hath divided it unto them by line: they shall possess it for ever, from generation to generation shall they dwell therein.

Chapter 35

The wilderness and the solitary place shall be glad for them; and the desert shall rejoice, and blossom as the rose.

2 It shall blossom abundantly, and rejoice even with joy and singing: the glory of Lebanon shall be given unto it, the excellency of Cär′mĕl and Shăr′ŏn; they shall see the glory of the LORD, *and* the excellency of our God.

3 ¶ Strengthen ye the weak hands, and confirm the feeble knees.

4 Say to them *that are* of a fearful heart, Be strong, fear not: behold, your God will come *with* vengeance, *even* God *with* a recompense; he will come and save you.

5 Then the eyes of the blind shall be opened, and the ears of the deaf shall be unstopped.

6 Then shall the lame *man* leap as a hart, and the tongue of the dumb sing: for in the wilderness shall waters break out, and streams in the desert.

7 And the parched ground shall become a pool, and the thirsty land springs of water: in the habitation of dragons, where each lay, *shall be* grass with reeds and rushes.

8 And a highway shall be there, and a way, and it shall be called The way of holiness; the unclean shall not pass over it; but it *shall be* for those: the wayfaring men, though fools, shall not err *therein*.

9 No lion shall be there, nor *any* ravenous beast shall go up thereon, it shall not be found there; but the redeemed shall walk *there*:

10 And the ransomed of the LORD shall return, and come to Zion with songs and everlasting joy upon their heads: they shall obtain joy and gladness, and sorrow and sighing shall flee away.

Chapter 5

And seeing the multitudes, he went up into a mountain: and when he was set, his disciples came unto him:

2 And he opened his mouth, and taught them, saying,

3 Blessed *are* the poor in spirit: for theirs is the kingdom of heaven.

4 Blessed *are* they that mourn: for they shall be comforted.

5 Blessed *are* the meek: for they shall inherit the earth.

6 Blessed *are* they which do hunger and thirst after righteousness: for they shall be filled.

7 Blessed *are* the merciful: for they shall obtain mercy.

8 Blessed *are* the pure in heart: for they shall see God.

9 Blessed *are* the peacemakers: for they shall be called the children of God.

10 Blessed *are* they which are persecuted for righteousness' sake: for theirs is the kingdom of heaven.

11 Blessed are ye, when *men* shall revile you, and persecute *you,* and shall say all manner of evil against you falsely, for my sake.

12 Rejoice, and be exceeding glad: for great *is* your reward in heaven: for so persecuted they the prophets which were before you.

13 ¶ Ye are the salt of the earth: but if the salt have lost his savor, wherewith shall it be salted? it is thenceforth good for nothing, but to be cast out, and to be trodden under foot of men.

14 Ye are the light of the world. A city that is set on a hill cannot be hid.

15 Neither do men light a candle, and put it under a bushel, but on a candlestick; and it giveth light unto all that are in the house.

16 Let your light so shine before men, that they may see your good works, and glorify your Father which is in heaven.

17 ¶ Think not that I am come to destroy the law, or the prophets: I am not come to destroy, but to fulfil.

18 For verily I say unto you, Till heaven and earth pass, one jot or one tittle shall in no wise pass from the law, till all be fulfilled.

19 Whosoever therefore shall break one of these least commandments, and shall teach men so, he shall be called the least in the kingdom of heaven: but whosoever shall do and teach *them,* the same shall be called great in the kingdom of heaven.

20 For I say unto you, That except your righteousness shall ex-

ceed *the righteousness* of the scribes and Phȧr'ĭ-sēes̩, ye shall in no case enter into the kingdom of heaven.

21 ¶ Ye have heard that it was said by them of old time, Thou shalt not kill; and whosoever shall kill shall be in danger of the judgment:

22 But I say unto you, That whosoever is angry with his brother without a cause shall be in danger of the judgment: and whosoever shall say to his brother, Rā'cȧ, shall be in danger of the council: but whosoever shall say, Thou fool, shall be in danger of hell fire.

23 Therefore if thou bring thy gift to the altar, and there rememberest that thy brother hath aught against thee;

24 Leave there thy gift before the altar, and go thy way; first be reconciled to thy brother, and then come and offer thy gift.

25 Agree with thine adversary quickly, while thou art in the way with him; lest at any time the adversary deliver thee to the judge, and the judge deliver thee to the officer, and thou be cast into prison.

26 Verily I say unto thee, Thou shalt by no means come out thence, till thou hast paid the uttermost farthing.

27 ¶ Ye have heard that it was said by them of old time, Thou shalt not commit adultery:

28 But I say unto you, That whosoever looketh on a woman to lust after her hath committed adultery with her already in his heart.

29 And if thy right eye offend thee, pluck it out, and cast *it* from thee: for it is profitable for thee that one of thy members should perish, and not *that* thy whole body should be cast into hell.

30 And if thy right hand offend thee, cut it off, and cast *it* from thee: for it is profitable for thee that one of thy members should perish, and not *that* thy whole body should be cast into hell.

31 It hath been said, Whosoever shall put away his wife, let him give her a writing of divorcement:

32 But I say unto you, That whosoever shall put away his wife, saving for the cause of fornication, causeth her to commit adultery: and whosoever shall marry her that is divorced committeth adultery.

33 ¶ Again, ye have heard that it hath been said by them of old time, Thou shalt not forswear thyself, but shalt perform unto the Lord thine oaths:

34 But I say unto you, Swear not at all; neither by heaven; for it is God's throne:

35 Nor by the earth; for it is his footstool: neither by Jerusalem; for it is the city of the great King.

36 Neither shalt thou swear by thy head, because thou canst not make one hair white or black.

37 But let your communication be, Yea, yea; Nay, nay: for whatsoever is more than these cometh of evil.

38 ¶ Ye have heard that it hath been said, An eye for an eye, and a tooth for a tooth:

39 But I say unto you, That ye resist not evil: but whosoever shall smite thee on thy right cheek, turn to him the other also.

40 And if any man will sue thee at the law, and take away thy coat, let him have *thy* cloak also.

41 And whosoever shall compel thee to go a mile, go with him twain.

42 Give to him that asketh thee, and from him that would borrow of thee turn not thou away.

43 ¶ Ye have heard that it hath been said, Thou shalt love thy neighbor, and hate thine enemy.

44 But I say unto you, Love your enemies, bless them that curse you, do good to them that hate you, and pray for them which despitefully use you, and persecute you;

45 That ye may be the children of your Father which is in heaven: for he maketh his sun to rise on the evil and on the good, and sendeth rain on the just and on the unjust.

46 For if ye love them which love you, what reward have ye? do not even the publicans the same?

47 And if ye salute your brethren only, what do ye more *than others?* do not even the publicans so?

48 Be ye therefore perfect, even as your Father which is in heaven is perfect.

Chapter 6

Take heed that ye do not your alms before men, to be seen of them: otherwise ye have no reward of your Father which is in heaven.

2 Therefore when thou doest *thine* alms, do not sound a trumpet before thee, as the hypocrites do in the synagogues and in the streets, that they may have glory of men. Verily I say unto you, They have their reward.

3 But when thou doest alms, let not thy left hand know what thy right hand doeth:

4 That thine alms may be in secret; and thy Father which seeth in secret himself shall reward thee openly.

5 ¶ And when thou prayest, thou shalt not be as the hypocrites *are:* for they love to pray standing in the synagogues and in the

corners of the streets, that they may be seen of men. Verily I say unto you, They have their reward.

6 But thou, when thou prayest, enter into thy closet, and when thou hast shut thy door, pray to thy Father which is in secret; and thy Father which seeth in secret shall reward thee openly.

7 But when ye pray, use not vain repetitions, as the heathen *do*: for they think that they shall be heard for their much speaking.

8 Be not ye therefore like unto them: for your Father knoweth what things ye have need of, before ye ask him.

9 After this manner therefore pray ye: Our Father which art in heaven, Hallowed be thy name.

10 Thy kingdom come. Thy will be done in earth, as *it is* in heaven.

11 Give us this day our daily bread.

12 And forgive us our debts, as we forgive our debtors.

13 And lead us not into temptation, but deliver us from evil: For thine is the kingdom, and the power, and the glory, for ever. Amen.

14 For if ye forgive men their trespasses, your heavenly Father will also forgive you:

15 But if ye forgive not men their trespasses, neither will your Father forgive your trespasses.

16 ¶ Moreover when ye fast, be not, as the hypocrites, of a sad countenance: for they disfigure their faces, that they may appear unto men to fast. Verily I say unto you, They have their reward.

17 But thou, when thou fastest, anoint thine head, and wash thy face;

18 That thou appear not unto men to fast, but unto thy Father which is in secret: and thy Father which seeth in secret shall reward thee openly.

19 ¶ Lay not up for yourselves treasures upon earth, where moth and rust doth corrupt, and where thieves break through and steal:

20 But lay up for yourselves treasures in heaven, where neither moth nor rust doth corrupt, and where thieves do not break through nor steal:

21 For where your treasure is, there will your heart be also.

22 The light of the body is the eye: if therefore thine eye be single, thy whole body shall be full of light.

23 But if thine eye be evil, thy whole body shall be full of darkness. If therefore the light that is in thee be darkness, how great *is* that darkness!

24 ¶ No man can serve two masters: for either he will hate the one, and love the other; or else he will hold to the one, and despise the other. Ye cannot serve God and mammon.

25 Therefore I say unto you, Take no thought for your life, what ye shall eat, or what ye shall drink; nor yet for your body, what ye shall put on. Is not the life more than meat, and the body than raiment?

26 Behold the fowls of the air: for they sow not, neither do they reap, nor gather into barns; yet your heavenly Father feedeth them. Are ye not much better than they?

27 Which of you by taking thought can add one cubit unto his stature?

28 And why take ye thought for raiment? Consider the lilies of the field, how they grow; they toil not, neither do they spin:

29 And yet I say unto you, That even Solomon in all his glory was not arrayed like one of these.

30 Wherefore, if God so clothe the grass of the field, which to-day is, and to-morrow is cast into the oven, *shall he* not much more *clothe* you, O ye of little faith?

31 Therefore take no thought, saying, What shall we eat? or, What shall we drink? or, Wherewithal shall we be clothed?

32 (For after all these things do the Gĕn'tīles seek:) for your heavenly Father knoweth that ye have need of all these things.

33 But seek ye first the kingdom of God, and his righteousness; and all these things shall be added unto you.

34 Take therefore no thought for the morrow: for the morrow shall take thought for the things of itself. Sufficient unto the day *is* the evil thereof.

Chapter 7

Judge not, that ye be not judged.

2 For with what judgment ye judge, ye shall be judged: and with what measure ye mete, it shall be measured to you again.

3 And why beholdest thou the mote that is in thy brother's eye, but considerest not the beam that is in thine own eye?

4 Or how wilt thou say to thy brother, Let me pull out the mote out of thine eye; and, behold, a beam *is* in thine own eye?

5 Thou hypocrite, first cast out the beam out of thine own eye; and then shalt thou see clearly to cast out the mote out of thy brother's eye.

6 ¶ Give not that which is holy unto the dogs, neither cast ye your pearls before swine, lest they trample them under their feet, and turn again and rend you.

7 ¶ Ask, and it shall be given you; seek, and ye shall find; knock, and it shall be opened unto you:

8 For every one that asketh receiveth; and he that seeketh findeth; and to him that knocketh it shall be opened.

9 Or what man is there of you, whom if his son ask bread, will he give him a stone?

10 Or if he ask a fish, will he give him a serpent?

11 If ye then, being evil, know how to give good gifts unto your children, how much more shall your Father which is in heaven give good things to them that ask him?

12 Therefore all things whatsoever ye would that men should do to you, do ye even so to them: for this is the law and the prophets.

13 ¶ Enter ye in at the strait gate: for wide *is* the gate, and broad *is* the way, that leadeth to destruction, and many there be which go in thereat:

14 Because strait *is* the gate, and narrow *is* the way, which leadeth unto life, and few there be that find it.

15 ¶ Beware of false prophets, which come to you in sheep's clothing, but inwardly they are ravening wolves.

16 Ye shall know them by their fruits. Do men gather grapes of thorns, or figs of thistles?

17 Even so every good tree bringeth forth good fruit; but a corrupt tree bringeth forth evil fruit.

18 A good tree cannot bring forth evil fruit, neither *can* a corrupt tree bring forth good fruit.

19 Every tree that bringeth not forth good fruit is hewn down, and cast into the fire.

20 Wherefore by their fruits ye shall know them.

21 ¶ Not every one that saith unto me, Lord, Lord, shall enter into the kingdom of heaven; but he that doeth the will of my Father which is in heaven.

22 Many will say to me in that day, Lord, Lord, have we not prophesied in thy name? and in thy name have cast out devils? and in thy name done many wonderful works?

23 And then will I profess unto them, I never knew you: depart from me, ye that work iniquity.

24 ¶ Therefore whosoever heareth these sayings of mine, and doeth them, I will liken him unto a wise man, which built his house upon a rock:

25 And the rain descended, and the floods came, and the winds blew, and beat upon that house; and it fell not: for it was founded upon a rock.

26 And every one that heareth these sayings of mine, and doeth them not, shall be likened unto a foolish man, which built his house upon the sand:

27 And the rain descended, and the floods came, and the winds blew, and beat upon that house; and it fell: and great was the fall of it.

28 And it came to pass, when Jesus had ended these sayings, the people were astonished at his doctrine:

29 For he taught them as *one* having authority, and not as the scribes.

O V I D

The Metamorphoses—Creation

TRANSLATED BY HORACE GREGORY

The first millennium was the age of gold:
Then living creatures trusted one another;
People did well without the thought of ill:
Nothing forbidden in a book of laws,
No fears, no prohibitions read in bronze,
Or in the sculptured face of judge and master.
Even the pine tree stood on its own hills,
Nor did it fall to sail uncharted seas;
All that men knew of earth were shores of home,
No cities climbed behind high walls and bridges;
No brass-lipped trumpets called, nor clanging swords,
Nor helmets marched the streets, country and town
Had never heard of war: and seasons travelled
Through the years of peace. The innocent earth
Learned neither spade nor plough; she gave her
Riches as fruit hangs from the tree: grapes
Dropping from the vine, cherry, strawberry
Ripened in silver shadows of the mountain,
And in the shade of Jove's miraculous tree,
The falling acorn. Springtide the single
Season of the year, and through that hour
The soft breath of the south in flowering leaf,
In white waves of the wheat across the meadows,
Season of milk and wine in amber streams
And honey pouring from the green-lipped oak.

After old Saturn fell to Death's dark country
Straitly Jove ruled the world with silver charm,

Less radiant than gold, less false than brass.
And it was then that Jove split up the year
In shifty Autumn, wild Winter, and short Spring,
Summer that glared with heat: the winter wind
Gleamed white with ice that streamed on field and river;
Then men built walls against both sun and wind—
Their elder shelters had been caves or boughs.
Now grain was planted and the plough pierced earth;
The driven ox whimpered beneath the yoke.

Third came the age of bronze, less soft than silver,
And men in bronze were quick with sword and spear,
Yet all feared Jove. Then came the age of iron
And from it poured the very blood of evil:
Piety, Faith, Love, and Truth changed to Deceit,
Violence, the Tricks of Trade, Usury, Profit;
Ignorant of contrary winds, men sailed the seas:
The mountain oak, the pine were felled and stripped,
Their long beams swaying above uncharted Ocean.
Then land, once like the gift of sunlit air,
Was cut in properties, estates, and holdings:
Not only crops were hoarded; men invaded
Entrails of earth down deeper than the river
Where Death's shades weave in darkness underground;
Where hidden from the sight of men Jove's treasures
Were locked in night. There, in his sacred mines,
All that drives men to avarice and murder
Shone in the dark: the loot was dragged to light
And War, inspired by curse of iron and gold,
Lifted blood-clotted hands and marched the earth.
Men fed on loot and lust; the guest feared host;
Neighbour looked warily with smiles at neighbour;
And fathers had good reasons to distrust
Their eager sons-in-law. If brothers loved
Each other, the sight was rare, and watchful
Husbands prayed for death of wives; stepmothers
Made poison a dessert at dinner—sons
Counted the hours that led to fathers' graves.
Piety was overthrown, and Astraea,
Last-born sister of the skies, left the blood-
Sweating earth to drink its blood, and turning
Lightly swiftly found her place in heaven.

CHRISTOPHER MARLOWE

The Passionate Shepherd to His Love

Come live with me and be my love,
And we will all the pleasures prove
That valleys, groves, hills, and fields,
Woods, or steepy mountain yields.

And we will sit upon the rocks,
Seeing the shepherds feed their flocks,
By shallow rivers to whose falls
Melodious birds sing madrigals.

And I will make thee beds of roses
And a thousand fragrant posies,
A cap of flowers, and a kirtle
Embroidered all with leaves of myrtle;

A gown made of the finest wool
Which from our pretty lambs we pull;
Fair linèd slippers for the cold,
With buckles of the purest gold;

A belt of straw and ivy buds,
With coral clasps and amber studs:
And if these pleasures may thee move.
Come live with me, and be my love.

The shepherds' swains shall dance and sing
For thy delight each May morning:
If these delights thy mind may move,
Then live with me and be my love.

SIR WALTER RALEGH

The Nymph's Reply to the Shepherd

If all the world and love were young,
And truth in every shepherd's tongue,
These pretty pleasures might me move
To live with thee and be thy love.

Time drives the flocks from field to fold
When rivers rage and rocks grow cold,
And Philomel becometh dumb;
The rest complains of cares to come.

The flowers do fade, and wanton fields
To wayward winter reckoning yields;
A honey tongue, a heart of gall,
Is fancy's spring, but sorrow's fall.

Thy gowns, thy shoes, thy beds of roses,
Thy cap, thy kirtle, and thy posies
Soon break, soon wither, soon forgotten,—
In folly ripe, in reason rotten.

Thy belt of straw and ivy buds,
Thy coral clasps and amber studs,
All these in me no means can move
To come to thee and be thy love.

But could youth last and love still breed,
Had joys no date nor age no need,
Then these delights my mind might move
To live with thee and be thy love.

WILLIAM BLAKE

The Shepherd

How sweet is the Shepherd's sweet lot!
From the morn to the evening he strays;
He shall follow his sheep all the day,
And his tongue shall be filled with praise.

For he hears the lamb's innocent call,
And he hears the ewe's tender reply;
He is watchful while they are in peace,
For they know when their Shepherd is nigh.

Night

The sun descending in the west,
The evening star does shine;
The birds are silent in their nest,
And I must seek for mine.
The moon like a flower
In heaven's high bower,
With silent delight
Sits and smiles on the night.

Farewell, green fields and happy groves,
Where flocks have took delight.
Where lambs have nibbled, silent moves
The feet of angels bright;
Unseen they pour blessing,
And joy without ceasing,
On each bud and blossom,
And each sleeping bosom.

They look in every thoughtless nest,
Where birds are cover'd warm;
They visit caves of every beast.
To keep them all from harm.
If they see any weeping
That should have been sleeping,
They pour sleep on their head,
And sit down by their bed.

When wolves and tygers howl for prey,
They pitying stand and weep;
Seeking to drive their thirst away,
And keep them from the sheep;
But if they rush dreadful,
The angels, most heedful,
Receive each mild spirit,
New worlds to inherit.

And there the lion's ruddy eyes
Shall flow with tears of gold,
And pitying the tender cries,
And walking round the fold,
Saying "Wrath, by his meekness,

"And by his health, sickness
"Is driven away
"From our immortal day.

"And now beside thee, bleating lamb,
"I can lie down and sleep;
"Or think on him who bore thy name,
"Graze after thee and weep.
"For, wash'd in life's river,
"My bright mane for ever
"Shall shine like the gold
"As I guard o'er the fold."

The Divine Image

To Mercy, Pity, Peace, and Love
All pray in their distress;
And to these virtues of delight
Return their thankfulness.

For Mercy, Pity, Peace, and Love
Is God, our father dear,
And Mercy, Pity, Peace, and Love
Is Man, his child and care.

For Mercy has a human heart,
Pity a human face,
And Love, the human form divine,
And Peace, the human dress.

Then every man, of every clime,
That prays in his distress,
Prays to the human form divine,
Love, Mercy, Pity, Peace.

And all must love the human form,
In heathen, turk, or jew;
Where Mercy, Love, & Pity dwell
There God is dwelling too.

A Divine Image

Cruelty has a Human Heart,
And Jealousy a Human Face;
Terror the Human Form Divine,
And Secrecy the Human Dress.

The Human Dress is forged Iron,
The Human Form a fiery Forge,
The Human Face a Furnace seal'd,
The Human Heart its hungry Gorge.

The Clod & the Pebble

"Love seeketh not Itself to please,
"Nor for itself hath any care,
"But for another gives its ease,
"And builds a Heaven in Hell's despair."

So sang a little Clod of Clay
Trodden with the cattle's feet,
But a Pebble of the brook
Warbled out these metres meet:

"Love seekth only Self to please,
"To bind another to Its delight,
"Joys in another's loss of ease,
"And builds a Hell in Heaven's despite."

The Garden of Love

I went to the Garden of Love,
And saw what I never had seen:
A Chapel was built in the midst,
Where I used to play on the green.

And the gates of this Chapel were shut,
And "Thou shalt not" writ over the door;
So I turn'd to the Garden of Love
That so many sweet flowers bore;

And I saw it was filled with graves,
And tomb-stones where flowers should be;
And Priests in black gowns were walking their rounds,
And binding with briars my joys & desires.

London

I wander thro' each charter'd street,
Near where the charter'd Thames does flow,
And mark in every face I meet
Marks of weakness, marks of woe.

In every cry of every Man,
In every Infant's cry of fear,
In every voice, in every ban,
The mind-forg'd manacles I hear.

How the Chimney-sweeper's cry
Every black'ning Church appalls;
And the hapless Soldier's sigh
Runs in blood down Palace walls.

But most thro' midnight streets I hear
How the youthful Harlot's curse
Blasts the new born Infant's tear,
And blights with plagues the Marriage hearse.

To Tirzah

Whate'er is Born of Mortal Birth
Must be consumed with the Earth
To rise from Generation free:
Then what have I to do with thee?

The Sexes sprung from Shame & Pride,
Blow'd in the morn; in evening died;
But Mercy chang'd Death into Sleep;
The Sexes rose to work & weep.

Thou, Mother of my Mortal part,
With cruelty didst mould my Heart,
And with false self-decieving tears
Didst bind my Nostrils, Eyes, & Ears:

Didst close my Tongue in senseless clay,
And me to Mortal Life betray.
The Death of Jesus set me free:
Then what have I to do with thee?

The Book of Thel

PLATE I

Thel's Motto.

Does the Eagle know what is in the pit?
Or wilt thou go ask the Mole?
Can Wisdom be put in a silver rod?
Or love in a golden bowl?

PLATE I

I

The daughters of Mne Seraphim led round their sunny
flocks,
All but the youngest: she in paleness sought the secret air,
To fade away like morning beauty from her mortal day:
Down by the river of Adona her soft voice is heard,
And thus her gentle lamentation falls like morning dew:

"O life of this our spring! why fades the lotus of the water,
"Why fade these children of the spring, born but to smile
& fall?
"Ah! Thel is like a wat'ry bow, and like a parting cloud;
"Like a reflection in a glass; like shadows in the water;
"Like dreams of infants, like a smile upon an infant's face;
"Like the dove's voice; like transient day; like music in the
air.
"Ah! gentle may I lay me down, and gentle rest my head,
"And gentle sleep the sleep of death, and gentle hear the
voice
"Of him that walketh in the garden in the evening time."

The Lilly of the valley, breathing in the humble grass,
Answer'd the lovely maid and said: "I am a wat'ry weed,
"And I am very small and love to dwell in lowly vales;
"So weak, the gilded butterfly scarce perches on my head.
"Yet I am visited from heaven, and he that smiles on all

"Walks in the valley and each morn over me spreads his
    hand,
"Saying, 'Rejoice, thou humble grass, thou new-born lilly
    flower,
" 'Thou gentle maid of silent valleys and of modest brooks;
" 'For thou shalt be clothed in light, and fed with morning
    manna,
" 'Till summer's heat melts thee beside the fountains and
    the springs
" 'To flourish in eternal vales.' Then why should Thel com-
    plain?

PLATE 2

"Why should the mistress of the vales of Har utter a sigh?"

She ceas'd & smil'd in tears, then sat down in her silver
    shrine.

Thel answer'd: "O thou little virgin of the peaceful valley,
"Giving to those that cannot crave, the voiceless, the o'er-
    tired;
"Thy breath doth nourish the innocent lamb, he smells thy
    milky garments,
"He crops thy flowers while thou sittest smiling in his face,
"Wiping his mild and meekin mouth from all contagious
    taints.
"Thy wine doth purify the golden honey; thy perfume,
"Which thou dost scatter on every little blade of grass that
    springs,
"Revives the milked cow, & tames the fire-breathing steed.
"But Thel is like a faint cloud kindled at the rising sun:
"I vanish from my pearly throne, and who shall find my
    place?"

"Queen of the vales," the Lilly answer'd, "ask the tender
    cloud,
"And it shall tell thee why it glitters in the morning sky,
"And why it scatters its bright beauty thro' the humid air,
"Descend, O little Cloud, & hover before the eyes of Thel."

The Cloud descended, and the Lilly bow'd her modest head
And went to mind her numerous charge among the verdant
    grass.

PLATE 3

II

"O little Cloud," the virgin said, "I charge thee tell to me
"Why thou complainest not when in one hour thou fade
    away:
"Then we shall seek thee, but not find. Ah! Thel is like to
    thee:
"I pass away: yet I complain, and no one hears my voice."

The Cloud then shew'd his golden head & his bright form
    emerg'd,
Hovering and glittering on the air before the face of Thel.

"O virgin, know'st thou not our steeds drink of the golden
    springs
"Where Luvah doth renew his horses? Look'st thou on my
    youth,
"And fearest thou, because I vanish and am seen no more,
"Nothing remains? O maid, I tell thee, when I pass away
"It is to tenfold life, to love, to peace and raptures holy:
"Unseen descending, weigh my light wings upon blamy
    flowers,
"And court the fair-eyed dew to take me to her shining tent:
"The weeping virgin, trembling kneels before the risen sun,
"Till we arise link'd in a golden band and never part,
"But walk united, bearing food to all our tender flowers."

    "Dost thou, O little Cloud? I fear that I am not like thee,
"For I walk thro' the vales of Har, and smell the sweetest
    flowers,
"But I feed not the little flowers; I hear the warbling birds,
"But I feed not the warbling birds; they fly and seek their
    food:
"But Thel delights in these no more, because I fade away;
"And all shall say, 'Without a use this shining woman liv'd,
" 'Or did she only live to be at death the food of worms?' "

The Cloud reclin'd upon his airy throne and answer'd thus:

"Then if thou art the food of worms, O virgin of the skies,
"How great thy use, how great thy blessing! Every thing that
    lives
"Lives not alone nor for itself. Fear not, and I will call
"The weak worm from its lowly bed, and thou shalt hear its
    voice.

"Come forth, worm of the silent valley, to thy pensive queen."

The helpless worm arose, and sat upon the Lilly's leaf,
And the bright Cloud sail'd on, to find his partner in the vale.

PLATE 4

III

Then Thel astonish'd view'd the Worm upon its dewy bed.

"Art thou a Worm? Image of weakness, art thou but a Worm?
"I see thee like an infant wrapped in the Lilly's leaf.
"Ah! weep not, little voice, thou canst not speak, but thou canst weep.
"Is this a Worm? I see thee lay helpless & naked, weeping,
"And none to answer, none to cherish thee with mother's smiles."

The Clod of Clay heard the Worm's voice & rais'd her pitying head:
She bow'd over the weeping infant, and her life exhal'd
In milky fondness: then on Thel she fix'd her humble eyes.

"O beauty of the vales of Har! we live not for ourselves.
"Thou seest me the meanest thing, and so I am indeed.
"My bosom of itself is cold, and of itself is dark;

PLATE 5

"But he, that loves the lowly, pours his oil upon my head,
"And kisses me, and binds his nuptial bands around my breast,
"And says: 'Thou mother of my children, I have loved thee
"'And I have given thee a crown that none can take away.'
"But how this is, sweet maid, I know not, and I cannot know;
"I ponder, and I cannot ponder; yet I live and love."
    The daughter of beauty wip'd her pitying tears with her white veil,
And said: "Alas! I knew not this, and therefore did I weep.

"That God would love a Worm I knew, and punish the evil
    foot
"That wilful bruis'd its helpless form; but that he cherish'd
    it
"With milk and oil I never knew, and therefore did I weep;
"And I complain'd in the mild air, because I fade away,
"And lay me down in thy cold bed, and leave my shining
    lot."

"Queen of the vales," the matron Clay answer'd, "I heard
    thy sighs,
"And all thy moans flew o'er my roof, but I have call'd them
    down.
"Wilt thou, O Queen, enter my house? 'Tis given thee to
    enter
"And to return: fear nothing, enter with thy virgin feet."

PLATE 6

IV

The eternal gates' terrific porter lifted the northern bar:
Thel enter'd in & saw the secrets of the land unknown.
She saw the couches of the dead, & where the fibrous roots
Of every heart on earth infixes deep its restless twists:
A land of sorrows & of tears where never smile was seen.

She wander'd in the land of clouds thro' valleys dark, list'n-
    ing
Dolours & lamentations; waiting oft beside a dewy grave
She stood in silence, list'ning to the voices of the ground,
Till to her own grave plot she came, & there she sat down,
And heard this voice of sorrow breathed from the hollow
    pit.

"Why cannot the Ear be closed to its own destruction?
"Or the glist'ning Eye to the poison of a smile?
"Why are Eyelids stor'd with arrows ready drawn,
"Where a thousand fighting men in ambush lie?
"Or an Eye of gifts & graces show'ring fruits & coined gold?
"Why a Tongue impress'd with honey from every wind?

"Why an Ear, a whirlpool fierce to draw creations in?
"Why a Nostril wide inhaling terror, trembling, & affright?

"Why a tender curb upon the youthful burning boy?
"Why a little curtain of flesh on the bed of our desire?"

The Virgin started from her seat, & with a shriek
Fled back unhinder'd till she came into the vales of Har.

PERCY BYSSHE SHELLEY

Declaration of Rights

I

Government has no rights; it is a delegation from several individuals for the purpose of securing their own. It is therefore just, only so far as it exists by their consent, useful only so far as it operates to their well-being.

II

If these individuals think that the form of government which they, or their forefathers constituted is ill adapted to produce their happiness, they have a right to change it.

III

Government is devised for the security of rights. The rights of man are liberty, and an equal participation of the commonage of nature.

IV

As the benefit of the governed, is, or ought to be the origin of government, no men can have any authority that does not expressly emanate from their will.

V

Though all governments are not so bad as that of Turkey, yet none are so good as they might be; the majority of every country have a right to perfect their government, the minority should not disturb them, they ought to secede, and form their own system in their own way.

VI

All have a right to an equal share in the benefits, and burdens of government. Any disabilities for opinion, imply by their existence, barefaced tyranny on the side of government, ignorant slavishness on the side of the governed.

VII

The rights of man, in the present state of society, are only to be secured by some degree of coercion to be exercised on their violator. The sufferer has a right that the degree of coercion employed be as slight as possible.

VIII

It may be considered as a plain proof of the hollowness of any proposition, if power be used to enforce instead of reason to persuade its admission. Government is never supported by fraud until it cannot be supported by reason.

IX

No man has a right to disturb the public peace, by personally resisting the execution of a law however bad. He ought to acquiesce, using at the same time the utmost powers of his reason, to promote its repeal.

X

A man must have a right to act in a certain manner before it can be his duty. He may, before he ought.

XI

A man has a right to think as his reason directs, it is a duty he owes to himself to think with freedom, that he may act from conviction.

XII

A man has a right to unrestricted liberty of discussion, falsehood is a scorpion that will sting itself to death.

XIII

A man has not only a right to express his thoughts, but it is his duty to do so.

XIV

No law has a right to discourage the practice of truth. A man ought to speak the truth on every occasion, a duty can never be criminal, what is not criminal cannot be injurious.

XV

Law cannot make what is in its nature virtuous or innocent, to be criminal, any more than it can make what is criminal to be innocent. Government cannot make a law, it can only pronounce that which was the law before its organization, viz. the moral result of the imperishable relations of things.

XVI

The present generation cannot bind their posterity. The few cannot promise for the many.

XVII

No man has a right to do an evil thing that good may come.

XVIII

Expediency is inadmissible in morals. Politics are only sound when conducted on principles of morality. They are, in fact, the morals of nations.

XIX

Man has no right to kill his brother, it is no excuse that he does so in uniform. He only adds the infamy of servitude to the crime of murder.

XX

Man, whatever be his country, has the same rights in one place as another, the rights of universal citizenship.

XXI

The government of a country ought to be perfectly indifferent to every opinion. Religious differences, the bloodiest and most rancorous of all, spring from partiality.

XXII

A delegation of individuals, for the purpose of securing their rights, can have no undelegated power of restraining the expression of their opinion.

XXIII

Belief is involuntary; nothing involuntary is meritorious or reprehensible. A man ought not to be considered worse or better for his belief.

XXIV

A Christian, a Deist, a Turk, and a Jew, have equal rights: they are men and brethren.

XXV

If a person's religious ideas correspond not with your own, love him nevertheless. How different would yours have been had the chance of birth placed you in Tartary or India!

XXVI

Those who believe that Heaven is, what earth has been, a monopoly in the hands of a favoured few, would do well to reconsider their opinion: if they find that it came from their priest or their grandmother, they could not do better than reject it.

XXVII

No man has a right to be respected for any other possessions, but those of virtue and talents. Titles are tinsel, power a corruptor, glory a bubble, and excessive wealth, a libel on its possessor.

XXVIII

No man has a right to monopolise more than he can enjoy; what the rich give to the poor, whilst millions are starving, is not a perfect favour, but an imperfect right.

XXIX

Every man has a right to a certain degree of leisure and liberty, because it is his duty to attain a certain degree of knowledge. He may before he ought.

XXX

Sobriety of body and mind is necessary to those who would be free; because, without sobriety a high sense of philanthropy cannot actuate the heart, nor cool and determined courage execute its dictates.

XXXI

The only use of government is to repress the vices of man. If man were to-day sinless, to-morrow he would have a right to demand that government and all its evils should cease.

Man! thou whose rights are here declared, be no longer forgetful of the loftiness of thy destination. Think of thy rights; of those possessions which will give thee virtue and wisdom, by which thou mayest arrive at happiness and freedom. They are declared to thee by one who knows thy dignity, for every hour does his heart swell with honourable pride in the contemplation of what thou mayest attain, by one who is not forgetful of thy degeneracy, for every moment brings home to him the bitter conviction of what thou art.

Awake!—arise!—or be for ever fallen.

The Bill of Rights

ARTICLE I

Congress shall make no law respecting an establishment of religion, or prohibiting the free exercise thereof; or abridging the freedom of speech or of the press; or the right of the people peaceably to assemble and to petition the Government for a redress of grievances.

ARTICLE II

A well-regulated militia being necessary to the security of a free State, the right of the people to keep and bear arms shall not be infringed.

ARTICLE III

No soldier shall, in time of peace, be quartered in any house without the consent of the owner, nor in time of war but in a manner to be prescribed by law.

ARTICLE IV

The right of the people to be secure in their persons, houses, papers, and effects, against unreasonable searches and seizures, shall not be violated, and no warrants shall issue but upon probable cause, supported by oath or affirmation, and particularly describing the place to be searched, and the persons or things to be seized.

ARTICLE V

No person shall be held to answer for a capital or other infamous crime unless on a presentment or indictment of a Grand Jury, except in cases arising in the land or naval forces, or in the militia, when in actual service, in time of war or public danger; nor shall any person be subject for the same offense to be twice put in jeopardy of life or limb; nor shall be compelled in any criminal case to be a witness against himself, nor be deprived of life, liberty, or property, without due process of law; nor shall private property be taken for public use without just compensation.

ARTICLE VI

In all criminal prosecutions, the accused shall enjoy the right to a speedy and public trial, by an impartial jury of the State and district wherein the crime shall have been committed, which districts shall have been previously ascertained by law, and to be informed of the nature and cause of the accusation; to be confronted with the witnesses against him; to have compulsory process for obtaining witnesses in his favor, and to have the assistance of counsel for his defense.

ARTICLE VII

In suits at common law, where the value in controversy shall exceed twenty dollars, the right of trial by jury shall be preserved, and no fact tried by a jury shall be otherwise reexamined in any court of the United States than according to the rules of the common law.

ARTICLE VIII

Excessive bail shall not be required, nor excessive fines imposed, nor cruel and unusual punishments inflicted.

ARTICLE IX

The enumeration in the Constitution of certain rights shall not be construed to deny or disparage others retained by the people.

ARTICLE X

The powers not delegated to the United States by the Constitution, nor prohibited by it to the States, are reserved to the States respectively, or to the people.

October 1966
BLACK PANTHER PARTY
PLATFORM AND PROGRAM

What We Want
What We Believe

1. We want freedom. We want power to determine the destiny of our Black Community.

We believe that black people will not be free until we are able to determine our destiny.

2. We want full employment for our people.

We believe that the federal government is responsible and obligated to give every man employment or a guaranteed income. We believe that if the white American businessmen will not give full employment, then the means of production should be taken from the businessmen and placed in the community so that the people of the community can organize and employ all of its people and give a high standard of living.

3. We want an end to the robbery by the CAPITALIST of our Black Community.

We believe that this racist government has robbed us and now we are demanding the overdue debt of forty acres and two mules. Forty acres and two mules was promised 100 years ago as restitution for slave labor and mass murder of black people. We will accept the payment in currency which will be distributed to our many communities. The Germans are now aiding the Jews in Israel for the genocide of the Jewish people. The Germans murdered six million Jews. The American racist has taken part in the slaughter of over fifty million black people; therefore, we feel that this is a modest demand that we make.

4. We want decent housing, fit for shelter of human beings.

We believe that if the white landlords will not give decent housing to our Black Community, then the housing and the land should be made into cooperatives so that our community, with government aid, can build and make decent housing for its people.

5. We want education for our people that exposes the true nature of this decadent American society. We want education that teaches us our true history and our role in the present-day society.

We believe in an educational system that will give to our people a knowledge of self. If a man does not have knowledge of himself and his position in society and the world, then he has little chance to relate to anything else.

6. We want all black men to be exempt from military service.

We believe that black people should not be forced to fight in the military service to defend a racist government that does not protect us. We will not fight and kill other people of color in the world who, like black people, are being victimized by the white racist government of America. We will protect ourselves from the force and violence of the racist police and the racist military, by whatever means necessary.

7. We want an immediate end to POLICE BRUTALITY and MURDER of black people.

We believe we can end police brutality in our Black Community by organizing black self-defense groups that are dedicated to defending our Black Community from racist police oppression and brutality. The Second Amendment to the Constitution of the United States gives a right to bear arms. We therefore believe that all black people should arm themselves for self-defense.

8. We want freedom for all black men held in federal, state, county and city prisons and jails.

We believe that all black people should be released from the many jails and prisons because they have not received a fair and impartial trial.

9. We want all black people when brought to trial to be tried in court by a jury of their peer group or people from their Black Communities, as defined by the Constitution of the United States.

We believe that the courts should follow the United States Constitution so that black people will receive fair trials. The Fourteenth Amendment of the U.S. Constitution gives a man a right to be tried by his peer group. A peer is a person from a similar economic, social, religious, geographical, environmental, historical and racial background. To do this the court will be forced to select a jury from the Black Community from which the black defendant came. We have been, and are being tried by all-white juries that have no understanding of the "average reasoning man" of the Black Community.

10. We want land, bread, housing, education, clothing, justice and peace. And as our major political objective, a United Nations-supervised plebiscite to be held throughout the black colony in which only black colonial subjects will be allowed to participate, for the purpose of determining the will of black people as to their national destiny.

When, in the course of human events, it becomes necessary for one people to dissolve the political bands which have connected them with another, and to assume, among the powers of the earth, the separate and equal station to which the laws of nature and nature's God entitle them, a decent respect to the opinions of mankind requires that they should declare the causes which impel them to the separation.

We hold these truths to be self-evident, that all men are created equal; that they are endowed by their Creator with certain unalienable rights; that among these are life, liberty, and the pursuit of happiness. That, to secure these rights, governments are instituted among men, deriving their just powers from the consent of the governed; that, whenever any form of government becomes destructive of these ends, it is the right of the people to alter or to abolish it, and to institute a new government, laying its foundation on such principles, and organizing its powers in such form, as to them shall seem most likely to effect their safety and happiness. Prudence, indeed, will dictate that governments long established should not be changed for light and transient causes; and, accordingly, all experience hath shown, that mankind are more disposed to suffer, while evils are sufferable, than to right themselves by abolishing the forms to which they are accustomed. But, when a long train of abuses and usurpations, pursuing invariably the same object, evinces a design to reduce them under absolute despotism, it is their right, it is their duty, to throw off such government, and to provide new guards for their future security.

PART D

SUGGESTIONS FOR
FURTHER READING

SUGGESTIONS FOR
FURTHER READING

ARISTOPHANES	*The Birds*
ARNOLD, MATTHEW	*Culture and Anarchy*
AUGUSTINE, SAINT	*The City of God*
BACON, FRANCIS	*New Atlantis,* "Of Plantations"
BAUDELAIRE, CHARLES	*Artificial Paradise*
BELLAMY, EDWARD	*Looking Backward*
BLAKE, WILLIAM	*The Marriage of Heaven and Hell*
BRADBURY, RAY	*Farenheit 451*
BROWN, NORMAN O.	*Life Against Death*
BUBER, MARTIN	*Paths in Utopia*
BULWER-LYTTON, EDWARD	*The Coming Race*
BUTLER, SAMUEL	*Erehwon*
CABET, ÉTIENNE	*A Voyage to Icaria*
CAMUS, ALBERT	*Le Juste*
CARLYLE, THOMAS	*Past and Present*
CATHERINE, SAINT	*Revelations of St. Catherine of Siena*
COMTE, AUGUSTE	*Western Republic*
DEFOE, DANIEL	*Robinson Crusoe*
DE TOCQUEVILLE, ALEXIS	*Democracy in America*
DOSTOEVSKY, FEDOR	*The Possessed*
ELIOT, T. S.	*Notes Toward a Definition of Culture*
ENGELS, FRIEDRICH	"On Authority," *Socialism: Utopian and Scientific*
FORSTER, E. M.	"The Machine Stops"
FREUD, SIGMUND	*Civilization and Its Discontents*
GOODMAN, PAUL AND PERCIVAL	*Communitas*
HARRINGTON, JAMES	*Oceana*
HAWTHORNE, NATHANIEL	*The Blithedale Romance*
HERTZKA, THEODOR	*Freeland*
HILTON, JAMES	*Lost Horizon*
HOWELLS, W. D.	*A Traveler From Altruria*
HUDSON, WALTER	*A Crystal Age*
HUXLEY, ALDOUS	*Brave New World*
JAMES, WILLIAM	"The Moral Equivalent of War"
JOHNSON, SAMUEL	*Rasselas*

KARP, DAVID	*One*
KRUTCH, JOSEPH	*The Measure of Man*
LEVI-STRAUSS, CLAUDE	*Tristes Tropiques*
LONDON, JACK	*The Iron Heel*
MALLOCK, WILLIAM H.	*New Republic*
MANNHEIM, KARL	*Ideology and Utopia*
MARCUSE, HERBERT	*One Dimensional Man*
MARX, KARL	*The Communist Manifesto*
MELVILLE, HERMAN	*Typee*
MILL, JOHN STUART	"On Liberty"
MONTAIGNE, MICHEL DE	"On the Cannibals"
MORE, THOMAS	*Utopia*
NIETZSCHE, FRIEDRICH	*Genealogy of Morals*
ORWELL, GEORGE	*Animal Farm, 1984*
PAINE, THOMAS	*The Rights of Man*
PLATO	*Republic*
POPPER, KARL	*The Open Society and Its Enemies*
RABELAIS, FRANÇOIS	"The Abbey of Theleme"
RAND, AYN	*Anthem*
ROUSSEAU, JEAN-JACQUES	*Emile, The Social Contract*
RUSKIN, JOHN	*Time and Tide, Unto This Last*
RUSSELL, BERTRAND	*Proposed Roads to Freedom*
SAINT-SIMON, CLAUDE DE	"The New Christianity"
SHAKESPEARE, WILLIAM	*The Tempest*
SHELLEY, MARY	*Frankenstein*
SHELLEY, PERCY BYSSHE	*Prometheus Unbound*
SKINNER, B. F.	*Walden Two*
SWIFT, JONATHAN	*Gulliver's Travels*
THOREAU, HENRY DAVID	*Walden*
VOLTAIRE	*Candide*
WELLS, H. G.	*A Modern Utopia, Men Like Gods, The Time Machine*
WHITMAN, WALT	*Song of Myself*
WILDE, OSCAR	"The Soul of Man Under Socialism"
WRIGHT, AUSTIN	*Islandia*
WYNDHAM, JOHN	*Re-Birth*
ZAMIATIN, EUGENE	*We*

B
C
D
E
F
G
H
I
J